Voice over IP First-Step

Kevin Wallace

Cisco Press
800 East 96th Street
Indianapolis, IN 46038

Voice over IP First-Step

Kevin Wallace

Copyright © 2006 Cisco Systems, Inc.

Published by:
Cisco Press
800 East 96th Street
Indianapolis, IN 46240 USA

Printed in the United States of America   1 2 3 4 5 6 7 8 9 0

First Printing   December 2005

Library of Congress Cataloging-in-Publication Number: 2005926125

ISBN: 1-58720-156-9

Warning and Disclaimer

This book is designed to provide information about the basics of Voice over IP (VoIP). Every effort has been made to make this book as complete and as accurate as possible, but no warranty or fitness is implied.

The information is provided on an "as is" basis. The authors, Cisco Press, and Cisco Systems, Inc., shall have neither liability nor responsibility to any person or entity with respect to any loss or damages arising from the information contained in this book or from the use of the disks or programs that might accompany it.

The opinions expressed in this book belong to the author and are not necessarily those of Cisco Systems, Inc.

Trademark Acknowledgments

All terms mentioned in this book that are known to be trademarks or service marks have been appropriately capitalized. Cisco Press or Cisco Systems, Inc. cannot attest to the accuracy of this information. Use of a term in this book should not be regarded as affecting the validity of any trademark or service mark.

Publisher
John Wait

Editor-in-Chief
John Kane

Executive Editor
Mary Beth Ray

Cisco Representative
Anthony Wolfenden

Cisco Press Program Manager
Nannette M. Noble

Production Manager
Patrick Kanouse

Senior Development Editor
Christopher Cleveland

Project Editor
Marc Fowler

Copy Editor
Ben Lawson

Technical Editors
Dave Goodwin
Graham Gudgin
Todd Stone

Team Coordinator
Tammi Barnett

Book/Cover Designer
Louisa Adair

Composition
Mark Shirar

Indexer
WordWise
Publishing Services

Feedback Information

At Cisco Press, our goal is to create in-depth technical books of the highest quality and value. Each book is crafted with care and precision, undergoing rigorous development that involves the unique expertise of members from the professional technical community.

Readers' feedback is a natural continuation of this process. If you have any comments regarding how we could improve the quality of this book, or otherwise alter it to better suit your needs, you can contact us through e-mail at feedback@ciscopress.com. Please make sure to include the book title and ISBN in your message.

We greatly appreciate your assistance.

Corporate and Government Sales

Cisco Press offers excellent discounts on this book when ordered in quantity for bulk purchases or special sales.

For more information please contact: U.S. Corporate and Government Sales
1-800-382-3419 corpsales@pearsontechgroup.com

For sales outside the U.S. please contact: International Sales international@pearsoned.com

CISCO SYSTEMS

Corporate Headquarters
Cisco Systems, Inc.
170 West Tasman Drive
San Jose, CA 95134-1706
USA
www.cisco.com
Tel: 408 526-4000
         800 553-NETS (6387)
Fax: 408 526-4100

European Headquarters
Cisco Systems International BV
Haarlerbergpark
Haarlerbergweg 13-19
1101 CH Amsterdam
The Netherlands
www-europe.cisco.com
Tel: 31 0 20 357 1000
Fax: 31 0 20 357 1100

Americas Headquarters
Cisco Systems, Inc.
170 West Tasman Drive
San Jose, CA 95134-1706
USA
www.cisco.com
Tel: 408 526-7660
Fax: 408 527-0883

Asia Pacific Headquarters
Cisco Systems, Inc.
Capital Tower
168 Robinson Road
#22-01 to #29-01
Singapore 068912
www.cisco.com
Tel: +65 6317 7777
Fax: +65 6317 7799

Cisco Systems has more than 200 offices in the following countries and regions. Addresses, phone numbers, and fax numbers are listed on the **Cisco.com Web site at www.cisco.com/go/offices.**

Argentina • Australia • Austria • Belgium • Brazil • Bulgaria • Canada • Chile • China PRC • Colombia • Costa Rica • Croatia • Czech Republic
Denmark • Dubai, UAE • Finland • France • Germany • Greece • Hong Kong SAR • Hungary • India • Indonesia • Ireland • Israel • Italy
Japan • Korea • Luxembourg • Malaysia • Mexico • The Netherlands • New Zealand • Norway • Peru • Philippines • Poland • Portugal
Puerto Rico • Romania • Russia • Saudi Arabia • Scotland • Singapore • Slovakia • Slovenia • South Africa • Spain • Sweden
Switzerland • Taiwan • Thailand • Turkey • Ukraine • United Kingdom • United States • Venezuela • Vietnam • Zimbabwe

About the Author

Kevin Wallace, CCIE No. 7945, CCSI, CCNP, CCDP, MCSE 4, CNE 4/5, is a full-time instructor for Thomson NETg. With 16 years of Cisco internetworking experience, Kevin has been a network design specialist for The Walt Disney World Resort and a network manager for Eastern Kentucky University. Kevin holds a bachelor of science degree in electrical engineering from the University of Kentucky. Among Kevin's other publication credits are *CCDA/CCDP Flash Cards* and *Exam Practice Pack* (coauthored with Anthony Sequeira), *CCIE Routing and Switching Flash Cards and Exam Practice Pack* (coauthored with Anthony Sequeira), and *Cisco IP Telephony Flash Cards and Exam Practice Pack*, all of which are available from Cisco Press. Additionally, Kevin authored the *Cisco Enterprise Voice over Data Design (EVoDD)* 3.3 course, was a contributing author for the *Cisco IP Telephony Troubleshooting (IPTT)* 2.0 course, and has written for the Cisco *Packet* magazine. Kevin also holds the IP Telephony Design Specialist and IP Telephony Support Specialist CQS certifications.

About the Technical Reviewers

Dave Goodwin, CCIE No. 4992 (Routing & Switching and Voice), is a customer support engineer for the Cisco Technical Assistance Center (TAC). He is responsible for providing escalation support to the Cisco TAC voice teams worldwide, as well as discovering and resolving issues in new and emerging Cisco IP Communications products. He also works closely with the Cisco engineering teams and is actively involved in the field trials of new products. Dave has been with Cisco for seven years and has worked as a network engineer for ten years.

Graham Gudgin, CCIE No. 2370, is a technical marketing engineer in the Voice Systems Engineering group at Cisco Systems. He is a member of the team responsible for IP Communications system designs and the creation of Solution Reference Network Designs posted at http://www.cisco.com/go/srnd. Previously, Graham worked in the field and at the Cisco TAC specializing in the development and design of packet, cell, time division multiplexing (TDM)- and voice-based systems.

Todd Stone is a Unity customer solutions architect for Cisco Systems. Todd was responsible for installing the very first versions of the product and has since become involved in the architectural aspects of Unity.

Dedications

This book is dedicated to Vivian, my bride of 11 years.

Acknowledgments

My family's support made this book possible. To my wife, Vivian, I feel so blessed to walk through life with you. To my daughter, Sabrina, your natural sense of humor keeps us all in stitches, and your caring for others warms our hearts. To my daughter, Stacie, your enthusiasm for life and the way you naturally attract new friends makes me proud to be your dad.

To the instructor team at Thomson NETg, lead by Tom Warrick and Michael Watkins, working with you pushes me to be my best and to continually grow. And, as always, I acknowledge my Heavenly Father for His blessings in my life.

This Book Is Safari Enabled

The Safari® Enabled icon on the cover of your favorite technology book means the book is available through Safari Bookshelf. When you buy this book, you get free access to the online edition for 45 days.

Safari Bookshelf is an electronic reference library that lets you easily search thousands of technical books, find code samples, download chapters, and access technical information whenever and wherever you need it.

To gain 45-day Safari Enabled access to this book:

- Go to http://www.ciscopress.com/safarienabled
- Enter the ISBN of this book (shown on the back cover, above the bar code)
- Log in or Sign up (site membership is required to register your book)
- Enter the coupon code TZKJ-MPII-SWAW-RNJR-BZ6Q

If you have difficulty registering on Safari Bookshelf or accessing the online edition, please e-mail customer-service@safaribooksonline.com.

Contents at a Glance

Contents

Icons Used in This Book

 PBX Switch

 CO Switch

 SS7 Switch

 CallManager

 IP Telephony Router

 Bridge

 Cisco Unity Server

 Directory Server

 PBX-IP Media Gateway (PIMG)

 Workgroup Switch

 Multilayer Switch without Text

 Voice-Enabled Workgroup Switch

 Cable Modem

 Router

 Voice-Enabled Router

 Phone

 Cisco IP Phone

 Phone Feature

 Fax

 PBX

 PC

 Camera PC/Video

 Camera PC/Video

 Relational Database

 File Server

 Line: Ethernet

 Line: Serial

 Network Cloud, White

 Headquarters

Introduction

Ever since Alexander Graham Bell invented the telephone in 1876, telephony systems have been a part of our life. More recently, with the advent of the Internet, much of our day-to-day communication (for example, e-mail) crosses an IP network (for example, the Internet). Today, these two worlds are merging, and companies can place phone calls over their existing data network infrastructures using a technology called *Voice over IP (VoIP)*.

The topic of VoIP attracts people of diverse backgrounds, from the private branch exchange (PBX) technician, to the network engineer, to the home user wanting to reduce his or her monthly phone bill. This book gets all readers on the same page by reviewing legacy telephony systems, and then it proceeds to delve into the brave new world of VoIP.

When I teach VoIP courses, I use plenty of metaphors to help anchor what can be complex concepts. The format of the Cisco Press *First-Step* Series allows me to talk with you and share stories, just as if you were attending one of my classes. So, expect plenty of metaphors, analogies, and even a little humor. Also, if you're like me, you learn best from examples. So, I've sprinkled multiple case studies and other examples throughout this book.

How This Book Is Organized

This book is organized in a logical, step-by-step approach to building a comprehensive understanding of VoIP. That approach is demonstrated in the following outline of the chapters:

- **Chapter 1, "Touring the History Museum of Telephony"**—Reviews the function and purpose of public switched telephone network (PSTN), PBX, and key system telephony networks. The chapter covers topics such as supervisory signaling, alert signaling, and address signaling. Near the end of Chapter 1, a case study is introduced. The scenario introduced in the case study is revisited and expanded upon in future chapters.

- **Chapter 2, "Making Waves: Turning Your Voice into Zeros and Ones"** — Explains how the human voice can be converted into a series of ones and zeros, and how bandwidth can be preserved on the Wide Area Network (WAN) by compressing voice traffic.

- **Chapter 3, "Paving the Pathway to a Voice over IP Network"** — Builds on the legacy telephony concepts established in Chapter 1, as well as the theory of digitizing voice covered in Chapter 2, by introducing the reader to an initial migration step away from traditional telephony systems, which involves sending calls across a WAN instead of the PSTN.

- **Chapter 4, "Meet the 'Brain' of the Voice over IP Network"** — Introduces you to the world of IP telephony, focusing on Cisco CallManager (CCM) solutions. Current CCM 4.x features (for example, security and video) are discussed.

- **Chapter 5, "Speaking the Gateways' Languages"** — Expands the IP telephony solution beyond a single "cluster" to the rest of the world via gateways. Gateway protocols (for example, H.323, MGCP, and SIP) are discussed as the potential gateway protocols of choice.

- **Chapter 6, "Why Quality Matters"** — Addresses quality of service (QoS) issues in a VoIP network. Some designers make the mistake of simply superimposing voice traffic on a data network. However, voice traffic needs high priority and has little tolerance for delay. Therefore, this chapter introduces a plethora of QoS technologies for treating special traffic (for example, voice) in a special way.

- **Chapter 7, "VoIP Supporting Roles"** — Introduces you to optional, value-added IP telephony components, such as Cisco Unity, which provides a unified messaging solution. Conferencing and contact center applications are also discussed.

- **Appendix A, "Answers to Chapter Review Questions"** — Each chapter ends with a "Chapter Review Questions" section. This appendix repeats the questions and lists answers as well.

- **Appendix B, "Next Steps: Where Do I Go From Here?"** — While this book introduces you to the theory surrounding VoIP, many readers might want to take the next step: learning how to configure VoIP equipment. This appendix recommends Cisco Press books and courses offered by Cisco Learning Partners that lead not only to a further understanding of VoIP, but also to Cisco certifications.

- **Glossary**—The world of VoIP requires its citizens to use often confusing lingo. This appendix gives clear and concise definitions for the most important terms introduced in the book.

Who Ought to Read This Book

If you work with data networks (perhaps to send e-mail or transfer files), if you work with telephony networks (perhaps with a corporate PBX system), if you're a home user interested in how VoIP can reduce your monthly phone bill, or if the concept of VoIP simply intrigues you, this book is for you. The concepts in this book are presented in plain language, so you don't need in-depth background knowledge to comprehend the technologies presented.

Stuff You'll Find in This Book

This book includes several features to help you digest the materials with minimal heartburn. With the solid foundation gained through this book, you can learn things about new VoIP technologies more easily, talk VoIP with others, or be better prepared to begin a career in VoIP:

- **Chapter objectives**—Every chapter begins with a list of objectives that are addressed in the chapter. The objectives are revisited in the chapter summary.

- **Highlighted keywords and Glossary**—Throughout this book, you will see terms formatted with italics. These terms are particularly significant. If you find you aren't familiar with the term or at any point need a refresher, simply look up the term in the Glossary toward the end of the book to find a full definition.

- **Case studies**—Every chapter concludes with a case study. The case study scenario is introduced at the end of Chapter 1 and expanded upon in all remaining chapters. The case studies give you the opportunity to take what you've learned in a chapter and put your newfound knowledge to work in a specific design scenario.

- **Chapter summaries**—Every chapter concludes with a comprehensive chapter summary that reviews chapter objectives, ensuring complete coverage, and discusses the chapter's relationship to future content.

- **Chapter review questions**—Every chapter concludes with review questions. These questions test the basic ideas and concepts covered in each chapter. You can find the answers to the questions in Appendix A.

- **Nontechie headings and titles**—The titles and headings throughout this book avoid the use of technical terms when possible, focusing instead on words that connote something about the underlying concepts.

For More Information...

If you have any comments about this book, you can submit them through the ciscopress.com website. Simply go to the website, select Contact Us, and type in your message.

I hope you enjoy your first step into a deeper knowledge of VoIP, and I trust that this first step will be a giant leap in your understanding of VoIP.

What You Will Learn

After reading this chapter, you should be able to

✔ Explain the differences between various types of telephone switches.

✔ Describe the operation of traditional telephony systems.

✔ Identify the advantages of a Voice over IP (VoIP) network.

CHAPTER 1

Touring the History Museum of Telephony

Welcome to the world of Voice over IP (VoIP)! Think of it, sending your company's voice traffic (or even your home's voice traffic) over a data network. When you place a call from your office to New York or Los Angeles, your voice travels across your company's network links, not through the telephone company's voice network. As a result, you avoid long-distance charges; however, that's just the tip of the iceberg. This book introduces you to the plethora of benefits VoIP offers.

Prior to getting into the nuts and bolts of VoIP, you need to have a firm understanding of traditional telephony networks. This chapter takes you on a tour through the history of telephony. Traditional telephony components introduced in this chapter are compared and contrasted in later chapters with today's VoIP components, providing you with the distinctions necessary to begin the migration to this exciting new world of telephony.

Dissecting a Telephony Network

When you pick up your home phone's handset and place a call to a friend, many operations occur in the background. This section walks through a basic phone call step by step, assuming you have a regular analog phone.

note

Traditional analog phones are called POTS devices. POTS stands for "Plain Old Telephone Service."

When you pick up the handset of your phone, you hear a *dial tone* in the receiver, and you can press keys on the touch-tone keypad to dial digits. However, on close inspection of your phone, you notice that there doesn't seem to be a battery in the phone, and it's not being powered from an alternating current (AC) wall outlet. So, the question is, "Where is the phone getting its power?" The answer is the phone company. The telephone switch at the phone company's *central office (CO)* applies -48 volts of direct current (DC) across the wires coming out of the telephone wall jack. That voltage enables the phone to dial digits or even illuminate the keypad (in case you need to dial in the dark), for example.

note

The telephone jack in the wall of your home (assuming you live in North America) is an RJ-11 jack, where RJ means Registered Jack. This RJ-11 jack has up to six conductors, although a phone that has only a single line uses just two of these wires.

You dial your friend's phone number of 555-1212. The tones created from the digits you dial travel over a pair of wires leaving your phone, into your RJ-11 wall jack, and back to the telephone switch at your local CO. These two wires leaving your phone are called the *tip* and *ring* wires.

note
Did you ever notice that in the movies or on television, almost all phone numbers begin with 555? That's because originally, there were no residential or business seven-digit phone numbers in the North American Dial Plan beginning with 555. (Although some numbers outside the 555-0100 through 555-0199 range are now released for actual assignment.) Examples include 555-1212 for the Brady Bunch's home and 555-0267 for the Townsend Agency in *Charlie's Angels*. (It doesn't work. I tried.) The producers don't want to create another situation like the one caused by the song "Jenny." Remember, eight six seven five three oh nine.

The names tip and ring come from the plug used by the operators of yesteryear to interconnect calls. As you can see in Figure 1-1, the plug used by these operators resembles the plug you might use to connect your headphones to your home stereo equipment. There are three conductors on this plug. The conductor (that is, wire) connected to the tip of the plug is called the tip, and the conductor connected to the ring in the middle of the plug is called the ring.

Figure 1-1   Tip and Ring

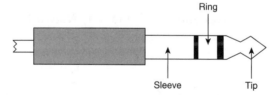

The tip and ring wires take on a new name after they leave your home. The connection from your home to the local CO is called the *local loop*. When your dialed digits, carried over the local loop, reach your local CO, the local loop connects into a phone switch. As the name suggests, a *phone switch* is responsible for interconnecting the endpoints (that is, the phones) that make up a phone call. The phone switch can recognize the digits you dialed by listening to the tones generated by your telephony keypad, or by interpreting pulses generated by a rotary phone. The phone switch can then determine to where your call should be forwarded, based on those dialed digits. If your friend lives just across town, perhaps your friend's phone connects into the same CO that your home phone connects to. If that's the case, then the phone switch sends ringing voltage over the local loop connecting to your friend's home. If your friend does not live nearby, then the phone switch might need to forward your call to a phone switch in a different CO. A connection from one phone switch to the other is called an *interoffice trunk*.

Your friend's phone begins to ring, and he picks it up. Your friend's local CO telephone switch notices that he picked up his phone's handset and stops sending ringing voltage. At this point, you and your friend can begin to talk with one another.

This chapter digs deeper into the inner workings of the phone call just described. For example, several types of *signaling* occurred to make the phone call possible. When you heard the dial tone and your friend heard his phone ringing, that was *information signaling*. When you dialed digits, that was *address signaling*.

Figure 1-2 illustrates some of the components that make up a traditional telephony network.

Figure 1-2   Components of a Telephony Network

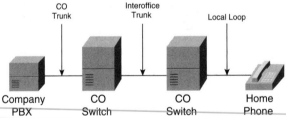
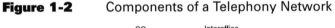

The list that follows defines the traditional telephony network components illustrated in Figure 1-2:

- **Edge devices** (for example, phones)—Connect into a telephony network.

- **Local loops**—Connect callers to a local CO over a pair of wires called tip and ring.

- **Phone switches**—Make it possible for one phone to connect to another phone by dialing a phone number. The switch interprets the dialed digits and interconnects the dialing phone's local loop with the destination phone's local loop.

- **Trunks**—Interconnect phone switches. Unlike a local loop, a trunk typically transports multiple simultaneous conversations.

The preceding example considered a phone switch located in your local CO. However, for businesses, that is not always the case. Businesses might have their own phone switches. The next few lessons in this chapter compare and contrast these various types of phone switches, beginning with phone switches that make up the *public switched telephone network (PSTN)*.

The Public Switched Telephone Network: The Phone System That You Grew Up With

The telephone that Alexander Graham Bell invented in 1876 did not have a touch-tone keypad. Nor did it have a rotary dial. In fact, for decades after the invention of the telephone, many callers could not directly dial the person they wanted to speak with. They first had to speak with an operator and ask the operator to connect them with the desired party.

You have probably seen this scene played out on the *Andy Griffith Show*. Andy picks up the receiver on his phone in the sheriff's office and asks Sara to connect him with Floyd's Barber Shop. Andy didn't have the option of dialing Floyd directly.

This was standard operation for the phone system until a Kansas City undertaker became fed up. Back in 1889, an undertaker named Almond Brown Strowger was losing business because the local Bell Telephone operator had a brother-in-law who was a competing undertaker. So, when someone called the operator wanting to speak with an undertaker, guess who they were connected with? That's right, the Bell Telephone operator's brother-in-law.

note

Different accounts of the story suggest relationships between the operator and the competing undertaker other than brother-in-law/sister-in-law (such as cousin or spouse). However, the various versions of the story do depict a close family relationship between the operator and the competing undertaker.

Mr. Strowger thought that callers should be able to call him directly, without a meddling operator. This frustration led to his invention of the first telephone switch. This switch, through a series of mechanical relays, could interpret a caller's dialed digits and form a pathway between the calling party's phone and the called party's phone. The Strowger Switch, also known as the Step-by-Step Switch, was adopted by AT&T in 1924 and was in widespread use in the United States into the 1980s.

Today's CO telephone switches are digital, as opposed to the mechanical Strowger Switch, and these switches are connected in a hierarchical manner. Your home phone probably connects to a *Class 5* CO (that is, your local CO), which then connects up to a *Class 4* CO, and so on. This hierarchical approach of inter-connecting telephone offices minimizes the number of interoffice trunks required to connect all of the nation's telephones together into what is called the PSTN.

The structure of the PSTN is composed of three different types of networks:

- **Local Network**—Local networks typically include local loop connections that provide a path for businesses and homes to connect back to their local central office.

- **Exchange Area Network**—Exchange area networks typically interconnect local exchanges (for example, Class 5 offices) and tandem exchanges (for example, an office that can act as an intermediary point, when two other switches do not have an available trunk between themselves).

- **Long-Haul Network**—Long-haul networks typically interconnect local exchanges (for example, Class 5 offices) with long-distance offices.

Private Branch Exchanges: How Big Businesses Talk

I used to work on the telephone system at a university, and the university had about 6000 telephones on campus. How much do you think it would cost for each one of those phones to have a direct connection back to the local CO? In those days (the early 90s), a business line had a recurring monthly charge of approximately $40. That comes out to $240,000 every month for local phone service for those 6000 phones! There must be a more economical approach.

One such approach was for the university to have its own phone switch. That's right. A private entity such as a business or university can have its internal phones connect to its own phone switch instead of the local CO. That private phone switch then connects to the local CO over a series of trunks (analog and/or digital, which are discussed Chapter 3, "Paving the Pathway to a Voice over IP Network"). The good news is that 6000 trunk connections back to the local CO were not required because statistically speaking, all 6000 phones would never be in use at exactly the same time. In fact, based on traffic studies (a topic covered in Chapter 2, "Making Waves: Turning Your Voice into Zeros and Ones"), we needed approximately 210 trunk lines (that is, voice paths) interconnecting the university's phone switch with the local CO, as illustrated in Figure 1-3.

Figure 1-3   University Telephone System

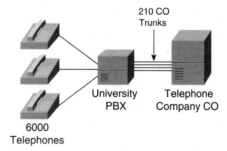

210 CO
Trunks

University
PBX

Telephone
Company CO

6000
Telephones

Admittedly, there are other costs associated with having a private phone switch. For example, we had to pay a maintenance contract to have a technician onsite, and we had to purchase the phone switch itself (which was approximately $3 million back in the late 1980s). However, when considering the vast discrepancy in recurring monthly phone line charges, the economies of scale are clear. Assuming each of those 210 trunk lines costs $40 per month, the total monthly "phone bill" would be $8400. When compared with an earlier calculation of $240,000 per month, that's a savings of $156,000 per month!

Large businesses typically select *private branch exchanges (PBXs)* to act as their privately owned phone switches. PBXs are available in a wide variety of shapes and sizes and typically support 20 to 20,000 phones. Most PBXs are "feature-rich," offering voice mail, music-on-hold, call transfer capabilities, and many other features. However, the relatively large initial cost of a PBX might not give a smaller business a satisfactory return on investment (ROI). The alternative for a smaller business is an entry-level phone switch called a *key system*, as described in the following section.

Key Systems: How Small Businesses Talk

Smaller businesses only needing to support 30 to 40 phones might not be able to justify the purchase of a PBX system and instead might rely on another option called a *key system*. Like a PBX, a key system can act as a phone switch for phones within the organization and provide trunk lines back to the local CO for call destinations outside of the business.

The distinction between a classic key system and a PBX is more than simply the number of supported phones. In a PBX environment, callers typically dial a 9 on the telephone keypad to access an outside line. In other words, after they dial a 9, they get a second dial tone. This second dial tone comes from the local CO.

In a key system environment, because the number of lines (that is, trunk connections) going back to the local CO is relatively small, these lines are directly accessible from the key system's key phones. For example, you might be using a key phone with five line buttons. If you want to call outside of the local business, instead of dialing a 9 to access an outside line, you can press an available line button right on the key phone.

You might have been visiting a car lot, as an example, and heard over the booming intercom, "Kevin, you have a call on line three. Kevin, please pick up line three." In that instance, Kevin could go to one of the key system's key phones, and press the line three button to access the call.

However, if you have been in the market for PBXs or key systems lately, you have probably realized that the line between the two is starting to blur. More and more key systems are starting to feel very PBX-like. For example, these days, you might need to dial a 9 to access an outside line on your key system. These phone switches that have characteristics of both PBXs and key systems are sometimes called *hybrid phone switches*.

Ringing, Dial Tone, and Other Bells and Whistles

Earlier in this chapter, you considered an end-to-end telephone call between you and a friend. In passing, you learned that various types of "signaling" occurred during that phone call. The following sections examine the various types of signaling:

- Supervisory signaling
- Address signaling
- Information signaling

Supervisory Signaling

Supervisory signaling indicates to the phone switch whether a connected phone is currently on-hook or off-hook and also when a phone receives an incoming call. Supervisor signaling includes:

- Loop Start Signaling

- Ground Start Signaling

- Ringing

Loop Start Signaling

In a home environment, the phone switch in the local CO can determine whether a phone is on-hook or off-hook based on whether current is flowing over the local loop connecting back to that phone. Because an on-hook phone mechanically has its tip and ring circuit open, the -48 volts of DC applied across the tip and ring wires isn't doing anything. The voltage is just sitting there, waiting for the circuit to close. After the handset goes off-hook, however, the tip and ring circuit is closed, and current can begin to flow through that circuit. When the telephone switch at the CO sees this current begin to flow, it knows that the phone has gone off-hook, and the telephone switch sends a dial tone to the caller, indicating that they can begin dialing digits. This type of supervisory signaling is called *loop start signaling*.

Loop start signaling has an issue with *glare*. Did you ever pick up the phone to call someone, but you didn't hear any dial tone and instead discovered that someone was on the other end of the line? If so, you experienced glare. Glare occurs when you beat the signaling and pick up your handset before your phone rings. What's really spooky is when the person you were about to call is the person on the other end of the line!

Glare may not be a major concern in a home environment, but what about a line connecting to a company's PBX system? Because the lines connected to a PBX experience a significantly higher call volume than you do on your home phone (unless you have teenagers), the probability of glare occurring with a PBX using loop start signaling is much higher than the probability of glare occurring on your home phone. Therefore, you often find another type of signaling used on PBX systems, and also on pay phones. That other type of signaling is *ground start*, and the good news is that ground start signaling prevents glare.

Ground Start Signaling

With ground start signaling, the phone switch monitors the voltage potential on the "ring" lead of a line, and when the ring lead has a ground potential, the line is seized. If you watched the 1983 movie *WarGames*, you witnessed an example of ground start signaling. Do you remember the scene? Matthew Broderick's character rides his bicycle up to a pay phone, but he doesn't have any money. So, he takes the pay phone handset and bangs it against the pay phone's chassis, which loosens the transmitter cover. He opens up the transmitter portion of the handset, pulls out one of the leads (the ring lead), and touches the lead to the chassis of the pay phone (which had a ground potential). By creating this off-hook ground start signal, he can place a call.

note
Circuits in today's pay phones prevent the falsification of ground start signals, as Matthew Broderick did in *WarGames*.

Ringing

Ringing is also considered to be supervisory signaling. Ringing voltage is sent from the telephone switch to alert the destination phone that it is receiving an incoming call. Here is a fun experiment: the next time your home phone rings, start counting (one thousand one, one thousand two, ...) to see how many seconds the ringing lasts and how many seconds of silence there are before the ringing begins again. In the United States, the pattern of ringing, called the *ring cadence*, is two seconds on and four seconds off, as Figure 1-4 illustrates. However, it seems that Hollywood isn't that patient. If a phone rings on a TV show or a movie, most of the time, they use a much shorter ring pattern (typically, one second on and two seconds off).

Figure 1-4   Ringing Pattern Examples

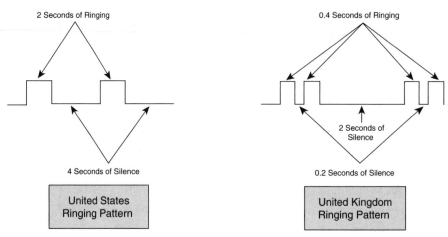

Pop quiz time! Who invented the telephone ringer? This is a question that I ask students in my classes, and the most popular answer is Alexander Graham Bell. However, it was Thomas Watson, Mr. Bell's assistant, who invented the mechanical ringer. Back in those days, the copper wiring over which the voice traffic and ringing voltage was sent wasn't manufactured to the quality standards that today's transmission is. As a result, Thomas Watson used significant voltage to go across this lower quality medium to cause a mechanical ringer to ring. Specifically, the original ringer required 75 volts of AC. Because today's signaling might be communicated over fiber optic cable, and the ringers are rarely the mechanical kind, you might assume that such high voltage levels would not be necessary. However, the tradition of using higher voltages for ringing is still observed today in the PSTN, which is why you shouldn't touch bare telephone wires.

Another mystery of ringing voltage goes back to an earlier statement. When discussing how the CO knows when a phone goes off-hook, you learned that the tip and ring circuit is open when the phone is on-hook. That leads to the question, "If the tip and ring circuit is open, how can ringing current flow through this open circuit?" Actually, the circuit is considered open to DC. However, the phone's internal circuitry has an electrical component called a *capacitor* between the tip and ring wires, and even though direct current does not flow through a capacitor, AC does. Ringing voltage uses AC. Therefore, this ringing current can flow through a phone in the on-hook condition, causing the ringer to ring, as shown in Figure 1-5.

Figure 1-5   Ringing Circuit

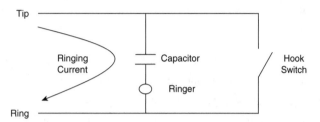

Address Signaling

Address signaling allows a phone to specify the "address" (phone number) of the destination phone by dialing digits. Most phones support two types of dialing. The older method, used by rotary phones, is *pulse dialing*. Pulse dialing opens and closes the tip and ring circuit very rapidly. This series of open and closed circuit conditions within specific timing parameters indicates a dialed digit to the telephone switch, as shown in Figure 1-6.

Figure 1-6   Pulse Dialing

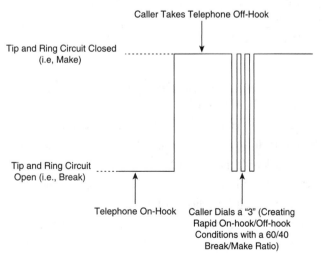

When a phone's handset is lifted off its cradle, the hook switch closes the tip and ring circuit. Similarly, when a phone's handset is placed back on its cradle, the hook switch opens the tip and ring circuit. In fact, as a child, I tried dialing phone numbers by rapidly tapping the hook switch, attempting to simulate pulse dialing. Admittedly, my timing wasn't perfect, and I didn't always dial the correct number, but I dialed someone!

A more efficient approach to address signaling is *dual tone multifrequency (DTMF)*, also known as "touch tone" dialing. With DTMF, two simultaneous frequencies are generated, and a phone switch interprets this combination of frequencies as a dialed digit. For example, the combination of a 697 Hz tone and a 1209 Hz tone indicates a dialed digit of 1, as shown in Table 1-1. You might be curious as to why "dual" tones are used instead of just a single tone; the answer is background noise. The phone company doesn't want the radio or your kids playing in the background to make a sound that may be interpreted as a dialed digit. So, specific combinations of two simultaneous frequencies are used to represent a dialed digit.

Table 1-1   Dual Tone Multifrequency (DTMF) Frequencies

Frequency	1209 Hz	1336 Hz	1477 Hz
697 Hz	1	2	3
770 Hz	4	5	6
852 Hz	7	8	9
941 Hz	*	0	#

Although pulse dialing served callers well for decades, DTMF dialing offers some significant advantages. Foremost of these advantages is speed. If you remember using an old rotary phone years ago (or even more recently—my mother still has one), think about how long it took to dial a 0. You positioned your finger in the 0 position, made a clockwise motion to dial the digit, and released the dial. The dial then very slowly rotated counter-clockwise back to its original position. Due to the mechanical inertia built into those rotary phones, it took a full second to dial that 0. DTMF enables you to dial digits much more rapidly. If your fingers are nimble enough, you can dial several digits in a second. The tones generated by a

DTMF keypad also enable a caller to interact with devices on the other side of the link. For example, suppose that you are away from home, and you want to check your messages, either on your home answering machine or on your voice mail. You dial your home number and then enter a series of DTMF tones to retrieve your messages. You would not be able to do that using pulse dialing.

Information Signaling

Similar to DTMF, information signaling uses combinations of frequencies, in this case to indicate the status of a call (that is, to provide information to the caller). For example, a *busy signal* is a combination of a 480-Hz tone and a 620-Hz tone, with on/off times of .5 sec/.5 sec. Another type of information signaling that you are probably familiar with is *ring back*. Ring back is the ringing sound heard by the caller to indicate that the dialed phone is ringing. Realize, however, that the ring back heard by the caller doesn't occur at exactly the same time as the ringing on the destination phone. Try it. The next time you call someone, ask them how many times their phone rang before they picked up. Compare that number with the number of times you heard ring back. In some instances, the numbers will differ. Table 1-2 lists several other types of information signaling used in North America that you might be familiar with, along with the corresponding frequencies used for each signal.

Table 1-2   Information Signaling

Information Signal	Description	Frequencies (Hz)
Dial tone	Heard by the caller after picking up the telephone handset	350 and 440
Ring back	Heard by the caller, indicating that the called phone is ringing	440 and 480
Busy signal	Heard by the caller, indicating that the called phone is off-hook	480 and 620
Reorder tone	Heard by the caller, indicating that the call cannot be completed successfully—perhaps due to all trunks being busy	480 and 620

A set of rules that determines how information is exchanged is called a *protocol*. You can think of a protocol as a "language of love" between two devices. The protocol that runs over the Internet, as you might guess, is called the *Internet Protocol (IP)*. For decades, IP has transmitted data, not just across the public Internet, but also across private networks.

Because voice can be digitized (converted to binary 1s and 0s), as described in Chapter 2, binary digits representing the voice can be transmitted across existing IP-based data networks. The process of sending voice traffic across an IP network is called *Voice over IP (VoIP)*.

As Figure 1-7 illustrates, a VoIP network has its own pieces and parts, just as a traditional telephony network does.

Figure 1-7   VoIP Components

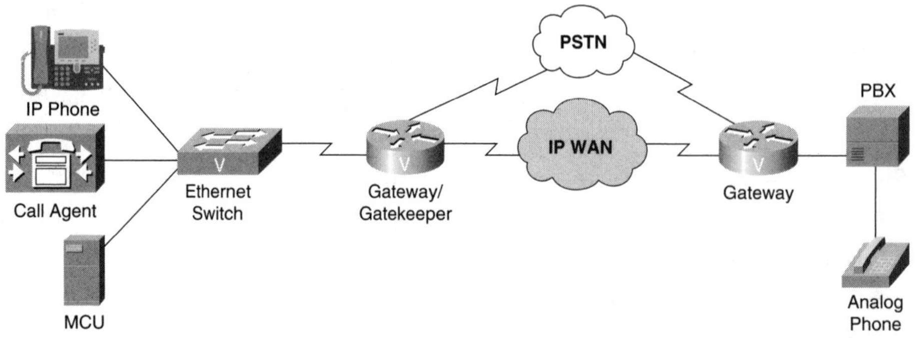

The list that follows defines the VoIP network components illustrated in Figure 1-7:

- **IP phones**—Have an Ethernet network connection used to send and receive voice calls.

- **Call agents**—Replace many of the features previously provided by PBXs. For example, a call agent can be configured with rules that determine how calls are forwarded. The *Cisco CallManager (CCM)* product is an example of a call agent.

- **Gateways**—Can forward calls between different types of networks. For example, you could place a call from an IP phone in your office, through a gateway to the PSTN, to call your home.

- **Gatekeepers**—Can be thought of as the traffic cops of the *wide-area network (WAN)*. For example, because bandwidth on a WAN is typically somewhat limited, a gatekeeper can monitor the available bandwidth on the WAN. Then, when there is not enough bandwidth to support another voice call, the gatekeeper can deny future call attempts.

- **Multipoint Control Units (MCUs)**—Are useful for conference calling. On a conference call, multiple people can be talking at the same time, and everyone on that conference call can hear them. It takes processing power to mix these audio streams together. MCUs provide that processing power. MCUs may contain digital signal processors (DSPs), which are dedicated pieces of computer circuitry that can mix those audio streams together.

- **Voice-enabled Ethernet switches**—Add quality of service features to traditional Ethernet switches, allowing voice packets to be stored in a separate area from data packets. Voice-enabled Ethernet switches can recognize an attached IP phone, provide the attached IP phone with subnet information, and optionally supply power to the IP phone.

note
The term *Ethernet switch* should not be confused with the term *phone switch*, discussed earlier in this chapter. Ethernet switches forward data, whereas phone switches forward phone calls.

With the maturity of PBX-centric phone systems, why might you consider migrating your existing tried and true PBX to a VoIP network? One of the first responses that comes to most people's minds is cost, and that is certainly a valid reason. Actually, you can achieve cost savings from more than one source. Perhaps your company's headquarters has a PBX, and that PBX connects to other PBXs or key systems at remote office locations. You might be paying a recurring monthly cost for the circuits interconnecting these privately owned phone switches. In addition to the circuits you have for your voice traffic, you might also have separate circuits for your data traffic between these offices. With VoIP, you could potentially eliminate the voice circuits, along with their monthly charges, and send your voice and data traffic over a single circuit.

As an example, consider the university where I used to work. We had a PBX at the main campus, and a key system at each of three remote campuses. These remote campuses were small, just some office space in strip malls located in surrounding communities. In fact, each remote campus only had about four telephones each. Still, we had a dedicated T1 circuit from the main campus's PBX to each of the three remote campuses' key systems. There were also separate T1 circuits connecting the main campus's data network to the data network at each remote campus. With a VoIP solution, the university could send both voice and data traffic over the existing data T1 circuits and eliminate the dedicated voice T1s.

note

A T1 is a digital circuit that sends traffic at a rate of 1.544 Mbps. T1s are often used to carry voice, video, or data traffic. A T1 circuit can be subdivided into 24 separate channels, and PBXs require a full channel to support a voice path. Not all 24 channels need to be used for a single application (for example, voice, video, or data), however. A T1 can connect into a channel bank, which is a device that takes a T1 connection and breaks it out into 24 separate connections. If a full T1 is not required for a connection, many service providers sell fractional T1s, which provide a specific number of channels (less than 24).

Another cost savings offered by VoIP technologies can come in the form of cable plant expenses. Consider a company with separate infrastructures (that is, fiber optic cabling) for the voice, data, and video networks, as illustrated in Figure 1-8.

With the high-speed data networking technologies available in today's campus environment, voice, data, and even video traffic can peacefully coexist on the same high-speed network, as shown in Figure 1-9. This *converged network* approach requires less hardware because multiple traffic types use the same hardware.

Figure 1-8   Voice/Video/Data Before Convergence

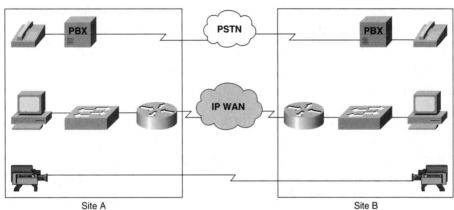

Figure 1-9   Voice/Video/Data After Convergence

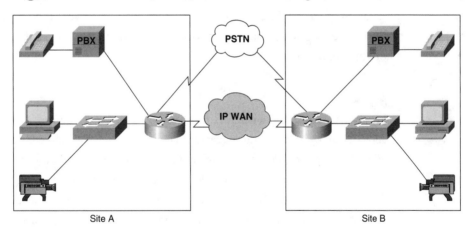

At this point, you can see that cost savings can be a major driving force in the migration to a VoIP network, and rightfully so. However, adopting a converged networking approach offers a number of other advantages. For example, a VoIP network not only mirrors the features offered by a PBX, but also offers a suite of new features.

Later chapters in this book describe many of these features, such as the ability to support converged messaging (that is, having a single repository for voice mail, fax messages, and e-mail), virtual call centers, and extension mobility (that is, the ability for a user to log into a phone and receive their personal telephone settings). You can even play video games on many of the Cisco IP Phones, although that's not one of the reasons you want to give management.

To be fair, however, consider a couple of common concerns that many people have with the idea of VoIP. One of the biggest concerns that often surfaces is the reliability of a VoIP telephony system. After all, PBXs have a reputation for being up and operational most of the time. In fact, many people in the PBX industry boast about the *five nines* of reliability that they enjoy with their PBX. The five nines of reliability means their PBX is up 99.999 percent of the time. If you considered that level of reliability over the period of a year, that would only be five minutes of downtime during the entire year! This is a measure of reliability not just during working hours, but rather 24 hours a day, 7 days a week, 365 days a year (and 366 in leap year!) of uptime. Sad to say, many corporate decision makers have a dimmer view of network reliability.

note

I experienced this skepticism personally. While working at a university, I approached my director and suggested that we might want to start considering the adoption of VoIP. My director became quite upset, pointing out that the PBX system "never" went down, whereas I was "always" doing something to the data network, bringing it to its knees. Many in management share this sentiment, and although it might have had some validity at one time, today's VoIP networks can offer comparable levels of reliability to PBXs, as you will learn in Chapter 3.

Another major concern is the quality of the voice calls. Most people have experienced a poor cell phone connection, and many fear a VoIP call might offer a similar level of quality. Voice quality is so critical, this book dedicates an entire chapter (Chapter 6, "Why Quality Matters") to addressing the variety of tools available to VoIP network designers to help them achieve fantastic voice quality.

These tools fall under a technology called *quality of service (QoS)*. So, while there are definite concerns with VoIP, these concerns can certainly be addressed through proper VoIP network design, and later chapters explore many of these design best practices.

As discussed in this section, a VoIP network can help businesses today literally do more with less, enjoying more features and more flexibility with less recurring cost. Even though you haven't yet learned all the specific components that interconnect to form a VoIP network, you do have enough information at this point to start making some fundamental design decisions for a voice network. The next section puts your knowledge to the test.

Case Study: Your Turn to Put the Pieces in Place

To help you get a better feel for voice network design, consider a sample high-level design scenario. A suggested solution is provided after the scenario. However, remember, when it comes to the design of a voice network, there is no one solution. The flexibility of voice technology allows many different design approaches to achieve the same goal. So, don't be concerned if your solution differs from the suggested solution.

Consider the following scenario:

The XYZ Company comes to you wanting your advice for designing a telephone network to interconnect the XYZ Company headquarters with two of its remote offices. Even though the XYZ Company already has a data network interconnecting these offices, at this point, it isn't completely convinced it should pursue a VoIP telephony network, as opposed to a traditional PBX/key system network. Therefore, you are asked to recommend a traditional telephony (PBX or key system) solution based on the criteria outlined in Table 1-3.

Table 1-3   XYZ Company Requirements for a Telephony System

Location	Number of Telephones	Required Features
Headquarters	4500	Voice mail A conference bridge capable of supporting a conference of 20 simultaneous participants
Remote Office 1	2000	Access to the corporate voice mail system Access to the corporate conference bridge Capability to support 72 simultaneous voice paths back to the headquarters
Remote Office 2	30	Access to the corporate voice mail system Access to the corporate conference bridge Capability to support 12 simultaneous voice paths back to the headquarters

Because you are such an advocate of VoIP technologies, as opposed to a traditional PBX/key system approach, the XYZ Company asks you to add to your traditional telephony design your arguments as to why a VoIP network would be preferable. Use the space provided to diagram and document your design. Also, write a paragraph describing why a VoIP network might be preferable.

Design Diagram for XYZ Company:

Design Description for XYZ Company:

_____

_____

_____

_____

_____

_____

_____

_____

_____

_____

_____

_____

_____

Rationale for a VoIP Solution:

_____

_____

_____

_____

_____

_____

_____

_____

_____

_____

_____

_____

_____

_____

Suggested Solution

Figure 1-10 illustrates a suggested solution for the case study. Remember, however, there isn't just a single solution to voice network designs. Don't be concerned if your design doesn't exactly match the suggested solution. Rather, read through the suggested solution to see whether it triggers any ideas you might be able to use to tweak your design.

Design Diagram for XYZ Company

Figure 1-10   XYZ Company Suggested Solution

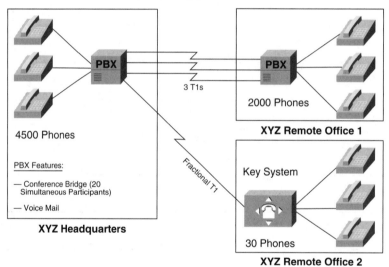

Design Description for XYZ Company

Due to the number of phones located at the company headquarters (4500), the headquarters requires a PBX. When selecting a PBX, prospective vendors need to specify the extra hardware and software required to support the stated conference bridge and voice mail requirements.

Remote Office 1 also requires a PBX because this site contains 2000 phones. Separate voice mail and conference systems are not required for this remote office, however. This remote office can simply access the voice mail and conferencing resources located at the company headquarters. Because the trunks connecting the remote office PBX to the headquarters PBX need to support 72 simultaneous voice paths, three T1 circuits will be used to interconnect these two PBXs (that is, 24 channels per T1 * 3 = 72 channels).

Remote Office 2 only requires a key system due to its relatively small number of phones (30 phones). Like Remote Office 1, there is no need for Remote Office 2 to have its own voice mail and conferencing systems. Remote Office 2 can access the resources that reside at the company headquarters. Because only 12 simultaneous voice paths are required between Remote Office 2 and the headquarters, a full T1 is not required. Instead, a fractional T1, containing 12 voice channels, will be used to interconnect Remote Office 2 to the company headquarters.

Rationale for a VoIP Solution

A VoIP solution might be able to use the existing data network to simultaneously send voice and data traffic, thus eliminating the need for the three T1s and one fractional T1 specified in the design, which saves on recurring monthly expenses.

A VoIP network would also lay the foundation for enhanced services. For example, instead of simply having a voice mail system, the XYZ Company may be able to use a product such as Cisco Unity (described in Chapter 7, "VoIP Supporting Roles"), which provides unified messaging. Unified messaging is more than just voice mail. It provides a single repository for voice mail, e-mail, and fax messages.

Chapter Summary

This chapter reviewed the history and operation of legacy telephony systems. Various flavors of telephone switches were discussed, including CO switches (which make up the PSTN), PBXs, and key systems. Both PBXs and key systems are privately owned telephone switches. Larger businesses use PBXs to support anywhere from 20 to 20,000 phones. Smaller businesses needing to support only 30 to 40 phones may opt for a key system.

Placing an end-to-end phone call involves different types of signaling, including supervisor signaling (which indicates to the CO switch that a phone has gone off-hook), information signaling (which provides information to the caller about the state of a call, such as a busy signal or ring back), and address signaling (which uses pulse dialing or DTMF dialing to communicate dialed digits to a telephone switch).

You also learned that migrating from a traditional PBX-centric (or key system-centric) telephony environment to a VoIP network offers several advantages. Cost savings is a primary motivator. Examples of these cost savings include reduced equipment and staffing expenses, in addition to the elimination of recurring monthly charges for dedicated voice circuits used to interconnect privately owned telephone switches. The advantages of VoIP, however, extend far beyond cost savings. A VoIP network lays the foundation for enhanced services that are not possible with legacy telephony solutions.

Chapter Review Questions

1. What are the names of the two wires used by a traditional home phone to carry voice traffic and signaling information? (Select two.)

   a. Ground

   b. Tip

   c. Magneto

   d. Ring

2. Who invented the first direct-dial telephone switch?

   a. Thomas Watson

   b. Almond Brown Strowger

c. Alexander Graham Bell

d. Harry Nyquist

3. Which type of telephone switch is most appropriate for a business needing to support 10,000 phones?

a. CO switch

b. Key system

c. PBX

d. Ethernet switch

4. Identify three types of signaling used on PSTN networks.

a. Information

b. Address

c. Fallback

d. Supervisory

5. How many voice channels can be carried over a T1 circuit in a traditional PSTN/PBX environment?

a. 16

b. 24

c. 30

d. 64

6. "Dial tone" is an example of which type of signaling?

a. Information

b. Address

c. Fallback

d. Supervisory

7. Which of the following are potential advantages of a VoIP network? (Select three.)

   a. Reduced dedicated circuit costs

   b. More mature technology than PBX/key system approaches

   c. Lays a foundation for more advanced services

   d. Reduced physical plant costs

8. How much voltage does a telephone switch apply across the tip and ring wires?

   a. -48 volts of DC

   b. -48 volts of AC

   c. +90 volts of DC

   d. +90 volts of AC

9. Which VoIP component is used to forward calls between different types of networks?

   a. Call agent

   b. Gatekeeper

   c. Gateway

   d. MCU

10. Which VoIP component is used to mix multiple audio streams?

   a. Call agent

   b. Gateway

   c. Gatekeeper

   d. MCU

What You Will Learn

After reading this chapter, you should be able to

- ✔ Explain how the spoken voice is digitized.

- ✔ Select an appropriate coder decoder (CODEC) to transmit digitized voice.

- ✔ Determine how much bandwidth is needed to support your voice calls.

CHAPTER 2

Making Waves: Turning Your Voice into 1s and 0s

Binary 1s and 0s don't come out of our mouths when we speak. However, if our voices are to be carried across a *Voice over IP (VoIP)* network, that's exactly how our voices need to look.

In their natural form, our voices are *analog*, meaning a continuously varying waveform. VoIP networks, on the other hand, transmit our voices digitally, using *binary* encoding, meaning a series of 1s and 0s, as shown in Figure 2-1. Obviously some conversion has to occur. We have to have some way of converting our analog voice waves into binary. Not only do we need to convert *to* binary, but there also has to be a way to convert from binary back to analog. Otherwise, the person at the other end of the call would not be able to understand what we were saying.

Figure 2-1   Analog and Digital Waveforms

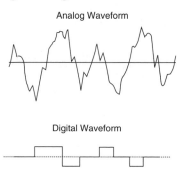

Analog Waveform

Digital Waveform

In this chapter, you will see how this conversion occurs, but we don't stop there. Once your voice is converted into 1s and 0s and is ready to be sent across the network, you want to make sure that you are not using too much of the network's bandwidth to transmit all of your voice calls. For example, on a *wide-area network* (*WAN*), which interconnects geographically separated offices, your company is charged a recurring monthly fee for the bandwidth (that is, the throughput capability) of that WAN link. To make the most efficient use of that link, you might want to take the binary data representing your voice and squeeze it down so that it doesn't take up as much bandwidth. After all, if you can send a voice call using less bandwidth, then you can place more voice calls across that same WAN link without paying any more money to your service provider. What a deal! Different approaches to doing that "squeezing" are covered in this chapter.

Because you might send several voice calls across the WAN at the same time, a critical design decision revolves around how much WAN bandwidth is needed for voice. Even though the required math to calculate this bandwidth can seem daunting, you won't need a math degree to successfully calculate the needed bandwidth. This chapter provides you with links to web-based calculators and shortcut methods for doing these calculations. So, let's get started by exploring how you can take the spoken voice (in analog) and convert it into a series of binary 1s and 0s.

Chopping Your Voice into "Byte"-Size Pieces

The job of converting analog voice into digital data begins with *sampling*. To better understand sampling, consider the movies you watch at your local theater. When you're watching your favorite actor or actress on the screen (Meg Ryan, in my case), you are not actually watching their continuous motion. Rather, you are watching still images of them played back very rapidly. Typically, movies show 24 frames every second, and when you see that many sequential frames that quickly, it appears to be smooth motion.

Digitizing voice uses a very similar concept. We take "snapshots" or "samples" of an analog voice wave very frequently. Those samples are then digitized (that is, represented as a series of 1s and 0s). Then, at the other end of the voice conversation, this digitized signal can be converted back into an analog wave, which the listener can understand.

One of the major issues with sampling is determining how often we should take those samples (that is, "snapshots") of the analog wave. We don't want to take too few samples per second because when the equipment at the other end of the phone call attempts to reassemble and make sense of those samples, a different sound (that is, a lower-frequency sound) signal might also match those samples, and the listener would hear an incorrect sound. This phenomenon is called *aliasing*, as show in Figure 2-2.

Figure 2-2   Aliasing

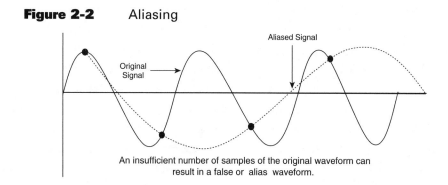

An insufficient number of samples of the original waveform can result in a false or alias waveform.

Now that you see the evils of undersampling, or aliasing, you might be tempted to say, "Let's take many more samples per second to avoid aliasing." Although that approach, sometimes called *oversampling*, does indeed eliminate the issue of aliasing, it also suffers from a major drawback. If we take far more samples per second than we actually need to accurately re-create the original signal, we are consuming more bandwidth than is absolutely necessary. Because bandwidth is a scarce commodity (especially on a WAN), we don't want to perform oversampling, as shown in Figure 2-3.

Figure 2-3   Oversampling

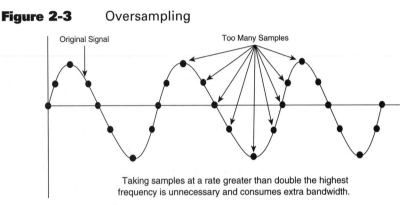

Taking samples at a rate greater than double the highest
frequency is unnecessary and consumes extra bandwidth.

At this point, you have seen that you do not want to take too few samples per second, nor do you want to take too many samples per second. So, where is the
"sweet spot?" What is the magic number of samples that allows equipment to
accurately reproduce the original signal, without consuming more bandwidth than
necessary? The answer was provided for us back in 1933 by Harry Nyquist. In
fact, the *Nyquist Theorem* is very popular among telephony professionals. Mr.
Nyquist said the sample rate needs to be at least twice as high as the highest frequency being sampled. For voice, in theory, the highest sampled frequency is
4 kHz (that is, 4000 cycles per second). Based on that information, the Nyquist
Theorem tells us that we need to take 8000 samples per second, which means that
we need to take a sample every 125 microseconds, as shown in Figure 2-4.

Figure 2-4   Sampling

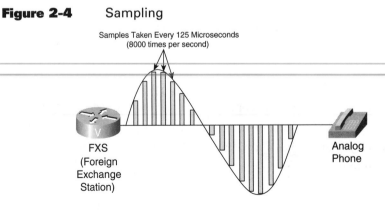

You might be wondering why we said that the highest frequency sampled for voice traffic is 4 kHz (that is, 4000 Hz or 4000 cycles per second). After all, if we measured the frequency range of the spoken voice with sophisticated test equipment, we would find that frequencies contained in the human voice go well above 4 kHz. The next time you are in one of those huge electronics stores, check out the frequency range (sometimes called the *frequency response*) on stereo speakers. Those speakers can typically reproduce sounds in the frequency range from 20 Hz at the low end to 20,000 Hz at the high end. Some of the really expensive speakers have an even greater frequency range. However, because most humans cannot hear frequencies above 20,000 Hz, I am not quite sure why customers pay extra money to reproduce sounds that they cannot even hear. Maybe they pay the extra money for the listening enjoyment of their household dog.

However, the question for our purposes is, "Why don't we attempt to reproduce the higher frequency components of the human voice?" The answer is twofold. First, if we sampled more times per second in order to reproduce higher frequencies (that is, frequencies above 4 kHz), the additional required samples would consume more bandwidth. Second, because our goal is to reproduce clear and understandable voice and not to reproduce the fidelity experienced in a concert hall, we don't need to reproduce signals in excess of 4 kHz. In fact, over 90 percent of *voice intelligence* (that is, frequencies used by human speech) is contained in the 0 to 4000 Hz frequency range.

A common misconception about these voice samples is that when we take a sample, the sample is immediately in digital form. The initial process of sampling is called *pulse amplitude modulation (PAM)*. Interestingly, after PAM is performed, the samples are still in an analog format. These samples, consisting of a single frequency, have *amplitudes* (that is, volumes) equaling the amplitudes of the sampled waveform at the instance of the sampling.

The next step in digitizing the voice waveforms is to take these PAM amplitudes and assign them a number, which can then be transmitted in binary form. The process of assigning a number to an amplitude is called *quantization*, as shown in Figure 2-5.

Figure 2-5   Linear Quantization

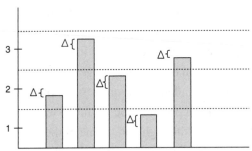

Once PAM samples have been taken, we need to quantize these samples (that is, assign numbers to represent their amplitudes). However, if we use a linear scale (as shown in Figure 2-5), the quantization error (as indicated by the deltas) causes distortion in the voice. This distortion is especially noticeable at lower volumes. Therefore, instead of a linear scale, we use a logarithmic scale, which has more measurement intervals at lower volumes.

In theory, these PAM samples might have an infinite number of amplitudes, and it would not be practical to try to assign a unique number to every sample. As a result, the quantization rounds off these amplitude values to the closest number on a scale, as shown in Figure 2-5 (represented by the deltas). The challenge with rounding off is that it causes *quantization error*, which sounds like a "hiss" on the line. The example in Figure 2-5 uses the linear scale on the left side to assign numbers to the various amplitudes.

Interestingly, quantization error is more noticeable at lower amplitudes (that is, lower volumes). This is because when the volume is louder, the volume of the speech tends to drown out the relatively quiet "hiss," and lower volumes occur more frequently than higher volumes. Based on these characteristics, taking more samples at lower volumes and fewer samples at higher volumes can help overcome the symptoms of quantization error, while still not using extra bandwidth. To accomplish this result, instead of a linear scale, a logarithmic scale is used, as shown in Figure 2-6.

Figure 2-6   Logarithmic Quantization

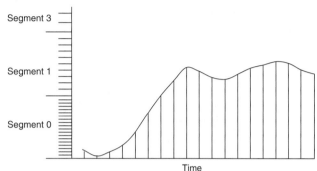

- A sample is taken every 1/8000th of a second.
- Each *segment* is divided into *steps*.
- Using a logarithmic scale, more accurate samples are taken at lower volumes.

There are a couple of popular approaches to defining this logarithmic scale, called *μ-Law* (pronounced "mu-Law" and sometimes written and pronounced as "u-Law") and *α-Law* (pronounced and sometimes written as "a-Law"). *μ*-Law is the approach most commonly used in North America and Japan, while *α*-Law is more commonly used in other countries. Although both approaches do a great job of defining a logarithmic scale, *μ*-Law has lower idle channel noise, while *α*-Law has a superior signal-to-noise (S/N) ratio for lower-volume samples. However, if VoIP equipment in a country using *μ*-Law connects to VoIP equipment in a country using *α*-Law, the common practice is for both sets of equipment to use *α*-Law. Now that we can measure PAM amplitudes more effectively, let's assign a number to these samples.

An 8-bit (that is, 1-byte) value represents each sample. The first bit of the byte determines the polarity (that is, positive or negative) of the sample. The byte's next 3 bits identify the segment (that is, the major division on the logarithmic scale), while the final 4 bits of the byte specify the step (that is, the minor division on the logarithmic scale), as shown in Figure 2-7.

Figure 2-7   Anatomy of an 8-Bit Sample

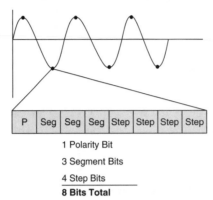

At this point, the spoken voice has been converted into a series of 1 and 0s, but the question is, "How much bandwidth is being used on my network to send this voice conversation?" Let's do the math:

> According to Mr. Nyquist, we need to take 8000 samples per second.
>
> Each sample uses 8 bits.
>
> 8000 samples per second * 8 bits per sample = 64,000 bits per second (that is, 64 kbps).

These calculations show us that we can transmit digitized voice using 64 kbps of bandwidth. However, in addition to the actual voice, header information also needs to be transmitted. The 64 kbps of bandwidth only represents the voice traffic.

Squeezing Your Voice into a Smaller Package

Once our analog waveforms have been digitized, we might want to save WAN bandwidth by compressing these digitized waveforms by encoding them. The processes of encoding and decoding these waveforms are defined by *coder decoders*, also known as *code decoder (CODEC)*. Let's consider a few forms of *waveform compression* used by various CODECs:

- **Pulse code modulation (PCM)** — Doesn't actually compress the analog waveform. Rather, PCM samples and performs quantization (as described earlier) without any compression. G.711 is the CODEC that uses PCM.

- **Adaptive Differentiated PCM (ADPCM)** — Uses a *difference signal*. Instead of encoding an entire sample, ADPCM can send the difference in the current sample, versus the previous sample. G.726 is an example of an ADPCM CODEC.

- **Conjugate Structure Algebraic Code Excited Linear Predication (CS-ACELP)** — Dynamically builds a codebook based on speech patterns. It then uses a *look ahead buffer* to see whether the next sample matches a pattern already in the *codebook*. If it does, then the codebook location can be sent instead of the actual sample. G.729 is an example of a CS-ACELP CODEC.

To help visualize how CS-ACELP works, imagine you and I are having a conversation across a digital circuit, and you notice that frequently in my speech pattern, I make the sound "ing" (for example, as in the words rout*ing*, compress*ing*, and read*ing*). Instead of digitizing the "ing" sound, you make an entry in a book that you have (called a codebook) that describes what "ing" sounds like. I also make the same entry in my codebook. In the future, instead of me having to digitize and transmit all of the 1s and 0s that describe how "ing" sounds, I simply send you the location of that sound in your codebook. For example, instead of sending the "ing" sound, I might tell you, as a metaphor, that I'm sending the sound located on page 51, line 30 in your codebook. You look up that location in your codebook and find the binary code for making the "ing" sound. The advantage is that instead of sending the actual sound, I'm only sending you the location of that sound in your codebook, which takes up far less bandwidth than sending the actual sound.

As mentioned earlier, this codebook is built dynamically, based on the speech patterns of the conversation. Therefore, it's probably safe to assume that the codebook built during a conversation with Barney the Purple Dinosaur would be significantly different from the codebook built during a conversation with the Osbourne family.

The purpose of the look-ahead buffer used by G.729 is to collect voice patterns in a buffer and attempt to match those voice patterns with a pattern already defined in the local codebook. In fact, in the Cisco VoIP environment, G.729 is the most popular CODEC for sending voice traffic over the WAN, primarily because of its high quality and low bandwidth requirements. To transmit the actual digitized voice, G.729 only requires 8 kbps, compared to the 64 kbps of bandwidth required by G.711. CS-ACELP is designed to encode speech patterns. Therefore, other audio sources (for example, music on hold) might experience more quality degradation than human speech.

■ **Low-Delay Conjugate Excited Linear Predication (LDCELP)**—Is very similar to CS-ACELP. However, LDCELP uses a smaller codebook, resulting in less delay, but it requires more bandwidth. The G.728 CODEC is an example of a LDCELP CODEC.

Working with Cisco products, you will normally use G.711 (which requires 64 kbps of bandwidth for voice payload) in the local area network (LAN) environment and G.729 (which requires 8 kbps of bandwidth for voice payload) over the WAN. G.729 does have a couple of variants. Although all flavors of G.729 require 8 kbps of bandwidth to transmit voice, G.729a uses a less complex algorithm, which saves processor resources with very slight quality degradation. G.729b enables voice activity detection (VAD).

What is VAD, and why do we need it? Let's say that you and I are talking with each other on the phone, and you step away for a moment. During that time, neither of us is talking. However, the VoIP networking is still carrying that "silence," and silence takes up just as much bandwidth as regular speech. However, VAD can detect when the conversation stops. By default on Cisco routers, after 250 milliseconds (ms) (that is, one-fourth of a second) of silence, the router stops sending the silence, thus freeing up bandwidth. To take a line from Simon and Garfunkel, VAD does not send "the sound of silence." Although the amount of bandwidth saved by VAD varies based on speech patterns, a 30 percent bandwidth savings is typical.

In addition to the type of compression used, the size of the final voice packet depends on several variables, such as:

- **Media**—Is the voice traffic being transmitted across a Frame Relay, Asynchronous Transfer Mode (ATM), or Ethernet network?

- **Tunnel**—Is the voice traffic being sent over a virtual private network (VPN)?

- **Header Compression**—Is the header information being compressed?

- **CODEC Selection**—Is the digitized voice being compressed? For example, G.711 does not compress voice, but other CODECs (for example, G.729 and G.723) do compress voice.

Although several Cisco course publications offer charts to aid in determining the required bandwidth for a call, I prefer to use the Cisco web-based *Voice Bandwidth Calculator* located at the following URL:

http://tools.cisco.com/Support/VBC/do/CodecCalc1.do

note

A Cisco Connection Online (CCO) account is required in order to use this tool. You can register for a CCO account by pointing your web browser to the Cisco home page at http://www.cisco.com and clicking the **Register** link.

Let's walk through how to use this incredibly valuable tool to determine the required bandwidth for a call:

1. Open up a web browser to

   http://tools.cisco.com/Support/VBC/do/CodecCalc1.do

   From the initial screen, as shown in Figure 2-8, select the CODEC being used (typically G.711 on a high-speed LAN or G.729 on a lower-speed WAN), the voice protocol (VoIP for our discussion), and the number of simultaneous calls you need to support. Then click the **Next** button.

Figure 2-8   Voice Bandwidth Calculator – Screen 1

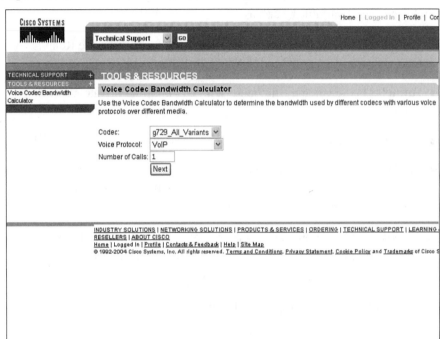

2. Complete the next screen, as shown in Figure 2-9, by entering the voice payload size (the number of bytes used to encode a single voice sample, which
   is typically 20 bytes for the G.729 CODEC), clicking a checkbox if you are
   using RTP header compression (discussed in Chapter 6, "Why Quality Matters"), selecting your media access (for example, Frame Relay, Ethernet, or
   PPP), and indicating any additional overhead that increases the size of the
   packet (for example, tunneling or security overhead). Then click the **Submit**
   button.

Figure 2-9   Voice Bandwidth Calculator – Screen 2

3. From the final screen, as shown in Figure 2-10, note the Total Bandwidth
   (including Overhead) value. This value gives you the amount of bandwidth
   required to support the number of simultaneous calls you indicated, with the
   network characteristics you specified.

Figure 2-10   Voice Bandwidth Calculator – Screen 3

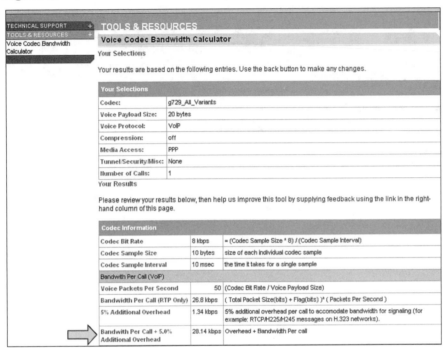

Thus far in the chapter, you have seen that when sending your voice traffic across the network, you can conserve bandwidth by using a CODEC that compresses the voice traffic. However, there is a tradeoff. If you reduce your bandwidth requirement, you might need to sacrifice some of the voice quality. To best determine whether this "bandwidth for quality" tradeoff is acceptable, you need a way to numerically compare quality. Fortunately, you have your choice of various voice quality measurements:

- **Mean Opinion Score (MOS)**—Uses a *trained ear* to judge the quality of voice after passing through the CODEC being tested. MOS values range from 1, for unsatisfactory quality, to 5, for no noticeable quality degradation. For toll-quality voice, however, an MOS value in the range of 4 is appropriate. The G.711 CODEC has an MOS value of 4.1. Accompanied by a significant bandwidth savings, G.729 has an MOS of 3.92, while the less processor intensive G.729a has a MOS of 3.9. However, the challenge with MOS is that at its essence, it is based on opinion.

- **Perceptual Speech Quality Measurement (PSQM)**—Digitally measures the difference in the original signal and the signal after it passes through a CODEC.

- **Perceptual Evaluation of Speech Quality (PESQ)**—Digitally measures quality, like PSQM, but attempts to match the more familiar MOS values. For example, if a particular CODEC has an MOS score of 4.1, then it should also have a PESQ value of approximately 4.1.

Deciding How Much Bandwidth Is Enough

Once you understand how to calculate the bandwidth needed to support a certain number of voice calls, using a certain CODEC with certain options (for example, payload size, media type, and any extra overhead for security), the next step is to determine how much bandwidth is needed to support the busiest telephone usage time of the day for a company. However, before you can determine the required bandwidth, you first need to know how many calls you need to support simultaneously. Then you can simply feed that number of calls into the Cisco web-based Voice Bandwidth Calculator discussed earlier.

You must first figure out how many telephone calls are going on during the busiest time of the day for your telephone network. If we dug into all of the nuts and bolts of doing this calculation, it could get very complicated. Voice professionals even have a name for this type of calculation: *traffic engineering*.

Traffic engineering gets deep into statistical analysis and very complex math. However, in this chapter, you're going to learn some great shortcuts, and these shortcuts provide excellent results, without having to dust off the scientific calculator you had in college. Here is the game plan:

Step 1 Calculate *Erlangs* based on monthly *private branch exchange (PBX) usage*.

Step 2 Determine the grade of service (GoS) (that is, how many rejected calls are acceptable during the busiest hour of the day).

Step 3   Calculate the number of required trunks, based on the Erlang value and the GoS value, using a web-based Erlang B calculator.

Step 4   Calculate the amount of required bandwidth, using the Cisco web-based Voice Bandwidth Calculator.

The following sections walk through each step.

Step 1: Calculating Erlangs

The call volume experienced by a company's telephone system (for example, PBX) is measured in Erlangs, where an Erlang is one solid hour of phone usage. For example, if you and three of your coworkers each use your company's phone system for 30 minutes during the same hour, that's a total of 120 *call minutes* (that is, 4 * 30) of phone system use. Because an Erlang is measured in hours, you can divide the *call minutes* by 60 to convert the call minutes to Erlangs. In this example, you and your coworkers had 2 Erlangs worth of phone system usage (that is, 120 / 60).

However, our traffic engineering goal for Step 1 is to determine the number of Erlangs of phone system usage your company experiences during the busiest hour of the day. There are various approaches to calculating the *busy hour* traffic, but let's consider an approach that only requires you to know the total number of minutes your company's phone system used during an entire month. This "call minutes" value could come from your company's internal Station Message Detail Recorder (SMDR) information or from your company's phone bill.

Statistically, the number of call minutes a corporate phone system experiences during the busiest hour of the day can be approximated using the following formula:

Busy_Hour_Call_Minutes = [Monthly_Call_Minutes / 22] * .15

The rationale for this formula is based on the observation that a month contains approximately 22 business days, and during a business day, approximately 15 percent of a day's call volume occurs during the busiest hour of the day. We can then calculate the busy hour Erlang value by dividing the Busy Hour Call Minutes by 60.

As an example, consider a scenario where a company's phone bill shows 50,000 minutes of phone usage during a month. We can calculate the company's busy hour call minutes as follows:

Busy_Hour_Call_Minutes = [50,000 / 22] * .15 = 340.9 call minutes

Next, we can convert the call minutes value into Erlangs by dividing the call minutes value by 60:

Erlangs = 341 / 60 = 5.7

Step 2: Determining the Grade of Service

Now that we know the call volume during your company's busy hour, we make the observation that we probably don't want to accommodate every single call during that busy hour. After all, if we purchased sufficient trunks (in the PBX world) or sufficient bandwidth (in the VoIP world) to handle every call during the busy hour, some trunks, or bandwidth, would go unused during the remainder of the day. Therefore, we need to determine an acceptable percentage of calls to reject during the busiest hour of the day. This percentage is defined as a *grade of service (GoS)*. Typically, telephone network designers use a GoS of P(.01), which is a one percent chance that a call will be rejected during the busiest hour of the day.

Step 3: Calculating the Number of Required Trunks

After calculating the call volume we need to support (measured in Erlangs) and determining the percentage of calls we're willing to reject during the busiest hour of the day (specified as a GoS), we can use an Erlang B calculator to determine how many trunks are required for a PBX to handle this call volume.

note
Erlang B is not the only Erlang model. Other models can be used for applications such as sizing a call center. However, for a company's telephone system, the Erlang B model is usually appropriate.

The web-based Erlang B calculator located at http://erlang.com/calculator/erlb takes our Erlang and GoS values and calculates the required number of trunks to accommodate the busy hour traffic with a specific GoS. Consider our example, with 5.7 Erlangs and a GoS of P(.01). We enter the 5.7 value in the **BHT (Erl.)** field of the Erlang B calculator (where BHT represents Busy Hour Traffic measured in Erlangs) and .01 in the **Blocking** field (which is the default value), as shown in Figure 2-11.

Figure 2-11   Erlang B Calculator – Inputting Busy Hour Traffic

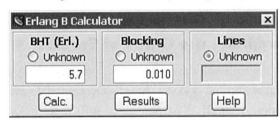

We then click the **Calc.** button, and the calculator displays the number of trunks needed to support the specified call volume, as shown in Figure 2-12. In our example, we require 12 trunks.

Figure 2-12   Erlang B Calculator – Calculating Lines

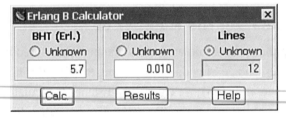

Step 4: Calculating the Amount of Required Bandwidth

PBX traffic engineers would be done at this point. They would know how many trunks the PBX needed. However, we need to take it a step further and determine how much bandwidth is required to support the specified call volume, and the good news is that we already know how to do it. Do you remember when we used the Cisco web-based Voice Bandwidth Calculator? We can use that same calculator again, inserting the number of required trunks (that is, 12 trunks), as calculated in Step 3, in the **Number of Calls** field, as shown in Figure 2-13.

Figure 2-13   Calculating the Required Bandwidth for 12 Trunks

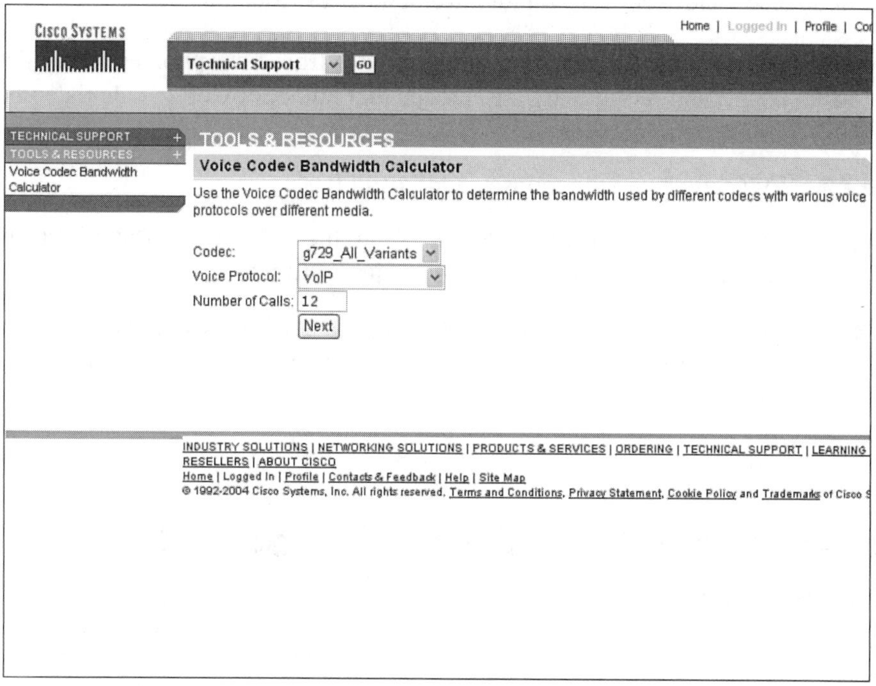

When sending these calls across the IP WAN, let us assume the following:

- CODEC: G.729a

- Voice Protocol: VoIP

- Voice Payload Size: 20 Bytes (default)

- RTP Header Compression: Disabled

- Media Access: PPP

- Tunnel/Security/Misc. Overhead: None

After entering these parameters into the Cisco Voice Bandwidth Calculator, we get a result of 337.68 kbps of bandwidth required to support the call volume in our example.

Admittedly, we went through this traffic engineering calculation slowly to demonstrate the details of each step. However, in the real world you can calculate the required voice bandwidth very rapidly. Remember the four steps:

Step 1 Determine your company's call minutes from your phone bill, divide by 22, and multiply by .15. Divide that number by 60 to calculate your Erlang requirements.

Step 2 Typically, you will choose a GoS of P(.01).

Step 3 Enter your Erlang and GoS values into the web-based Erlang B calculator to determine the number of required trunks.

Step 4 Enter the number of trunks and your specific VoIP call parameters in the Cisco Voice Bandwidth Calculator to determine the required voice bandwidth.

Case Study: Your Turn to Choose the Bandwidth

The XYZ Company, in the previous chapter's case study, asked for a design based on PBX and key system technology. The suggested solution from Chapter 1, "Touring the History Museum of Telephony," is shown in Figure 2-14. However, you were such a proponent of VoIP technology, XYZ Company is considering interconnecting the proposed PBXs and key system over the IP WAN, as opposed to dedicated T1 and fractional T1 lines, which were specified in Chapter 1's original proposal.

Figure 2-14   XYZ Company's Suggested Solution

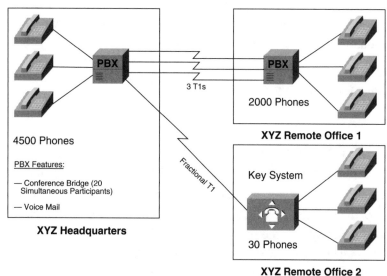

We saw in the previous case study that we need to support 72 simultaneous calls between the XYZ Company headquarters and XYZ Remote Office 1. The connection between the XYZ Company headquarters and XYZ Remote Office 2 needed to support 12 simultaneous calls.

Therefore, your task in this case study is to determine the required WAN bandwidth between the XYZ Company headquarters and each of the remote offices. Use the Cisco Voice Bandwidth Calculator located at the following URL:

    http://tools.cisco.com/Support/VBC/do/CodecCalc1.do

When calculating the required bandwidth amounts, make the following assumptions:

- CODEC: G.729a
- Voice Protocol: VoIP
- Voice Payload Size: 20 Bytes (default)
- RTP Header Compression: Disabled
- Media Access: PPP
- Tunnel/Security/Misc. Overhead: None

Enter your answers below:

- How much bandwidth is required on the link between the XYZ Company headquarters and XYZ Remote Office 1? _____

- How much bandwidth is required on the link between the XYZ Company headquarters and XYZ Remote Office 2? _____

Case Study Suggested Solution

Let's walk through the steps to calculate the bandwidth required for the two links in this scenario. First, we log in to the Cisco Voice Bandwidth Calculator, using our CCO login credentials. We select **g729_All_Variants** as the **Codec** and **VoIP** as the **Voice Protocol**. For the link between the XYZ Company headquarters and the XYZ Remote Office 1, we enter **72** as the **Number of Calls** parameter. After filling out this initial screen, we click the **Next** button, as shown in Figure 2-15.

Figure 2-15   Case Study: Voice Bandwidth Calculator – Screen 1

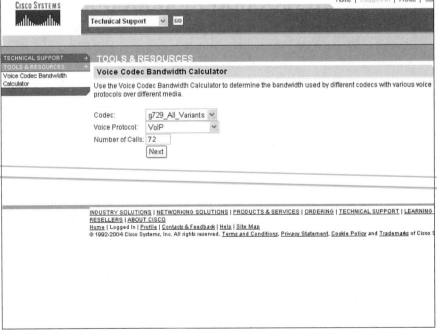

From the next screen, we select **PPP** for the **Media Access** parameter. In this scenario, we leave all other parameters at their default settings, as shown in Figure 2-16.

Figure 2-16   Case Study: Voice Bandwidth Calculator – Screen 2

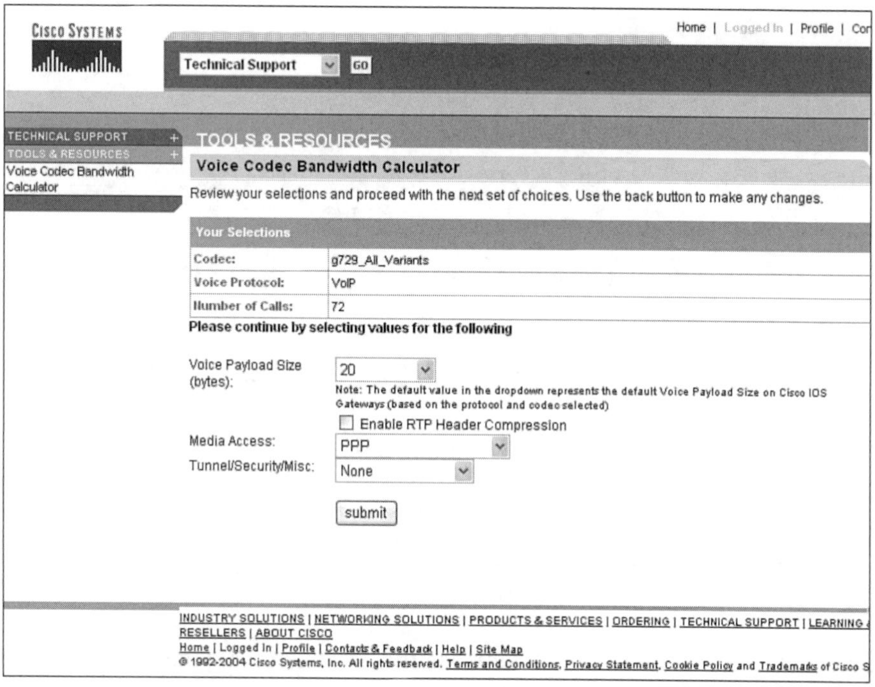

After clicking the **Submit** button, we are presented with a screen showing us a breakdown of the VoIP calculation. The Total Bandwidth (including Overhead) value tells us the amount of bandwidth that we should provision. In this example, the bandwidth is 2026.08 kbps, as shown in Figure 2-17.

Figure 2-17   Case Study: Voice Bandwidth Calculator – Screen 3

Your Selections	
Codec:	g729_All_Variants
Voice Payload Size:	20 bytes
Voice Protocol:	VoIP
Compression:	off
Media Access:	PPP
Tunnel/Security/Misc:	None
Number of Calls:	72

Your Results

Please review your results below, then help us improve this tool by supplying feedback using the link in the right-hand column of this page.

Codec Information		
Codec Bit Rate	8 kbps	= (Codec Sample Size * 8) / (Codec Sample Interval)
Codec Sample Size	10 bytes	size of each individual codec sample
Codec Sample Interval	10 msec	the time it takes for a single sample
Bandwith Per Call (VoIP)		
Voice Packets Per Second	50	(Codec Bit Rate / Voice Payload Size)
Bandwidth Per Call (RTP Only)	26.8 kbps	(Total Packet Size(bits) + Flag(bits))* (Packets Per Second)
5% Additional Overhead	1.34 kbps	5% additional overhead per call to accomodate bandwidth for signaling (for example: RTCP/H225/H245 messages on H.323 networks).
Bandwith Per Call + 5.0% Additional Overhead	28.14 kbps	Overhead + Bandwidth Per call
Total Bandwith Required (VoIP)		
Bandwidth Used for All Calls (RTP Only)	1929.6 kbps	(Bandwidth per Call) * (Number of Calls)
Total Bandwidth (including Overhead)	2026.08 kbps	Same as above + 5.0% Overhead
Packet Size Calculation		

We repeat the process for the link between the XYZ Company headquarters and XYZ Remote Office 1, this time specifying **12** as the **Number of Calls**. This calculation gives us a result of 337.68 kbps. Finally, you can enter your results in the case study as follows:

- How much bandwidth is required on the link between the XYZ Company headquarters and XYZ Remote Office 1?

2026.08 kbps

- How much bandwidth is required on the link between the XYZ Company headquarters and XYZ Remote Office 2?

337.68 kbps

Chapter Summary

This chapter explained how analog waveforms generated by the human voice are converted into digital data, which can then be sent across a network. Specifically, samples of an analog wave are taken at a rate of twice the highest frequency. For example, if the highest frequency being sampled is 4000 Hz, then 8000 samples (that is, 4000 * 2) are taken every second. This sampling is called (PAM. However, PAM does not digitize the signal. So, the next step is to assign numeric values to each of the PAM samples, based on the samples' volume (that is, amplitude). Each of these values can be represented numerically using 8 bits. Therefore, voice often requires 64,000 bits per second (that is, 4000 * 2 * 8) of bandwidth, not including additional overhead. This process is called PCM, which is how the G.711 CODEC operates.

To conserve bandwidth, especially over relatively slow-speed WAN links, VoIP network designers often use a CODEC other than G.711 in order to compress the voice samples and to reduce bandwidth demands. In the Cisco VoIP environment, the G.729 CODEC, which only requires 8 kbps of bandwidth (not including overhead), is commonly used.

Calculating the total bandwidth (including overhead) required by a VoIP call can be done using the Cisco web-based Voice Bandwidth Calculator. Because voice compression does somewhat sacrifice voice quality in favor of reduced bandwidth, being able to measure and quantify voice quality is critical. This chapter described three voice quality measurements: MOS, PSQM, and PESQ.

Finally, this chapter delved into traffic engineering, which calculates the total amount of bandwidth needed to support peak traffic loads in a VoIP network. However, we do not typically purchase enough bandwidth to handle *all* calls occurring during that peak usage time. Otherwise, we would pay for bandwidth that was only used for brief periods.

Chapter Review Questions

1. Which of the following best describes an *analog* waveform?

   a. A waveform represented by a series of 1s and 0s

   b. A continuously varying waveform

   c. A waveform after it passes through the G.711 CODEC

   d. A waveform after it passes through the G.729 CODEC

2. According to the *Nyquist Theorem*, if you are digitizing music, and the highest frequency being sampled is 20 kHz, what is the minimum number of samples that should be taken per second?

   a. 10,000

   b. 20,000

   c. 40,000

   d. 80,000

3. Undersampling an analog wave (that is, not taking enough samples to accurately reproduce the wave) can result in:

   a. Aliasing

   b. Glare

   c. Gaussian distribution

   d. Linear quantization

4. G.711 is an example of which type of CODEC?

   a. PCM

   b. ADPCM

   c. CS-ACELP

   d. LD-CELP

5. Which of the following CODECs includes VAD (Voice Activity Detection)?

   a. G.729

   b. G.729a

   c. G.729b

   d. G.711

6. Which of the following is a voice quality measurement that uses a "trained ear?"

   a. MOS

   b. PSQM

   c. GoS

   d. PSQM

7. The process of assigning numeric values to PAM (pulse amplitude modulation) samples is called:

   a. Aliasing

   b. Oversampling

   c. Glare

   d. Quantization

8. A solid hour of voice conversation is the definition of which of the following terms?

   a. GoS

   b. PSQM

   c. Erlang

   d. Centum Call Second

9. A company's monthly phone bill indicates that the company's total phone usage for the month was 10,000 minutes. Estimate the number of call minutes during the "busy hour."

   a. 68 call minutes

   b. 87 call minutes

   c. 360 call minutes

   d. 22 call minutes

10. Which of the following CODECs produces the best voice quality?

   a. G.723

   b. G.711

   c. G.729

   d. G.726

What You Will Learn

After reading this chapter, you should be able to

- ✔ Describe how VoIP can compete with the reliability of traditional PBX systems.

- ✔ Explain how to replace PBX-to-PBX connections with a VoIP network.

- ✔ Identify router interfaces used for connecting various analog devices (for example, phones and fax machines).

- ✔ Describe how voice-enabled routers connect to digital circuits (for example, T1 and E1 circuits).

- ✔ Explain how dial peers allow voice-enabled routers to forward calls to the appropriate destination.

- ✔ Discuss how VoIP can be used in the home, as opposed to traditional telephone service.

CHAPTER 3

Paving the Pathway to a Voice over IP Network

The transition from a traditional private branch exchange (PBX)-based telephony system to a *Voice over IP (VoIP)* system is not usually an overnight (or over-the-weekend for that matter) process. Instead, we usually take "baby steps," as they said in *What About Bob?* A first step might be to replace the trunk line that interconnects PBXs at remote sites with an IP *wide area network (WAN)* connection. A next step could be to connect existing analog phones, fax machines, and speaker phones to voice-enabled routers.

The end result of these baby steps is a telephony network, without a PBX, where voice traffic is transmitted over an IP network. In this chapter, we'll explore how to begin this migration and pave the pathway to a VoIP network.

Competing with the Reliability of Existing Phone Systems

The perception of many in business today is that VoIP simply isn't reliable enough to support the telecommunication demands of a corporate environment. After all, corporate PBX systems are considered highly reliable, but how many times in a month do you hear users say, "My e-mail isn't working," "The Internet is down," or "I can't print to the network printer"? Because of such past frustrations with data network applications, this perception of unreliability has unfortunately carried forward to any new application running on the data network, such as VoIP.

Many PBX administrators like to boast, even though they are not always correct, that their PBX has the "five nines" of availability. By the "five nines" they mean that their PBX is available (that is, up and running) 99.999 percent of the time, and this availability isn't just during regular business hours—it's 24 hours a day, 365 days a year. If we were to do the math, we would see that if a network is up and available 99.999 percent of the time, then it would only be unavailable for five minutes a year. Consider Table 3-1, which illustrates the yearly downtime associated with various availability levels.

Table 3-1   Availability and Downtime

Availability	Maximum Yearly Downtime
99.000 percent (two nines)	3 days, 15 hours, and 36 minutes
99.900 percent (three nines)	8 hours, and 46 minutes
99.990 percent (four nines)	53 minutes
99.999 percent (five nines)	5 minutes
99.9999 percent (six nines)	30 seconds

Before discussing how a VoIP network can be designed to be more available, we need to distinguish between *reliability* and *availability*. A *reliable* network, as an example, does not drop many packets, whereas an *available* network is up and functioning. Availability is a function of the *mean time to repair (MTTR)* and the *mean time between failures (MTBF)*.

As the names suggest, the MTTR is the average time it takes to repair a failed network component, and the MTBF is the average time between the failures of a network component. A network's availability can be improved by reducing the MTTR and increasing the MTBF. When purchasing network hardware (for example, an Ethernet switch), many manufacturers, such as Cisco, provide MTBF information; and you can determine the MTTR as part of your network design. For example, you might have spare parts on-site to quickly swap out failed equipment, or you might have redundant components within a chassis (for example, redundant supervisor engines in a Cisco Catalyst switch). These network components can also be interconnected in a redundant fashion (for example, having multiple connections between multiple devices). Let's consider some of these design approaches in a bit more detail.

One approach is to have fault tolerance built into the network components. So, even though the perception of VoIP reliability is still growing, we can actually design VoIP networks that are just as reliable as legacy PBX systems. Notice in Figure 3-1 that there are dual physical connections between all network components.

Figure 3-1   Redundant Devices with Single Points of Failure

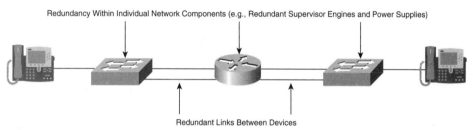

As an example, we might have a Cisco Catalyst 6500 multilayer switch with redundant features built into the chassis itself, including:

- Two supervisor engines (the "brains" of the switch)

- Two power supplies

- Two switch fabric modules (which increase the throughput of the switch)

Not only do these modules help minimize the MTTR, but they are also hot-swappable. For example, if one supervisor engine were to fail, the other supervisor engine could step in and take over that responsibility, and the failed supervisor engine could be removed from the chassis and replaced without powering down the chassis.

Instead of having redundancy built into the router or switch itself, another design approach is to have redundancy between devices, as shown in Figure 3-2. Notice that in this topology, any single network link or network infrastructure device (for example, switch or router) can fail (with the exception of the wiring closet switch where the IP phone attaches); and a path will still exist from the host to the server.

Redundant design approaches such as these benefit not only voice networks but also data networks. In fact, many network redundancy features were available well before the introduction of VoIP. However, the critical nature of voice traffic is causing many network designers to beef up the redundancy in their existing data networks.

Figure 3-2 No Single Points of Failure

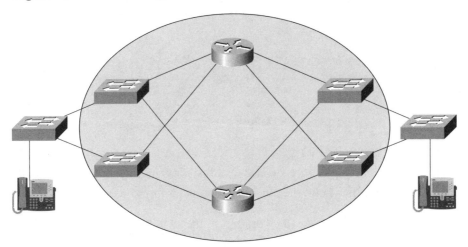

End systems not running a routing protocol point to a default gateway. The default gateway is traditionally the IP address of a router on the local subnet. However, if the default gateway router fails, the end systems are unable to leave their subnet. Two approaches to Layer 3 redundancy include *Hot Standby Router Protocol (HSRP)* and *Virtual Router Redundancy Protocol (VRRP)*. With both of these technologies, the *Media Access Control (MAC) address* and the IP address of the default gateway can be serviced by more than one router. Therefore, if a default gateway router goes down, then another router can take over, still servicing the same MAC and IP addresses:

- HSRP is a Cisco-proprietary approach to Layer 3 redundancy.

- VRRP is a standards-based approach to Layer 3 redundancy.

Layer 3 redundancy is also achieved by having multiple links between devices and selecting a routing protocol that load balances over the links. EtherChannel is another way to load balance across multiple links. With EtherChannel, you can define up to eight physical links that are logically bundled together, such that the bundle appears as a single link to the route processor.

Although having multiple links between switches is great for redundancy, these links can cause loops in the Layer 2 (that is, switching) network. These Layer 2 loops can cause *broadcast storms*, where broadcast packets circle the network forever, consuming bandwidth and switch processor resources. The IEEE 802.1D standard is the legacy approach for Layer 2 loop avoidance. IEEE 802.1D is better known as the *Spanning Tree Protocol (STP)*. By default, in the event of a link failure, STP takes 50 seconds to recover and start forwarding traffic over a backup link (that is, to *converge*). Cisco added proprietary enhancements to speed up the convergence time. These Cisco-proprietary STP enhancements include:

- **PortFast**—Used on ports connecting to end stations

- **UplinkFast**—Used on building access switches

- **BackboneFast**—Used on all switches in the topology

Each *virtual LAN (VLAN)* can run its own instance of STP. This Per-VLAN STP approach allows different VLANs (that is, subnets) to have different *root bridges* (that is, switches in the Layer 2 network that serve as the points to which other switches forward traffic). However, with the Cisco Per-VLAN STP, every VLAN must run its own instance of STP, which might place unnecessary overhead on the switches.

The best of both worlds is achieved with the new IEEE 802.1w and 802.1s protocols. IEEE 802.1w (that is, Rapid Spanning Tree Protocol) dramatically reduces convergence times in the event of a failure. IEEE 802.1s (that is, Multiple Spanning Tree) allows you to create a set of STP instances. Then VLANs might be assigned to appropriate STP instances. This eliminates the Per-VLAN STP requirement that each VLAN run its own instance of STP.

Replacing PBX Trunks: Out with the Old, In with the New

PBX systems often span a company's geographic locations, as shown in Figure 3-3. The connections used to tie the PBXs together are *trunks*, and a company pays monthly recurring charges to its telephone carrier for these trunk connections. However, more than calls are carried over these trunks. PBXs have *signaling protocols* used to communicate call setup information between them. For example, dialed digits and on-hook/off-hook conditions are sent across these trunk connections, too.

Figure 3-3 PBXs Before Convergence

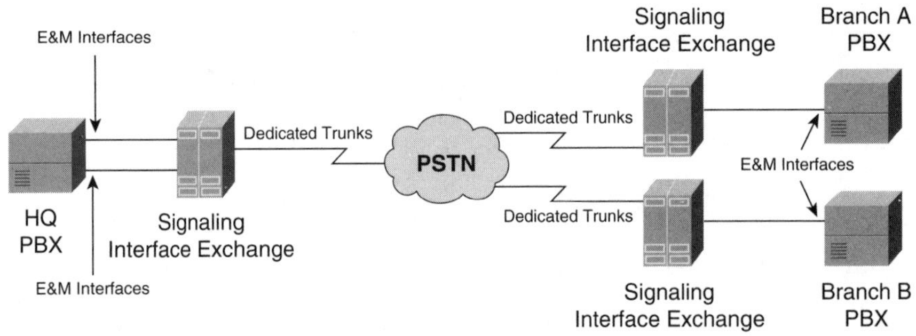

These trunks are likely candidates for replacement as a company begins its migration toward a VoIP network. This initial migration step doesn't necessitate throwing out the PBXs. The PBXs can continue to service the telephony needs of the company. However, the difference, as shown in Figure 3-4, is that the PBXs are interconnected by the IP WAN instead of the trunk lines. By eliminating these trunk lines, the company can eliminate the recurring cost of the dedicated trunk lines.

Figure 3-4   PBXs After Convergence

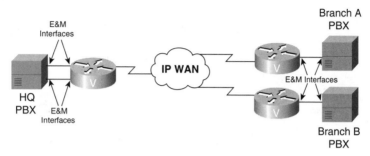

The connection from a PBX to a local router can take one of several approaches. In Figure 3-4, notice that the PBX connects to the router using an *Ear and Mouth (E&M)* connection. An E&M interface is an analog interface present in many of today's PBX systems. Many say that the E stands for Ear, and the M stands for Mouth. Other authorities say that the E stands for Earth, and the M stands for Magneto. You might also read that the E is the E in rEceive, and the M is the M in transMit. Personally, I use the Ear and Mouth definition because it gives me a great visual image of the E lead being used for the receive function, and the M lead being used for the transmit function.

Note that the actual voice path doesn't use the E or M leads (that is, wires). The E&M leads are used for call signaling (that is, setting up and tearing down a call), but an E&M connection still uses *tip and ring* wires to transmit the actual voice. Instead of always having a single tip wire and a single ring wire, in some instances, two wires are used for "tip," and two wires are used for "ring," as shown in Figure 3-5.

Figure 3-5   E&M Connections

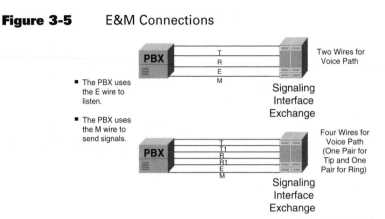

If a company already has an E&M interface in its PBX being used to form a trunk with a remote PBX, we can help preserve the company's original investment in its PBX E&M interface by connecting the PBX's E&M interface to an E&M interface in a router. The router then connects into the IP WAN using a traditional WAN interface, such as a serial interface. We don't have to use an E&M interface, however, to interconnect a PBX and a router. Other analog and digital interfaces are also available, as we'll discuss in the next couple of sections.

Connecting a Router to a Phone Line

As voice travels from a LAN to a PBX or to the *public switched telephone network (PSTN)*, it needs a "translator" to convert back and forth between those two environments. Voice on a LAN-based VoIP network takes the form of packets, whereas voice traveling to the PBX or PSTN might be analog waves or digital signals. The job of this translator can be performed by a voice-enabled router. When a router acts in this capacity, it is called a *gateway*.

A gateway typically has at least one interface that connects to the LAN (for example, an Ethernet or Fast Ethernet interface) and at least one interface that connects to the PBX/PSTN environment. These PBX/PSTN interfaces might be either analog or digital, as shown here:

Analog Interfaces:

- *FXS (Foreign Exchange Station)*

- *FXO (Foreign Exchange Office)*

- E&M

Digital Interfaces:

- T1

- E1

- Basic rate interface (BRI) /primary rate interface (PRI) (which use *Integrated Services Digital Network [ISDN]* technology)

First, let's consider what connects to an FXS port. A FXS port connects to a *station*, such as an analog phone, fax machine, or speaker phone, as shown in Figure 3-6. Consider the analog phone you have in your home. Just as you can connect that analog phone into your RJ-11 wall jack (which goes back to the telephone company), you can also connect that phone into an FXS port. The FXS port can provide the attached device with -48 VDC to power the phone. Ringing voltage can be sent from the FXS port to the device, and the FXS port can recognize digits dialed by the attached device.

Figure 3-6   FXS Connections

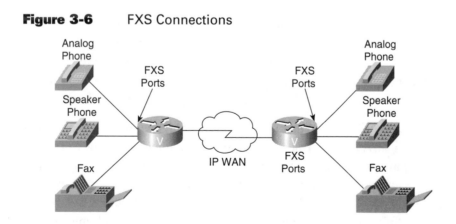

A Cisco router is configured using the Cisco Internetwork Operating System (IOS). Using the IOS, we can configure the characteristics of an FXS port, including the following parameters:

- **Signal type**—An FXS port on a Cisco router defaults to *loop start signaling*. However, for some applications, such as connecting a PBX trunk port into an FXS port, we might prefer to use *ground start signaling*.

- **Call progress tones**—A call progress tone gives the caller an idea of how the call is progressing. For example, if you call your friend, before your friend answers the phone, you hear *ring back* in your ear, indicating that your friend's phone is indeed ringing. If your friend is already on the phone when you call, you might instead hear a *busy signal*. Both ring back and a busy signal are examples of call progress tones. However, these call progress tones might vary from country to country. A Cisco router defaults to call progress tones heard in the United States. However, we can alternately configure the FXS to ports to use call progress tones common to other countries.

- **Ringing pattern**—If you live in the United States, chances are, when your home phone rings, the ringing lasts for two seconds, followed by a four-second pause, followed by two seconds of ringing, and so on. This ring pattern (sometimes called the *ring cadence*) might vary in different countries. Fortunately, the Cisco IOS allows us to configure a predefined ringing pattern to be sent out of an FXS port, or we can define a unique ringing pattern.

  If you are configuring several phones in an office (for example, in a cubicle environment), it might be wise to configure different ringing patterns for different phones. Then, when all of the employees are gathered around the water cooler, and a phone rings, an employee will be able to know that it is his phone ringing due to the distinctive ringing pattern you configured.

- **Ringing frequency**—When I was five years old, my family's home phone was on a *party line*. (No, not one of those 900 number party lines.) The party line allowed more than one home to share the tip and ring wires going back to the *central office (CO)*. As a result, only one home could use its phone at any one time (unless the homes were talking with each other). But the question is, "If we have more than one phone on the same tip and ring circuit, how can we make only one phone (the phone that was called) on that party line ring?" Back in those days, phones belonged to the phone company. We could not just go down to the local Wal-Mart and buy one like we can today. Because the telephone company controlled who got which phone, it could give a phone with one ring frequency to one party line member and a phone with another ring frequency to another party line member. These phones had a mechanical ringer, and these ringers were tuned to only ring at a specific frequency. If any of these phones are still being used in your VoIP environment, you might need to adjust the ringing frequency used by an FXS port to make the phone ring. However, this is not a concern for most modern phones, which use piezoelectric speakers. These ringers sound the same, regardless of the ringing frequency we specify.

- **Caller-ID information**—A popular feature on many home telephones today is *caller-ID*, which allows a called party to see who is calling them. On an FXS port, we can configure the caller-ID information that the router transmits over the VoIP network to the destination phone.

An FXO port connects to an *office* (that is, a phone switch such as a PBX or a switch in the local CO). For example, you could connect a router's FXO port to the RJ-11 wall jack in your home (which goes back to the telephone company). Or, you could connect an FXO port into the station side of a PBX, as shown in Figure 3-7. Therefore, we could say that an FXO port acts like a phone. It can place calls, receive calls, and dial digits (using either *dual tone multifrequency [DTMF]* or pulse dialing).

Figure 3-7   FXO Connections

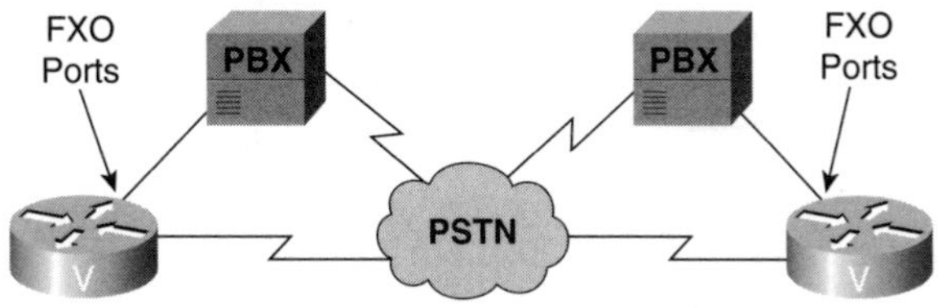

Using the IOS on a Cisco router, we can configure the characteristics of an FXO port including:

- **Signal type**—Just as we can select between loop start and ground start signaling on an FXS port, we can also select the signal type of an FXO port. Like the FXS port, the FXO port defaults to loop start signaling.

- **Ring number**—When I was first learning about VoIP, I connected a router's FXO port to my home telephone line, and set the router up so that a phone connected to an FXS port could call out to the PSTN. What I didn't consider, however, was that an FXO port can answer a call, and, by default, an FXO port answers a call after only one ring. So, when I had that FXO port connected into the phone wall jack in my home, if someone called my home, the FXO port on the router answered. As soon as the router answered, the caller would hear the dial tone, which was understandably confusing for the caller. The reason a caller would hear the dial tone was the FXO's *ring number* (that is, the number of rings received on an FXO port before the port answers the call) was at the default value of one. By default, an FXO port plays the dial tone when it answers a call, allowing the caller to call another number known to the router. However, the FXO port supports other options. For example, an FXO port can be configured to forward a call to a predetermined number after it answers, or the FXO port could look at the dialed digits and forward the incoming call based on those dialed digits.

- **Dial type**—On your home phone, you probably have an option of selecting either pulse dialing or DTMF dialing. Most locations in the United States now have COs that support DTMF dialing. However, in some parts of the world, we might need to use pulse dialing (that is, the type of dialing used by older rotary phones); and we have the option of changing the dial type on our Cisco FXO port from the default of DTMF dialing to pulse dialing.

Connecting a Router to a Digital Circuit

Although analog connections are great for connecting a router to a phone, a PBX, or even to the PSTN, as the need for more connections grows, so does the expense associated with adding more and more interfaces to the router. Digital connections are often a more cost-effective solution when we have more than approximately eight connections, because a single digital connection can carry multiple conversations over a single circuit.

Whereas analog interfaces send and receive analog waveforms that continually vary, digital interfaces send binary 1s and 0s, which are represented on the wire as the presence or absence of voltage. Examples of digital circuits include T1, E1, and ISDN circuits, as shown in Figure 3-8.

Figure 3-8   Digital Connections

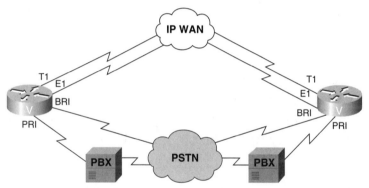

The question is, "How can multiple conversations be sent across a single connection?" Just like we learned to do as children, the multiple conversations share and take turns. Specifically, they share the bandwidth by taking turns sending data on the wire.

Consider a T1 circuit, which has 24 separate channels. With a T1, we can do *time-division multiplexing (TDM)*. With TDM, a T1 circuit can send an 8-bit sample from its first channel, followed by an 8-bit sample from its second channel, followed by an 8-bit sample from its third channel, and so on. Each channel, which means each conversation, gets its own time slice in which it can transmit its voice, represented as binary 1s and 0s. In fact, we could say that with TDM, each voice conversation has, to borrow a line from Whitney Houston, *one moment in time*, as shown in Figure 3-9.

Figure 3-9   Time-Division Multiplexing (TDM)

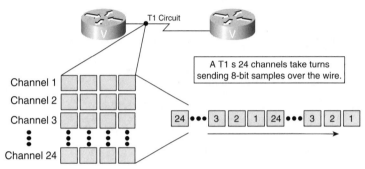

For years I heard that a T1 had 1.544 Mbps of bandwidth, and I knew a T1 had 24 channels, where each channel had 64 kbps of bandwidth. Then, one day I did the math. I multiplied 24 and 64,000, but to my surprise, I did not get 1,544,000 as a result. Instead, the result was 1,536,000. That really confused me. What happened to the extra 8000 bits?

What I did not consider were the *framing bits*. A framing bit is a single bit that indicates the end of the frame, and a frame contains an 8-bit sample from each of a T1's 24 channels. Once I accounted for the framing bit, the math worked out beautifully.

Each frame is 193 bits in size:

24 channels * 8 bits per channel + 1 framing bit = 193 bit frames

The Nyquist Theorem requires that we send 8000 samples per second:

Samples per second = 2 * the highest frequency being sampled

= 2 * 4000

= 8000

The total bandwidth on a T1 is 1.544 Mbps:

193 bit frames * 8000 samples per second = 1.544 Mbps

However, in a T1 environment, we don't typically send just one frame at a time. Instead, we connect multiple frames together and send them all at once. Two popular approaches to grouping these frames together are:

- **SF**—Combines 12 standard 193-bit frames into a *Super Frame*

- **ESF**—Combines 24 standard 193-bit frames into an *ESF*

When configuring a T1 interface (also known as a *T1 controller* on a Cisco router), the T1 interface defaults to SF as the framing type. The good news is that we do not have to be concerned with selecting a particular framing type. Because our T1 connects to a service provider, the service provider tells us what framing type to use, and we simply configure our router to match the service provider's parameters.

Another piece of T1 configuration information given to us by our service provider is the *line coding*. A T1 circuit's line coding is the set of rules that dictates how binary 1s and 0s are represented over the wire.

We normally think of binary 1s being the presence of voltage and binary 0s being the absence of voltage. Although that is true, the goal on a T1 line is to keep the average voltage on the line 0 volts, which means when we send a binary one using a positive voltage, the next binary 1 uses a negative voltage. Therefore, on average, the voltage on the wire is 0. Personally, if I put one hand in a bucket of boiling water and the other hand in a bucket of freezing water, on average, I'm not going to be comfortable, but I concede this approach does work for digital circuits.

If two consecutive voltages have the same polarity, an error, called a *bipolar violation*, occurs. The approach of representing binary 1s as alternating voltages is called *alternate mark inversion (AMI)*, as shown in Figure 3-10.

Figure 3-10   Alternate Mark Inversion (AMI)

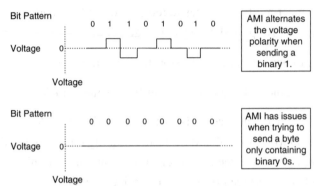

Although AMI does meet the goal of maintaining an average of 0 volts on the circuit, it has a major challenge. AMI has issues when it attempts to send a byte containing all 0s (that is, eight binary 0s in a row). Although there are various workarounds that address this issue, errors can occur when sending eight 0s in a row over a T1 circuit using generic AMI line coding.

Due to AMI's limitation, another type of line coding was developed. *Bipolar 8-zero substitution (B8ZS)* can represent a byte containing all 0s by creating a couple of bipolar violations. If a T1 circuit using B8ZS line coding experiences two bipolar violations at very specific bit positions, as shown in Figure 3-11, the equipment the T1 connects to (for example, a router) knows that a byte containing eight 0s is being transmitted. Therefore, in the case of B8ZS, two wrongs really do make a right. While T1 circuits commonly use B8ZS, you might see something called High Density Binary 3 (HDB3) used on E1 circuits. Like B8ZS, HDB3 overcomes the limitations of AMI.

Figure 3-11   Bipolar 8-Zero Substitution (B8ZS)

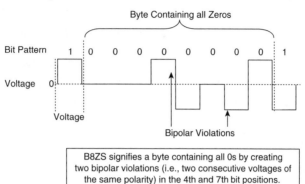

B8ZS signifies a byte containing all 0s by creating two bipolar violations (i.e., two consecutive voltages of the same polarity) in the 4th and 7th bit positions.

Just as an FXS port needs some type of signaling (for example, loop start or ground start) to determine when a phone is on-hook or off-hook, a T1 circuit also needs a signaling mechanism. Two approaches to sending signaling across a T1 circuit include:

- **Common Channel Signaling (CCS)** — With CCS, one or more channels are dedicated to sending a signaling protocol, while each of the other channels carry, for example, a voice conversation.

- **Channel Associated Signaling (CAS)** — With CAS, framing bits are "robbed" from the Super Frame or Extended Super Frame and used for signaling bits. This approach is sometimes referred to as *robbed-bit signaling*. Because none of the 24 channels are dedicated to just sending signaling information, unlike CCS, all 24 channels can be used.

Let us consider each of these approaches in a bit more detail. The simplest approach to understand is CCS. As the name suggests, all of the channels used for sending voice, video, or data use the same channel (that is, a "common channel") to send signaling information. A signaling protocol is sent over this dedicated channel.

A popular technology that leverages CCS is ISDN. An ISDN circuit is made up of *B-channels* and a *D-channel*. A B-channel is a "bearer" channel, which carries the voice, data, or video. These bearer channels typically carry information at a rate of

64 kbps. The D-channel acts as the "signaling" channel, meaning that the D-channel carries the data necessary to set up and tear down calls on the B-channels. Depending on your bandwidth needs, you might select either the BRI or the PRI flavor of ISDN.

- **BRI**—BRI ISDN connections contain two 64-kbps B-channels and one 16 kbps D-channel, for a total usable bandwidth of 128 kbps.

- **PRI**—A PRI ISDN connection can use the channels on either a T1 or an E1 circuit. If the PRI is based on a T1 circuit, 23 of the T1's 24 channels are used as B-channels, and the remaining channel serves as the D-channel, for a total usable bandwidth of 1.472 Mbps. However, if the PRI is based on an E1 circuit, 30 of the E1's 32 channels are used as B-channels. One of the 32 channels carries framing and synchronization information, while the remaining channel acts as the D-channel, carrying the signaling information for the 30 B-channels.

The D-channel in each of these instances uses *Q.931* as its signaling protocol. PRI ISDN connections are often used to connect a company's PBX to the PSTN. However, we might see BRI ISDN used in a small office/home office (SOHO) environment.

ISDN was developed during the 1980s and is, therefore, a very mature protocol. When I was first introduced to ISDN, back in 1988, web browsers were not available yet, and the thought of having 128 kbps of bandwidth in a home seemed to be overkill. In fact, we used to say that the acronym ISDN stood for "I Still Don't Need it."

Next, consider how CAS carries signaling information for a T1. Recall that a T1 doesn't send individual frames. Rather, a T1 sends a Super Frame (containing 12 standard frames) or an Extended Super Frame (containing 24 standard frames). Therefore, an Extended Super Frame contains 24 framing bits, one bit from each standard frame it contains. The Extended Super Frame does not need all 24 of these framing bits. So, some of those bits can be used to send signaling information. Specifically, every sixth bit in a Super Frame or an Extended Super Frame can be used as a signaling bit, as shown in Figure 3-12.

Figure 3-12   "Robbed-Bit" Signaling

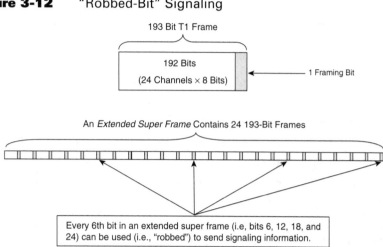

Because the CAS approach takes these unneeded framing bits and uses them for signaling, this approach is often referred to as "robbed-bit signaling." With CAS, all 24 of a T1's channels can be used for voice, data, or video because none of the channels are dedicated solely to signaling.

Just as T1 circuits are popular in North America, E1 circuits are commonplace in Europe. An E1 circuit has 32 channels, as opposed to the 24 channels available in a T1. The first of those 32 channels is dedicated to framing and synchronization, while the seventeenth channel is dedicated to signaling. Coming off our discussion of how a T1 can free up its signaling channel using CAS, it might be tempting to think we could do the same with an E1 circuit, giving us 31 usable channels to send our voice, video, and data. However, an E1 circuit approaches CAS very differently than a T1.

On a standard E1 circuit, the seventeenth channel is always used for signaling, regardless of whether we are doing CAS or CCS. The good news at this point is that you don't have to relearn how CCS is performed, because like a T1, a signaling protocol (for example, Q.931) is sent over an E1's signaling channel.

We should spend some time, however, delving into how an E1 CAS functions. To begin with, you need to understand that an E1 doesn't use the Super Frames or Extended Super Frames you saw in the T1 world. Rather, an E1 combines 16 frames together in a *multiframe*. If we examine the first frame in a multiframe and look at its seventeenth channel, we discover that the seventeenth channel indicates the beginning of this multiframe. But then if we take a close look at the second frame in a multiframe, we see that its seventeenth channel is used to send signaling information. Specifically, 4 bits of signaling information for channel number 2 and 4 bits of signaling information for channel number 18 are carried in the seventeenth channel of the second frame in an E1 multiframe. Similarly, the seventeenth channel of the third frame in a multiframe carries 4 bits of signaling information for channel 3 and 4 bits of signaling information for channel 19, as shown in Figure 3-13. This process continues for each of the remaining frames in the multiframe, such that the multiframe sends signaling information for 30 channels, which is exactly the number of channels we use in an E1 to send voice, video, and data.

Figure 3-13   E1 Multiframe

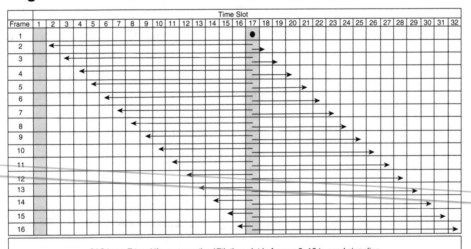

CAS in an E1 multiframe uses the 17th time slot in frames 2–16 to send signaling information for two time slots at a time. The 17th time slot in the first frame indicates the beginning of a multiframe. The first time slot is used for framing and synchronization. The arrows indicate which timeslot's signaling information is being transmitted in the 17th timeslot, for frames 2–16.

Thus far in this chapter, we examined how an IP WAN can replace a PBX-to-PBX trunk connection and how our Cisco router can connect to various analog and digital ports. Let's put all the pieces together by considering a sample VoIP migration scenario.

In this scenario, our company currently has a main office in Austin, TX and two branch offices, in San Jose, CA and Knoxville, TN. The Austin location has a PBX system, and each branch office has a key system. The key systems each have a dedicated T1 trunk connection back to the PBX in Austin. To support the Austin office's relatively high call volume, an ISDN PRI connection connects the Austin PBX to the local telephone company's CO. The branch offices each have four Plain Old Telephone Service (POTS) telephone lines connecting to their local COs to support local calls, as show in Figure 3-14.

Figure 3-14   Scenario Topology – Before Migration

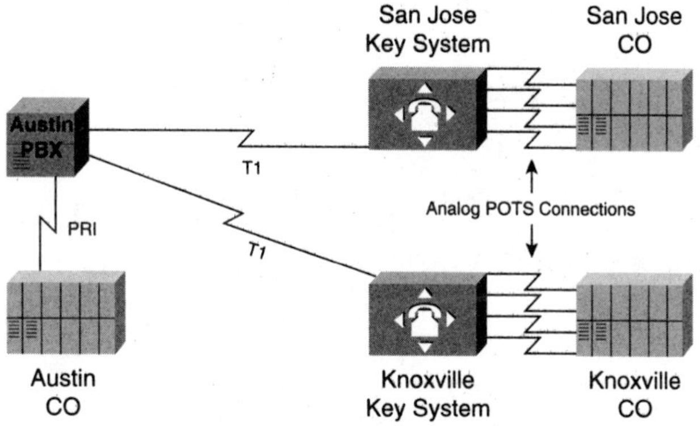

Our goal in this scenario is to replace the key system-to-PBX trunk connections with VoIP connections and, in preparation for removing the PBX, to have the Austin, San Jose, and Knoxville CO connections terminate on a router, as opposed to a PBX or a key system.

As a first step, we can replace the existing trunk connections from the branch offices to the main office with VoIP connections over the IP WAN. Because the PBX and key systems already have T1 interfaces, we can leverage the company's existing investment in these interfaces and purchase T1 interfaces for our Cisco routers. The PBX at the main office (that is, the Austin office) can then connect to a router located at the Austin location via a T1 connection. Similarly, the key systems at the San Jose and Knoxville locations can connect to local routers using T1 connections. The routers at these locations all connect into a service provider's IP WAN. For this scenario, assume the routers connect into a Frame Relay network using a hub-and-spoke topology, where each of the branch offices has a Frame Relay *permanent virtual circuit (PVC)* connecting back to the main office, as shown in Figure 3-15.

Figure 3-15   Scenario Topology – Migration Step 1

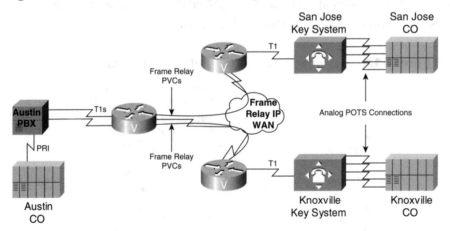

Our VoIP migration already eliminated the recurring cost of the dedicated PBX-to-key system trunk connections. However, another requirement was to take the CO connections at each location and terminate those connections on a router. At the main site, the PBX currently connects to the local CO using an ISDN PRI circuit. Therefore, we can install a T1 interface in our Cisco router, and configure that interface to function as an ISDN PRI interface. Then we can move the PRI connection from the PBX to the router. In a similar fashion, we can move the existing POTS telephone lines from the key systems at the branch office locations and terminate those lines on FXO ports in the local routers, as shown in Figure 3-16.

Figure 3-16   Scenario Topology – Migration Step 2

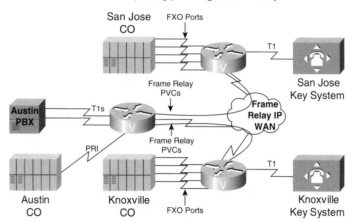

Even though this scenario did not involve converting any of the company's phones to IP phones or connecting any phones directly to a router, we did eliminate recurring costs for trunk lines and simultaneously laid the foundation for an IP telephony network that can, in the future, replace the PBX at the headquarters with a Cisco CallManager cluster; and replace the key systems at the branch offices with, perhaps, a *CallManager Express (CME)* router. Also, this future IP telephony network can replace existing analog and digital phones, currently connecting to the PBX and key systems, with IP phones.

note

The Cisco CallManager cluster and the Cisco CME router mentioned in this section are discussed in the next chapter.

At this point, we have seen how voice ports are used on our voice-enabled routers. However, the routers are not yet trained to reach specific destinations. In order to give our routers call routing intelligence, we create *dial peers* that inform our routers how to reach specific phone numbers. Consider the topology in Figure 3-17.

Figure 3-17   Dial Peers and Call Legs

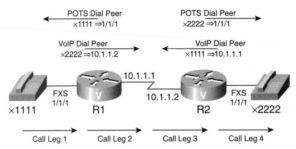

Routers R1 and R2 each have a POTS dial peer that points to their locally attached phone, and a VoIP dial peer that points to the IP address of the remote router.

Therefore, when extension 1111 dials extension 2222, router R1 searches for a dial peer that matches a destination pattern of 2222. In this case, R1 has a VoIP dial peer that points to R2's IP address of 1.1.1.2. R1 then forwards the call to R2. R2 then receives the incoming call destined for extension 2222. R2 searches for a dial peer that matches a destination of 2222, and it finds a POTS dial peer that specifies FXS port 1/1/1. The FXS port then sends ringing voltage out port 1/1/1. Extension 2222 rings and goes off-hook, and the end-to-end connection is complete.

Notice that there are a total of four dial peers, which allow a call in the opposite direction. Also, notice that four stages of the call (that is, *call legs*) are defined—two call legs from the perspective of each router:

- Call Leg 1: The call comes into R1 on FXS port 1/1/1

- Call Leg 2: The call is sent from R1 to IP address 1.1.1.2

- Call Leg 3: R2 receives an incoming call destined for x2222

- Call Leg 4: R2 forwards the call out FXS port 1/1/1

Voice over IP in the Home

Now that we have examined how we can begin to migrate our corporate telephony systems to VoIP, let's bring the conversation home, literally. After all, many homes today have broadband connections, such as digital subscriber line (DSL) or cable modem connections, and many service providers are beginning to offer telephone service over these broadband connections.

You can purchase a small router for your home that has one or more analog telephone jacks and sign up for VoIP service with a carrier, such as *Vonage* (http://www.vonage.com). Cisco makes a router that can be used with the Vonage service. This router also has an Ethernet connection, allowing you to connect it into your existing home network, or directly into your DSL router or cable modem, as shown in Figure 3-18. When you pick up your phone to place a call, the router supplies your phone with dial tone, and it can interpret the phone's dialed digits.

Figure 3-18   VoIP in the Home

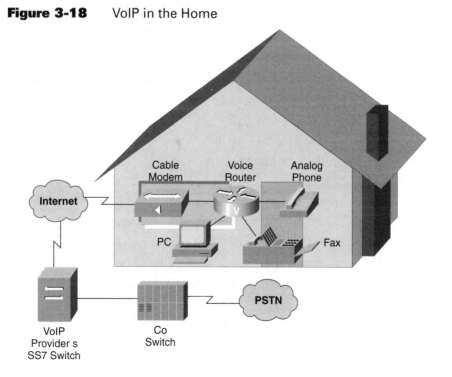

The router in your home forwards the dialed digits over the Internet to the carrier's equipment located in a telephone company's CO. Often times, the carrier leases space for its equipment in the CO. This type of leasing arrangement is called a *co-lo* (that is, "co-location"). The carrier's equipment in the CO connects into the traditional telephone company's network, using *Signaling System 7 (SS7)* as a signaling protocol.

Once an end-to-end call is set up, the router in your home converts your voice (that is, analog waveforms) into packets. These packets are transmitted over the Internet to the carrier's equipment in the CO, which sends your voice into the PSTN.

You can, in some cases, keep your current phone number if you convert your existing telephone service to a VoIP-based telephone service. However, because these services are not installed in every local CO, if your home is in a more rural location, the nearest CO you can connect to over the Internet might be in another city, which might mean that you cannot keep your existing phone number. Your friends and family might also need to pay a long-distance charge to reach your new number in the other city. These are just a couple of caveats to watch out for when subscribing to one of these residential VoIP services.

Another critical consideration when signing up for VoIP in your home is 911 emergency service. Please check with your VoIP carrier for the specifics of how its 911 service functions. You might, for example, need to activate 911 service for your line, and you might need to specify the physical location associated with your VoIP phone. Not all residential VoIP services offer Enhanced 911 (E-911), which can automatically send the caller's location to the 911 operator. Therefore, a caller might need to clearly state his location to the 911 operator. Because 911 service can literally mean life or death, and because 911 services with VoIP carriers vary, be sure you understand the specifics of how 911 services are provided by any VoIP carrier that you consider signing up with. Also, if communication between your home phone and the PSTN flows through a VoIP router, consider what would happen if you experienced a power outage. Without some sort of power backup, you would not be able to place any calls, because your VoIP router (and any other broadband router/switch equipment) would be unpowered.

Case Study: Your Turn to Put the Pieces of the Puzzle Together

You designed a telephony network for the XYZ Company in the case study in Chapter 1, "Touring the History Museum of Telephony." This design was based on traditional PBX and key system technologies. Then, in Chapter 2, "Making Waves: Turning Your Voice into Zeros and Ones," you calculated the bandwidth required to interconnect the XYZ Company's headquarters with two of its remote offices.

Based on your previous recommendations, the XYZ Company has decided to interconnect its PBXs and key system over the IP WAN, as opposed to using the T1 and fractional T1 connections specified in Chapter 1's case study. Therefore, your goal in this case study is to create a design that places a router at each XYZ Company location and to specify the router interfaces used to connect remote routers. Also, each XYZ Company location needs connections to its local CO as follows:

- Headquarters—48 connections to local CO

- Remote Office 1—24 connections to local CO

- Remote Office 2—5 connections to local CO

In addition to the required voice bandwidth you calculated in Chapter 2's case study, the links in this converged network solution also need to transport data. The data bandwidth requirements are as follows:

- Link from HQ to Remote Office 1: 768 kbps for data

- Link from HQ to Remote Office 2: 128 kbps for data

Demonstrate in your design how the router at each XYZ Company location connects into its local CO. This VoIP design lays the foundation for eventually replacing the PBXs and key system units with IP telephony components such as the Cisco CallManager, as discussed in the next chapter.

Use the following area to sketch your design.

Design for XYZ Company:

Suggested Solution

Although multiple solutions exist for the design scenario presented, the following is a suggested solution that meets the design criteria. The router located at the XYZ Company HQ needs WAN connectivity with each remote office. Based on the bandwidth requirements calculated in Chapter 2's case study, we have the following voice bandwidth requirements for each of these WAN links:

- Link from HQ to Remote Office 1: 2026.08 kbps for voice

- Link from HQ to Remote Office 2: 337.68 kbps for voice

In addition to voice, these intersite links need to carry data. The data requirements specified in the case study were:

- Link from HQ to Remote Office 1: 768 kbps for data

- Link from HQ to Remote Office 2: 128 kbps for data

To accommodate both voice and data, we sum the required bandwidth (that is, the voice bandwidth plus the data bandwidth) for these links to calculate each link's total required bandwidth:

- Link from HQ to Remote Office 1: 2794.08 kbps total

- Link from HQ to Remote Office 2: 465.68 kbps total

Although we could select from various WAN technologies to interconnect these sites (for example, Frame Relay, Point-to-Point Protocol [PPP], or Asynchronous Transfer Mode [ATM]), this suggested solution uses PPP links. The headquarters connects to Remote Office 1 using two T1s. Two T1s actually provide more bandwidth than the required 2.794 Mbps. However, these two T1s allow room for future growth. In this design, the two T1s are combined into a single logical link, using *Multilink PPP (MLPPP)*.

The headquarters connects to Remote Office 2 using a fractional T1, running at 512 kbps. Again, the allocated bandwidth is a little more than the required 465.68 kbps, thus allowing for future growth.

The routers at each site should also connect to their local CO. As a best practice, once we exceed eight connections, we should choose digital interfaces instead of analog interfaces, due to cost considerations. Therefore, this suggested design selected the following CO connections for the XYZ Company routers:

- Headquarters Router: Two T1 connections

- Remote Office 1 Router: One T1 connection

- Remote Office 2 Router: Five FXO connections

These suggested design solutions result in the design shown in Figure 3-19.

Figure 3-19   XYZ Company's Suggested Solution

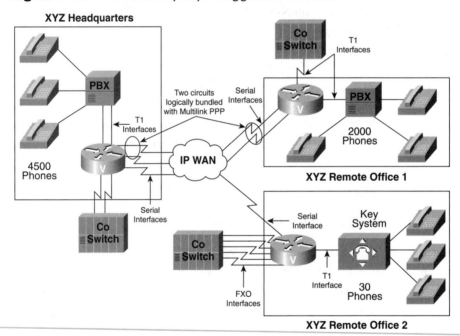

Chapter Summary

This chapter presented a major design challenge for VoIP: achieving high availability. Specifically, our VoIP availability design goal is the "five nines," 99.999 percent of availability, which equates to approximately five minutes of downtime per year.

Most companies perform a phased migration to VoIP, as opposed to a *forklift upgrade.* Interconnecting existing PBX/key system units over the IP WAN is often the first step in a phased migration, and it offers *toll bypass* cost savings.

We then considered various analog and digital interfaces available for our routers and what could connect to those interfaces. Analog phones, for example, can connect to FXS interfaces. The telephone wall jack in our home can connect to an FXO interface. Also, PBXs in our company might connect to remote PBXs using E&M interfaces. We can leverage our company's existing investment in those interfaces by connecting the PBX's E&M interfaces to E&M interfaces on our routers.

Whereas FXS, FXO, and E&M are examples of analog interfaces, digital interfaces include T1, E1, and ISDN. Recall that a T1 circuit has 24 channels, and we can use all 24 channels to send voice traffic if we use CAS, which is sometimes called "robbed-bit" signaling. However, the CCS option uses one of the 24 channels just for signaling.

An E1 interface has 32 channels. However, we only use 30 of those channels for voice. The first channel is used for framing and synchronization. The seventeenth channel is used for signaling, and it's interesting that the seventeenth channel is used for signaling in both the CAS and CCS modes.

ISDN comes in two flavors, BRI and PRI. The BRI flavor (which includes two 64-kbps B-channels) might be appropriate for a SOHO environment, whereas PRI (which includes 23 64-kbps B-channels on a T1-based PRI interface) would be more appropriate for a larger environment.

This chapter included an overview of VoIP in the home. Several service providers have equipment in telephone COs scattered across the country. If we have a broadband (for example, DSL or cable modem) connection in our home along with a router that allows us to connect phones, our phones can connect to the service provider's equipment over the Internet (that is, over our broadband connection) and from there connect to the PSTN. VoIP in the home has the potential to offer comparable features to our existing phone service. However, because VoIP in the home is an emerging technology, subscribers should understand exactly how their service provider handles 911 calls.

Chapter Review Questions

1. Approximately how many minutes of downtime per year does a network experience if it has the "five nines" of availability?

   a. 53 minutes

   b. 46 minutes

   c. 16 minutes

   d. 5 minutes

2. Which of the following offer Layer 3 redundancy in a network? (Select the two best answers.)

   a. 802.1w

   b. VRRP

   c. HSRP

   d. RSTP

3. An analog phone can connect to which of the following router interfaces?

   a. BRI

   b. FXO

   c. E&M

   d. FXS

4. The wall jack in your home, where you plug in your analog telephone, can connect to which of the following router interfaces?

   a. BRI

   b. FXO

   c. E&M

   d. FXS

5. Identify two valid framing types for a T1 circuit.

   a. AMI

   b. SF

   c. B8ZS

   d. ESF

6. Select the type of line coding that replaces a byte containing eight zeros with two bipolar violations.

  a. AMI

  b. SF

  c. B8ZS

  d. ESF

7. How many channels does a T1 circuit have?

  a. 16

  b. 24

  c. 30

  d. 32

8. What channel on an ISDN circuit carries signaling information?

  a. A

  b. B

  c. C

  d. D

9. Which of the following parameters are configurable on an FXS interface? (Select the two best answers.)

  a. Signal type

  b. Ring number

  c. Ring frequency

  d. Dial type

10. An ISDN BRI circuit has how much usable bandwidth (that is, not including the D channel)?

  a. 56 kbps

  b. 64 kbps

  c. 128 kbps

  d. 256 kbps

What You Will Learn

After reading this chapter, you should be able to

- ✔ Explain how Cisco CallManager can replace existing PBX functions.

- ✔ Describe options for grouping Cisco CallManagers together in "clusters."

- ✔ List various features available on Cisco IP Phones.

- ✔ Identify features to secure an IP telephony network.

- ✔ Describe how Cisco CallManager supports video calls.

- ✔ Explain how Cisco CallManager secures voice transmissions.

- ✔ Discuss how Cisco CallManager Express and Cisco Unity Express provide call processing, voice mail, and auto attendant features for smaller environments.

CHAPTER 4

Meet the "Brain" of the Voice over IP Network

Do you remember the scene from *2001: A Space Odyssey* where Dave Bowman is attempting to deactivate the HAL 9000 computer? A very concerned HAL says, "Just what do you think you're doing Dave?" If our *private branch exchanges (PBXs)* could speak, I imagine they might say something similar when we begin unpacking our *Cisco CallManager (CCM)* servers, because Cisco CallManager serves as a PBX replacement in an IP telephony environment.

This chapter explores CallManager's role in the *Voice over IP (VoIP)* network and how groups of CallManager servers work together. You then get to apply this knowledge in a design scenario. We also discuss CallManager features. For example, perhaps we don't want users sitting in the lobby to be able to place long-distance calls. CallManager's *partitions* and *calling search spaces* allow us to dictate which IP phones can call which phone numbers. New CallManager features include video and security, allowing us to see the person we're talking with and transmit our voice packets securely protected from would-be eavesdroppers.

Cisco IP Phones offer a variety of styles and features, and this chapter helps you become a better comparison shopper of these phones. Cisco CallManager also comes in an *Express* version, which runs on a Cisco router, as opposed to a server. This chapter explains how not only CallManager features but also voice mail features and auto attendant features are optionally serviced from a router.

Replacing Your Old Phone Switch with Cisco CallManager

CCM is a software component running on Cisco-approved server platforms. The CCM makes call-forwarding decisions, controls IP phones, and can support other optional features (for example, conference calling and call transfer). You can think of the CCM as the "brains" of your IP telephony network.

Consider the following scenario. A Cisco IP Phone goes off-hook. The IP phone tells the CCM server that the handset is off-hook using *Skinny Client Control Protocol (SCCP)*. The CCM server, seeing this off-hook condition, instructs the IP phone to play dial tone. The caller dials digits on the IP phone, and SCCP sends these dialed digits to the CCM server.

The CCM server contains a *dial plan*, a set of instructions for reaching various phone numbers. After the CCM examines the dialed digits and determines which dial plan entry to use, the CCM server signals the destination IP phone that the phone is receiving a call. After the destination phone goes off-hook, a *Real-Time Transport Protocol (RTP)* stream is set up directly between the IP phones, as shown in Figure 4-1.

Figure 4-1   Call Setup

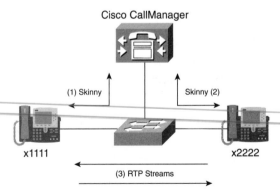

Administrators configure the CCM server through the *Cisco CallManager Administration* web interface. If you know the IP address or domain name of a CCM server, you can access the CCM administration interface at the following URL:

http://*server_IP_or_name*/ccmadmin

note
In CallManager 4.1 and later, https is used instead of http, thus providing a more secure connection.

The various menu options under the administration interface, as shown in Figure 4-2, make configuration intuitive for an administrator. You can even create different administrator accounts, each with a different subset of permissions. For example, you might want help desk personnel to view but not modify IP phone settings, while other personnel might need add/delete/edit permissions.

Figure 4-2   Cisco CallManager Administration Interface

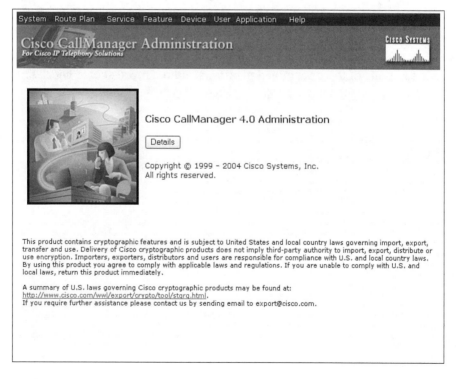

Cisco CallManager is software. Therefore, it needs to run on a server. Specifically, version 4.x (and also version 3.x) of the CCM software runs on a Windows 2000 server. CCM also needs to maintain a database. This database stores information about the CallManager system, such as IP phone configuration and call routing information. Instead of trying to create its own proprietary database, Cisco decided to use a well-established database application, Microsoft's SQL 2000.

Aside from the SQL 2000 database, CCM also leverages a directory containing user information. An attendant can, for example, query this directory to find the phone number associated with a specific user. Cisco includes the *Data Connection (DC) Directory* with the CCM software. However, if your network already has users entered in Microsoft's *Active Directory (AD)* or iPlanet (Netscape Directory), the CCM software can leverage either of those directories.

For disaster recovery, we also need some sort of backup application to maintain archival backups of the data contained in the CCM servers. The Cisco *Backup and Restore System (BARS)* offers one option.

Although the CCM 4.x software runs on a Windows 2000 server, Cisco limits the server platform that can run the CCM software. Supported servers are called *Media Convergence Servers (MCS)*. Although many of these approved servers are Cisco branded, the hardware is often manufactured by IBM or HP. Table 4-1 provides a sampling of these supported platforms, although you should check the Cisco website for the latest specifications before you make a purchase.

note
You do not have to purchase Cisco MCS servers. You can alternately purchase IBM or HP servers if they meet the specifications provided at http://www.cisco.com/go/swonly.

Table 4-1   Media Convergence Servers

Server Model	RAM	Hard Drive(s)	Number of IP Phones Supported	Redundant Power
Cisco 7815I	512 MB	One 40 GB ATA	Up to 300	No
Cisco 7825H	1 GB	One 40 GB SATA	Up to 1000	No
Cisco 7825I	1 GB	One 80 GB SATA	Up to 1000	No
Cisco 7835H	2 GB	Two 36 GB SCSI	Up to 2500	Yes
Cisco 7835I	2 GB	Two 36 GB SCSI	Up to 2500	Yes
Cisco 7845H	4 GB	Four 72 GB SCSI	Up to 7500	Yes

To achieve a PBX environment's level of availability, you can take multiple CCM servers and logically group them together. These groupings of CCMs are called *clusters*. All CCM servers in a cluster need the same database information, because at any time one server might be called upon to back up another server. To keep the servers' databases in sync (if you'll pardon the boy band reference), Microsoft's SQL 2000 designates a single server in the cluster as the *publisher*. New database information can only be written to the publisher. The publisher server then sends updates to *subscriber* servers. These subscriber servers have a *read-only* copy of the database.

The process of copying database information from the publisher server to subscriber servers is called *replication*. Database replication includes such information as registration and logging data.

When you make a configuration change, the change is written to the publisher. You can still access the CCM web interface even if the publisher is down. However, you cannot write any changes to the database. When a publisher is again available, it immediately sends configuration changes out to the subscribers. Even though the subscribers only have a read-only copy of the database, there is one instance when we can write information to a subscriber. Specifically, if the publisher is unavailable, *call detail records* (*CDRs*) can be stored temporarily on a subscriber. These CDRs are replicated to the publisher when the publisher comes back online.

The CCMs in a cluster also communicate *run-time* data directly to each other, using a "logical" full-mesh topology. This run-time data includes such information as details of the calls in progress, gateway and IP phone registration, and information about digital signal processor (DSP) resources.

As an example of run-time data, consider an IP phone registering with a CCM. The CCM lets all other CCMs in the cluster know about the registration. Then, the IP phone sends a *keepalive* message to its "primary" CCM, which it registered with, every 30 seconds. For redundancy, the IP phone also sends a *TCP connect* message to a backup CCM, so that the IP phone can failover to the backup CCM. The IP phone can also be configured with a third (that is, *tertiary*) CCM to which it can fallback if both the primary and backup CCMs fail.

There Is Power in Numbers: Grouping Cisco CallManagers Together

When you create a cluster of CCM servers, part of the design process involves identifying the roles played by the various CCMs. For example, because the publisher plays such a vital role, you probably do not want IP phones registering with the publisher. Also, the IP phones' configuration files are stored on a Trivial File Transfer Protocol (TFTP) server, and you might wish to use the publisher for that function. Finally, you might wish to designate which CCMs are going to be *backup CCMs* for *primary CCMs*.

You also need to select your redundancy design approach, either *1:1 redundancy* or *2:1 redundancy*. With 1:1 redundancy, you designate a dedicated backup CCM server for each primary CCM server, to take over in the event of a primary CCM server failure. When you look at the bottom line, however, you might realize that a 1:1 redundancy approach can be cost prohibitive, due to the purchase of so many backup CCM servers.

To reduce costs, you might opt for a 2:1 redundancy model, where one CCM server acts as a backup for two primary CCM servers. Although a 2:1 redundancy model does offer cost savings, you sacrifice an extra layer of redundancy, as shown in Figure 4-3. Specifically, consider a scenario where CCM Server A serves as a backup to both CCM Server B and CCM Server C. Also assume that each CCM server supports 2500 IP phones. If CCM Server B failed, no big deal. The 2500 IP phones registered with CCM Server B simply reregister with CCM Server A (that is, the backup CCM server). The issue we might face, however, is in the unlikely event that both CCM Server B and C simultaneously fail. In that instance, a total of 5000 IP phones try to reregister with CCM Server A, which only supports 2500 IP phones. This potential oversubscription scenario reduces the overall fault tolerance of the 2:1 redundancy model.

Figure 4-3   Redundancy Design Options

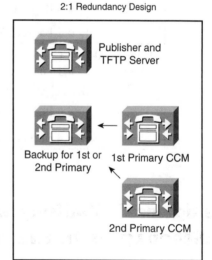

Table 4-2 indicates the number of CCM servers Cisco recommends to support a specific number of IP phones (with an MCS platform supporting 2500 IP phones per server).

Table 4-2   Redundancy Models

IP Phones	1:1 Redundancy	2:1 Redundancy
Up to 2500	3 CCM Servers ■ 1 Publisher and TFTP server (for 1o00 or more IP phones) ■ 1 Primary CCM ■ 1 Backup CCM	3 CCM Servers ■ 1 Publisher and TFTP server (for 1000 or more IP phones) ■ 1 Primary CCM ■ 1 Backup CCM
Up to 5000	5 CCM Servers ■ 1 Publisher and TFTP server ■ 2 Primary CCMs ■ 2 Backup CCMs	4 CCM Servers ■ 1 Publisher and TFTP server ■ 2 Primary CCMs ■ 1 Backup CCM
Up to 10000	9 CCM Servers ■ 1 Publisher and TFTP server ■ 4 Primary CCMs ■ 4 Backup CCMs	7 CCM Servers ■ 1 Publisher and TFTP server ■ 4 Primary CCMs ■ 2 Backup CCMs

Designers' Challenge: Placing Cisco CallManagers in the Network

Some companies might only need CCM servers at one location, while other companies might have IP phones at multiple geographic locations. A major CCM design decision revolves around how to deploy CCM servers across the company's locations. Based on a company's design requirements, you can select from one of four possible design models:

- **Single-Site**—IP phones and CCMs located at a single site

- **Centralized Call Processing**—IP phones at multiple sites and all CCMs at a single site

- **Distributed Call Processing**—IP phones and CCMs at multiple sites

- **Clustering over the WAN**—IP phones and CCMs at multiple sites, with all CCMs logically assigned to the same cluster

The sections that follow review each model in a bit more detail.

Single-Site Model

An IP telephony deployment at a single location (for example, a college campus or a company headquarters), as shown in Figure 4-4, uses the high-speed LAN at that location. The *public switched telephone network (PSTN)* is used for all calls to the outside world. Therefore, voice bandwidth usage is not a major design consideration, and the G.711 is typically the *coder decoder (CODEC)* of choice.

Figure 4-4   Single-Site Model

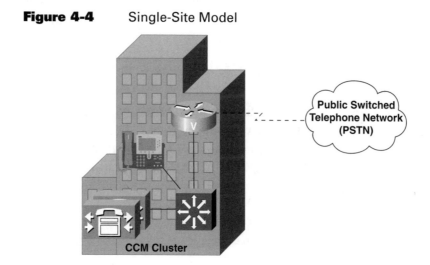

Hopefully, the single site's existing data network already uses a high availability design, with redundant links between switches and routers. Because all IP telephony components connect to that existing data network, these added IP telephony components also enjoy high availability.

Because a single-site deployment typically consists of a single cluster, all IP phones register with this same cluster. Therefore, the dial plan is simplified.

Centralized Call Processing Model

Sometimes, companies wish to extend their IP telephony network beyond the headquarters, reaching out to remote offices. However, often times the relatively small size of these remote offices does not justify the purchase of CallManager servers. A centralized call processing model, as shown in Figure 4-5, allows IP phones located at the remote sites to register with a CallManager cluster located at a central site (that is, at the headquarters). The central site not only houses the CallManager cluster but also contains DSPs that the remote IP phones use for features including conferencing and transcoding (that is, converting back and forth between different CODECs). A centralized deployment model typically uses the G.729 CODEC, which only requires 8 kbps of bandwidth for the voice payload, over the IP WAN for bandwidth conservation.

Maintenance at the remote sites is minimized because no CallManager servers reside at these sites. However, consider what might happen if the IP WAN became inaccessible. Because the IP phones at the remotes sites rely on the CCM cluster located at the headquarters, if the IP WAN goes down, those IP phones lose connectivity with their CallManager. To accommodate for such an IP WAN failure, we can use the Cisco *Survivable Remote Site Telephony* (*SRST*) feature at these remote sites, as shown in Figure 4-6.

Figure 4-5   Centralized Call Processing Model

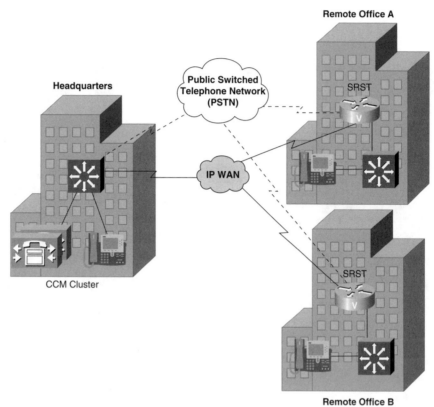

Figure 4-6   Survivable Remote Site Telephony (SRST)

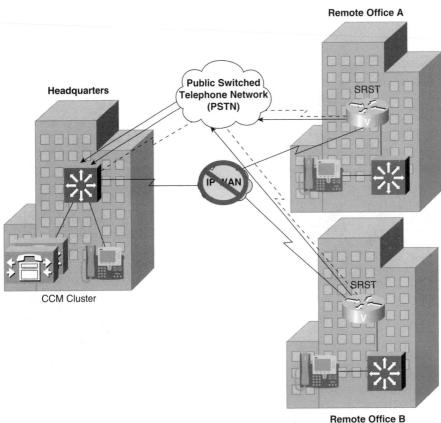

SRST allows a Cisco IOS router to step in and take over call processing tasks for IP phones at the remote sites in the event of a WAN failure. Even though an SRST router doesn't provide all the bells and whistles available on a CCM server, an SRST router does support basic functions and allows IP phones at the remote site to not only call each other but also call out to the PSTN. The number of IP phones supported by an SRST router varies based on the router platform, but as an example, a Cisco 7200 Series router supports up to 480 IP phones.

Centralized deployments, however, suffer from low scalability when remote sites have more than 1000 users. As a company adds more and more remote offices, the added IP phones place an increased burden on the centralized CCM cluster. The remote IP phones' call setup traffic also uses precious IP WAN bandwidth. Therefore, for larger deployments, designers might opt for a distributed deployment design.

Distributed Call Processing Model

Companies with multiple remote locations, or even a few large remote locations, might select a distributed call processing model, as shown in Figure 4-7, as opposed to a centralized call processing model. Distributed deployments place CCM clusters at all remote locations.

Figure 4-7   Distributed Call Processing Model

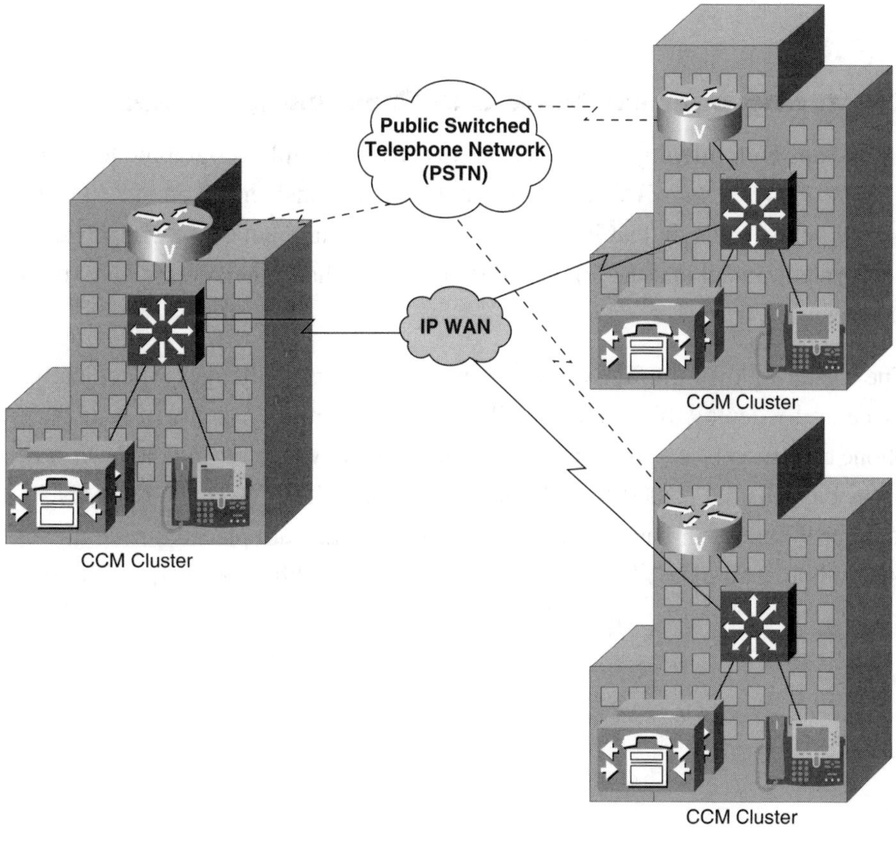

Because each remote location contains its own CCM cluster, remote sites are minimally impacted by IP WAN outages. The potential exists, however, for the IP WAN's bandwidth to become saturated with too many voice calls. Therefore, a distributed deployment model often uses a *gatekeeper* to keep track of the number of calls being placed between sites. As the IP WAN bandwidth usage approaches capacity, a gatekeeper can deny additional call attempts. Think of a gatekeeper as a traffic cop with a GO/STOP sign in hand, letting calls know whether or not they are allowed to cross the IP WAN.

A distributed deployment model can scale to multiple sites (that is, over 100 sites). However, additional expense is incurred, as compared to the centralized deployment model, due to the extra hardware and maintenance required for the remote sites. However, for large enterprise-wide IP telephony deployments, the distributed deployment model is usually the design of choice.

Clustering over the WAN Call Processing Model

A final option for deploying CCM servers across multiple geographic locations is a *clustering over the WAN* model. Some designers consider this model to be the best of both worlds, in that it offers the simplified dial plan of the centralized deployment model and the high availability of the distributed deployment model, as shown in Figure 4-8.

The clustering over the WAN model is not without its challenges. Specifically, to successfully deploy this model, you'll need bandwidth and plenty of it. If 10,000 phone calls are placed on the company's telephony system during the busiest hour of the day (that is, 10,000 *Busy Hour Call Attempts* [*BHCAs*]), the IP WAN requires 900 kbps of bandwidth. If 20,000 phone calls are placed during the busiest hour of the day, 1.8 Mbps of IP WAN bandwidth is needed, and so on.

Figure 4-8   Clustering over the WAN Model

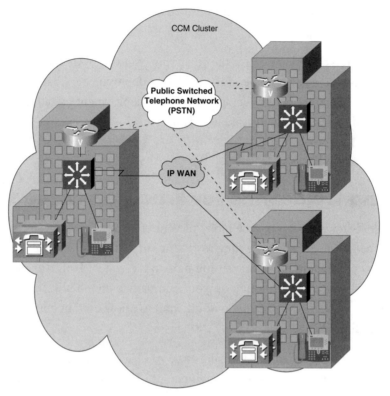

Besides plenty of bandwidth, the delay between the sites needs to be very low. At a maximum, a packet should travel from one site across the IP WAN and back again in 40 milliseconds (ms). Just for fun, you can try a PING from your computer while connected to the Internet to see what sort of *round trip delay* you're experiencing. On a Windows platform, click on the **START** button. Then click **RUN**. In the OPEN dialog box, type **ping www.ciscopress.com**, and press **ENTER**. Notice the round trip delay in the time = field. On my home computer, connected to the Internet via digital subscriber line (DSL), I get a round trip delay of about 82 ms, not even close to the clustering over the WAN requirement of 40 ms.

With the advent of *metropolitan-area networks (MANs)*, which use high-speed fiber optics to interconnect locations scattered across large cities, clustering over the WAN is gaining popularity.

As a final design consideration for the clustering over the WAN model, only four sites can belong to a cluster. Therefore, for larger deployments (that is, more than four sites), designers should select the distributed deployment model, even over a WAN with plenty of bandwidth and low delay.

Setting Guidelines for Who Can Make Calls

Imagine a visitor walking into the lobby of your company. The visitor checks in with the receptionist, and while they're waiting in the lobby, they decide to make a few calls using the phone sitting next to the couch. Unfortunately, they make long-distance calls, running up your company's phone bill. In addition to avoiding this situation, perhaps you don't want to allow certain employees to make long-distance calls.

PBXs restrict such unwanted calls using *class of service* settings. For example, when I worked at a university, we configured our PBX extensions with four different classes of service, as shown in Table 4-3.

Table 4-3   University Class of Service Example

Class of Service	Allowed Destinations
2	On-campus calls only (A calling card was required to call off-campus.)
3	On-campus calls Local calls
8	On-campus calls Local calls Long-distance calls
20	On-campus calls Local calls Long-distance calls International calls

At the university, we assigned a class of service of 2 to student phones in residence halls, and a class of service of 3 to most faculty and staff. Managers received a class of service of 8, and only a few designated phones in the telecommunications department received a class of service of 20.

The Cisco CallManager environment offers a similar solution to controlling which phones can call which destinations. The CCM environment uses partitions and calling search spaces to restrict calls.

- **Partition**—A partition defines a set of route patterns and/or directory numbers. Phones that can reach one route pattern within a partition can reach all route patterns within the partition.

- **Calling Search Space**—A calling search space is a list of partitions in which a device (for example, an IP phone) is allowed to look when matching dialed digits.

Visualize a partition as a "cookie jar." Different cookie jars represent different categories of destinations we can call. For example, imagine that you have four cookie jars, labeled *Internal*, *Local*, *Long-Distance*, and *International*, as shown in Figure 4-9.

Figure 4-9   Partitions are "Cookie Jars"

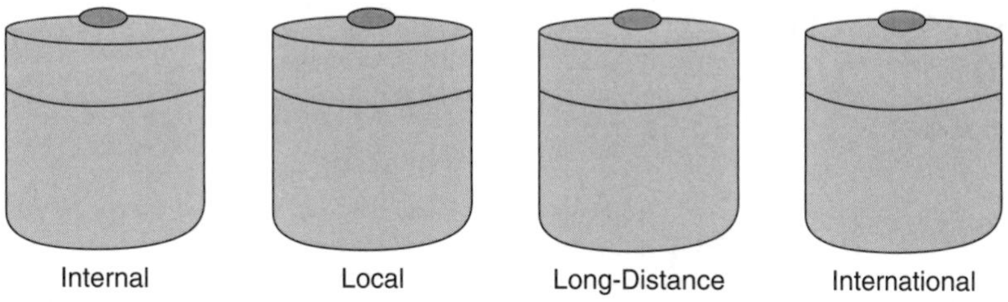

Internal   Local   Long-Distance   International

These "cookie jars" contain numbers (or number patterns) callers can dial. For example, the *Internal partition* might contain a pattern representing all four-digit internal extensions ranging from 2000 through 5999, while the *Local partition* contains seven-digit numbers beginning with the local office code of 624. The *Long-Distance partition* contains ten-digit numbers, and the *International partition* contains numbers of any length (because different countries might use country codes of different lengths), as shown in Figure 4-10.

Figure 4-10 Partitions Contain Destination Numbers

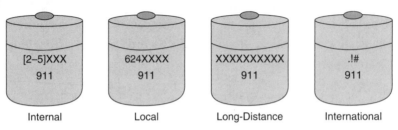

[2–5]XXX	624XXXX	XXXXXXXXXX	.!#
911	911	911	911
Internal	Local	Long-Distance	International

> The dial patterns shown in the "cookie jars" illustrate Cisco
> CallManager wildcards used to represent a range of numbers.

Partitions by themselves do not restrict calls, however. We use partitions in conjunction with Calling Search Spaces (CSSs). A calling search space is a list of partitions in which a particular extension is allowed to look when it tries to find the dialed number. In our example, you might have a *Lobby* CCS and an *Executive* CCS. The Lobby CCS might contain the Internal partition, and the Executive CCS might contain the Internal, Local, Long-Distance, and International partitions, as shown in Figure 4-11.

Figure 4-11 Calling Search Spaces

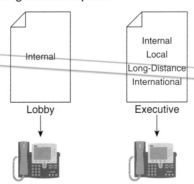

After defining calling search spaces, we assign these CSSs to extension numbers on specific IP phones. For example, if a lobby phone uses directory number 2020, we assign the Lobby calling search space to the directory number 2020.

When a visitor wanders into the lobby and picks up the lobby phone, they only have permission to call internal numbers (and of course 911 for emergency situations). Meanwhile, executives might call anywhere in the world using their IP phones because their directory numbers have the Executive CCS assigned.

note

All partitions, even those being used to restrict calls to internal extension numbers, should allow 911 calls.

Partitions and calling search spaces also offer the ability to route calls by the geographic location of a phone (for example, to help prevent a 911 call from being routed to an incorrect location). Consider the challenge with 911 emergency services. Let's say your company deployed a centralized call processing model across three cities. Louisville serves as the headquarters, and Cincinnati and Lexington act as branch offices. In this centralized model, the IP phones located in the Lexington and Cincinnati offices connect back to a centralized CCM cluster in Louisville. However, by default, if someone in Lexington or Cincinnati dialed 911, the Louisville location would forward the call to the Louisville 911 service, and the emergency response personnel would show up at the wrong location!

Partitions and calling search spaces can help prevent such a scenario. For example, if you install one or more *Foreign Exchange Office (FXO)* ports into the Lexington router and connect those ports to local phone lines coming from the Lexington *central office (CO)*, as shown in Figure 4-12, 911 calls placed from Lexington could be forwarded out to the local 911 authorities. In this example, let's say you create a partition named *Lex_911*, which contained a dial pattern that pointed 911 calls out a local FXO port. We then assign the *Lex_911* partition to each of the Lexington's calling search spaces (for example, *Lex_Internal*, *Lex_Local*, *Lex_Long-Distance*, and *Lex_International*), which are then assigned to IP phones. You configure the Cincinnati and Louisville locations similarly. As a result, when a caller in the Lexington office dials 911, the 911 call goes to the Lexington 911 authorities. Similarly, when a caller in Cincinnati dials 911, the call goes to the Cincinnati 911 authorities.

Figure 4-12   911 Services Using Partitions and Calling Search Spaces Example

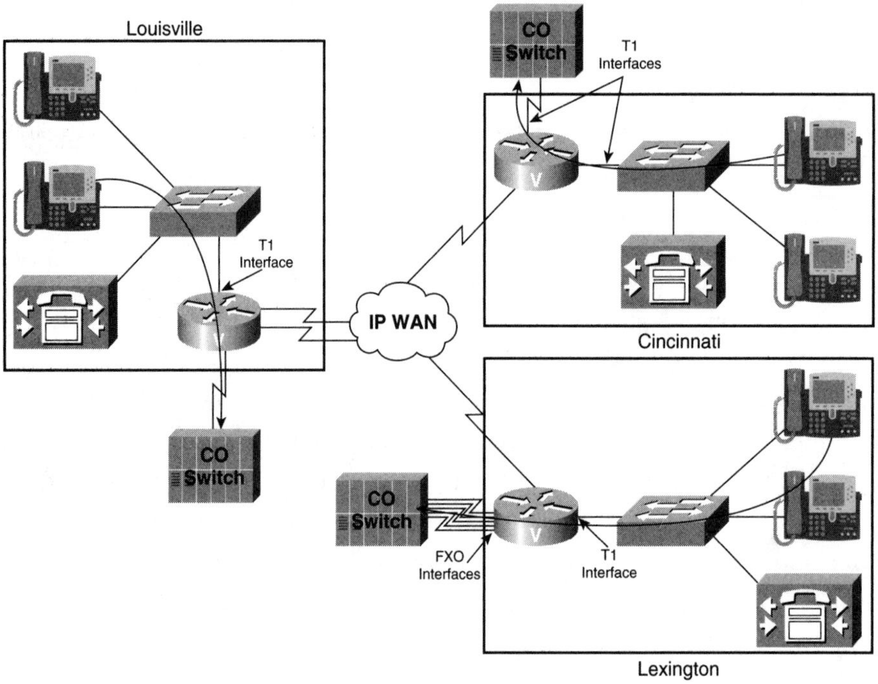

For larger environments, we might want to implement the *Cisco Emergency Responder* (*CER*) software, as opposed to using partitions and calling search spaces to direct 911 calls. CER synchronizes the CCM cluster's phone database with the 911 *Public Safety Answering Point* (*PSAP*), which can identify the caller's approximate physical location.

One of the major benefits of IP phones is the ability to move those phones from location to location. However, if we move a phone to another location, we need the CER to still know where the phone is located. The challenge is how to locate an IP phone that might be moved from location to location.

The Cisco endpoint location technologies can locate an IP phone even though we unplug it from one switch and plug it into another switch on another floor or in another building. Here's the logic. Although your IP phone is portable, Catalyst switches are not typically moved. So, if your IP phone connects to a Catalyst switch known to be on the second floor of Building A, your IP phone (that is, your current location) can be assumed to also be on the second floor of Building A. These Ethernet switches learn the *Media Access Control (MAC) address* of devices connected to them. A MAC address is a 48-bit address physically burned into the circuitry in a network interface. Therefore, an Ethernet switch learns the MAC addresses of IP phones connecting to that switch. The CER software communicates with the switches to determine which MAC addresses are connected to which switch. Because the CER software knows the phones associated with these IP phone MAC addresses, and because it knows where each switch is physically located (for example, in the third floor wiring closet in a building at a certain address), the CER software can provide the approximate location of each IP phone to 911 authorities.

note

Different areas of the country have different legal regulations regarding 911 support. Please check with your local authorities when deploying a 911 solution.

Replacing Old Phones with IP Phones

One of the first things a company's users notice after a migration to IP telephony is the cool new phone sitting on their desk. Cisco IP Phones come in a variety of shapes and sizes, and these IP phones come with a plethora of features.

When an IP phone boots up, the phone learns what *virtual LAN (VLAN)* it belongs to (that is, the voice VLAN) via a *Cisco Discovery Protocol (CDP)* message sent from the switch to the IP phone. The IP phone then sends out a Dynamic Host Configuration Protocol (DHCP) request, asking a DHCP server for an IP address that the IP phone can use. The DHCP server responds with not only the IP phone's IP address, but also subnet mask information, default gateway information, and the address of a Trivial File Transfer Protocol (TFTP) server. The IP phone needs the address of the TFTP server because the TFTP server contains the IP phone's configuration file. The configuration file contains such information as a listing of up to three CCM servers the IP phone can register with. The IP phone downloads its configuration file from the TFTP server and registers with a CCM server from the configuration file's listing of CCM servers. The IP phone can now place and receive calls.

Although Cisco continually introduces new IP phone models, to establish a frame of reference, consider some of the features to look for in Cisco IP Phones.

Inline Power

Just like an analog phone needs -48 volts of direct current (VDC), a Cisco IP Phone also requires -48 VDC to power up. Cisco IP Phones can be powered in one of three ways:

- **External Power Supply**—Just as many of the electronic devices in your home (for example, cordless phone or desktop computer) have an external power supply that plugs into the AC outlet in your wall, you can purchase an external power supply for a Cisco IP Phone. Sometimes called a *power brick*, this external transformer provides power to your IP phone from an AC wall outlet. However, in a corporate environment, this power option might not provide the highest level of availability. For example, if your company experiences a power outage, chances are your phone will stop working. You might even accidentally kick the power supply out of the already over-crowded power strip underneath your desk. Also, many locations might not be in close proximity to a power outlet. Therefore, purchasing an external power supply for your IP phone is not considered a best practice.

- **Inline Power from a Catalyst Switch**—Because your Cisco IP Phone plugs into a Cisco Catalyst Ethernet switch (typically located in a wiring closet), wouldn't it be great if the -48 VDC required by your phone could be provided directly by the Catalyst switch? That's exactly what inline power does. Cisco has multiple Catalyst switches capable of sending the required voltage over the same connection used to transmit voice and data packets.

If you take a close look at the RJ-45 connector (where "RJ" stands for Registered Jack) that plugs into your IP phone, you see eight separate conductors (indicating that eight wires are contained in the network cable). However, the Ethernet connection used by the IP phone (or any other Ethernet-connected device, such as a PC) only needs four of those eight wires in a network cable. Those four wires correspond to pins 1, 2, 3, and 6 on the RJ-45 connector. When a Cisco Catalyst switch provides inline power to an IP phone, the switch uses the same four wires used by Ethernet to power the phone.

Because the Catalyst switch resides in a wiring closet, by providing *Uninterruptible Power Supply (UPS)* or even generator power protection to that Catalyst switch, even if the company experiences a power outage, the IP phones continue to function because they receive power from the Catalyst switch, which is running on backup power.

note

Some Cisco routers support switch modules that support inline power.

- **Inline Power from a Midspan**—Perhaps none of the switches in your wiring closets support inline power. Fortunately, Cisco still allows us to use inline power by connecting our Cisco IP Phones and wiring closet switches to a *midspan*. A midspan is a patch panel typically containing 96 ports. Half of those ports (that is, 48 ports) allow Cisco IP Phones to connect to the midspan. The remaining 48 ports connect to the wiring closet switch. The midspan injects power on the non-Ethernet wires going back to the IP phone (that is, the wires using pins 4, 5, 7, and 8 on the RJ-45 connector). Therefore, a Cisco IP Phone can draw power from either the Ethernet or non-Ethernet wires.

The IEEE 802.3af standard describes how inline power, sometimes called *Power over Ethernet (PoE)*, functions. However, Cisco developed its own proprietary inline power approach prior to the IEEE 802.3af standard. Modern Cisco IP

Phones support both the Cisco prestandard inline power approach and IEEE 802.3af. Let's consider both inline power implementations:

- **Cisco Proprietary Inline Power**—The Cisco prestandard approach involves the switch port sending a tone, called a *Fast Link Pulse* (*FLP*), to the attached device. If the attached device is a Cisco IP Phone, the FLP loops back to the switch port. When the switch port sees the FLP coming back, it knows a Cisco IP Phone is attached to that port, and the switch applies -48 VDC to power the IP phone.

- **IEEE 802.3af**—The IEEE 802.3af standard says the switch port applies -2.8 VDC to -10 VDC across the Ethernet leads. If the switch port sees a current level indicating that the attached device contains a 25,000-Ohm resistor, the switch determines that a PoE device is connected, and the switch port provides power to the PoE device.

Some Cisco Catalyst switches/router switch modules only support the Cisco prestandard proprietary approach, while some Catalyst switches support both the Cisco prestandard approach and the IEEE 802.3af standard, as shown in Table 4-4.

Table 4-4   Inline Power Support

Cisco Device	Cisco Prestandard Inline Power Support	IEEE 802.3af (PoE) Support
Catalyst 6500	X	X
Catalyst 3560	X	X
Catalyst 4500	X	X
Catalyst 3750	X	X
EtherSwitch Network Module	X	
Catalyst 3550	X	

CODECs

CODECs (coder decoders) take analog voice waves and convert them into binary 1s and 0s. All Cisco IP Phones support the G.711 CODEC. G.711 does not compress the voice (that is, reduce the amount of bandwidth required for voice).

Rather, G.711 simply converts analog waves into binary using *pulse code modulation (PCM)*. High-speed LANs commonly use G.711 because the 64 kbps of bandwidth for voice payload required by G.711 presents an insignificant bandwidth impact on the LAN.

However, on the relatively slow-speed WAN, just a few G.711 calls might quickly eat up the available bandwidth. Therefore, you typically use the G.729 CODEC on WAN connections. G.729 only requires 8 kbps of bandwidth for voice payload. Second-generation Cisco IP Phones (that is, the Cisco IP Phones on the market today) support both G.711 and G.729. However, you might encounter an older first-generation Cisco IP Phone, such as the 12SP+ or 30VIP phone models. These first-generation phones support G.723, as opposed to G.729. G.723, like G.729, compresses the voice packets to preserve bandwidth, and G.723 only requires 6.3 kbps of bandwidth for the voice payload. However, G.723 suffers from more voice quality degradation than G.729. As a result, Cisco decided to only offer the G.711 and G.729 CODECs in current IP phone models. To be technically accurate, Cisco IP Phones use a variant of G.729, called *G.729a*. The "a" variant reduces the processor overhead required to compress voice samples.

Additional Switch Port

Suppose you want to place IP phones on the desktops of users in a cubicle environment. A single Ethernet connection currently runs to each of these cubicles for PC connections. However, if you install an IP phone in each cubicle, two devices (that is, the IP phone and the PC) now need connectivity back to the wiring closet. Do you have to run an additional Ethernet wire from the wiring closet to each cubicle? Maybe not. Some Cisco IP Phones contain an Ethernet switch port, allowing you to connect a PC to the IP phone and then connect the IP phone back to the wiring closet, as shown in Figure 4-13. As a result, a single, and hopefully existing, Ethernet connection can serve both a PC and a Cisco IP Phone. An IP phone containing an additional switch port acts as a three-port switch, with one port connecting to the internals of the IP phone, one port connecting to the wiring closet switch, and one port allowing a PC connection into the phone.

Figure 4-13   Additional Switch Port on IP Phone

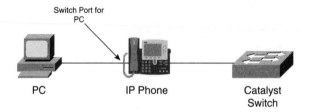

XML Support

Extensible Markup Language (XML) offers an alternative method of sending text and pictures over a network, as opposed to the *Hypertext Markup Language (HTML)* we're accustomed to when viewing web pages from the Internet. Some Cisco IP Phones contain *liquid crystal display (LCD)* screens that display XML pages. Users can interact with these XML pages using the buttons on IP phones. Examples of XML applications I've seen on Cisco IP Phones include

- Stock quotes

- Airport reports

- Headline news reports

- Class roster (with pictures of students)

As another example, you can even retrieve weather reports from a Cisco IP Phone using an XML application, as shown in Figure 4-14.

Figure 4-14 XML Application Example Weather Report

Auxiliary VLAN

If an IP phone contains an extra Ethernet port (used to connect a PC to the IP phone), both data and voice traffic flow over the Ethernet cable to the wiring closet switch. Cisco IP Phones can send the voice packets in one VLAN (that is, the *voice VLAN* or the *auxiliary VLAN*) and data packets in a separate VLAN (that is, the *data VLAN*), as shown in Figure 4-15.

Figure 4-15 Auxiliary VLAN

When an Ethernet connection carries traffic for more than one VLAN, we call that connection a *trunk*. The technical name for the type of trunk set up between the IP phone and the wiring closet switch is an *IEEE 802.1Q* trunk, meaning that the type of trunk is an industry standard and not Cisco proprietary.

Softkeys

Cisco IP Phones support so many features (for example, hold, transfer, conference, etc.) that an IP phone with a specific button for every feature would be massive. Fortunately, many Cisco IP Phones support *softkeys*, which serve different functions at different times. For example, when an IP phone is on-hook, a particular softkey might act as a Redial key, while the very same button might act as a Hold key when the IP phone is off-hook.

Line/Speed Dial Buttons

Many users need more than a single line on their phone. These users need to handle multiple incoming calls, perform call transfers, and set up conference calls. Therefore, some models of Cisco IP Phones offer multiple *line buttons*, where each button can represent a different extension number. However, let's say a user's IP phone has six buttons that can be used for line buttons, but the user only needs two line buttons. In that case, the four remaining buttons can serve as *speed dial buttons*. A caller can lift an IP phone's handset and press a speed dial button to dial a preconfigured number.

note

Although multiple lines are not required to make multiple calls, extra lines can be configured on an IP phone.

Either the Cisco CallManager administrator or a user can configure a phone's speed dial buttons. By empowering users to make their own speed dial modifications, administrators are not burdened, for example, with making changes every time someone gets a new boyfriend or girlfriend.

Now that you know some of the bells and whistles to look for when selecting a Cisco IP Phone, let's reinforce this discussion by examining a few specific Cisco IP Phone models.

Cisco 7902G

The Cisco 7902G IP Phone, as shown in Figure 4-16, serves as an entry-level IP phone. Because the 7902G acts as a single line phone and because it lacks many of the higher-end features (for example, softkeys and an extra Ethernet switch port) present in some IP phones, the 7902G might be appropriate for a company's break room. The Cisco 7902G offers the following characteristics:

- Inline power

- G.711 and G.729a CODEC support

- Single switch port

- No XML support

- Auxiliary VLAN support

- Four fixed-feature keys (that is, no softkeys)

- Single line

Figure 4-16　　Cisco 7902G IP Phone

Cisco 7905G and 7912G

The Cisco 7905G and 7912G, as shown in Figure 4-17, are entry-level Cisco IP Phones offering similar features. The 7905G and 7912G differ in one feature, however. The 7912G contains an extra Ethernet switch port, allowing a PC to connect directly into the 7912G. The features offered by these phones include

- Inline power

- G.711 and G.729a CODEC support

- Single switch port (7905G)

- Extra switch port (7912G)

- Limited XML support

- Auxiliary VLAN support

- Four softkeys

- Single line

Figure 4-17   Cisco 7905G/7912G IP Phone

Cisco 7910G+SW

The Cisco 7910G+SW, as shown in Figure 4-18, serves as an entry-level Cisco IP Phone. Like other entry-level Cisco IP Phones, the 7910G+SW offers basic functions commonplace in common-use areas within a company. Cisco 7910G+SW features include

- Inline power

- G.711 and G.729a CODEC support

- Extra switch port

- No XML support

- Auxiliary VLAN support

- No softkeys

- Single line

Figure 4-18   Cisco 7910G+SW IP Phone

Cisco 7940G and 7960G

The Cisco 7940G and 7960G IP phones, as shown in Figure 4-19, feature multiple line/speed dial buttons. Unlike the entry-level phones previously described, the 7940G and 7960G contain a large LCD display, which allows a caller to interact with XML applications. The 7960G offers the same features as the 7940G, with one exception. The 7960G contains six line/speed dial buttons, as opposed to the 7940G's two line/speed dial buttons. 7940G and 7060G features include

- Inline power

- G.711 and G.729a CODEC support

- Extra switch port

- XML support

- Auxiliary VLAN support

- Four softkeys

- Two line/speed dial buttons (7940G)

- Six line/speed dial buttons (7960G)

Figure 4-19   Cisco 7960G IP Phone

If you require additional line/speed dial buttons for a 7940G or 7960G IP phone, you can purchase the Cisco 7914 Expansion Module, as shown in Figure 4-20. The 7914 adds 14 additional buttons, which can be used as either line or speed dial buttons. In fact, two 7914s can be added to a 7940G or 7960G IP phone,

giving you 28 additional buttons at your disposal. However, you need to purchase a power brick for each 7914, because the 7914s do not support inline power.

Figure 4-20   Cisco 7914 Expansion Module

Cisco 7970G and 7971G-GE

Cisco introduced a color display in its 7970G IP phone model, as shown in Figure 4-21. Users can interact with XML applications via the color display's touch screen feature. Cisco recommends the 7970G for executives and decision makers.

Figure 4-21   Cisco 7970G IP Phone

Did you ever watch the NBC TV show *Las Vegas*? If so, you probably saw a 7970G sitting on Big Ed Deline's desk, with a big red Montecito logo on the phone's display. An updated version of the 7970G, the 7971G-GE contains a gigabit Ethernet switch port allowing a PC with a gigabit network interface card to plug into the IP phone, as compared to the 10/100 Mbps Ethernet switch port on the 7970G. Other than the different Ethernet switch port interface speed, the 7970G and 7971G-GE have identical features. Specifically, these IP phones feature:

- Inline power
- G.711 and G.729a CODEC support
- Extra switch port (1 Gbps port on 7971G-GE)
- XML support (with color touch screen)
- Auxiliary VLAN support
- Five softkeys
- Eight line/speed dial buttons

Cisco IP SoftPhone

Cisco offers software-based IP phones, which allow a user to install software on their laptop, as an example, and carry their laptop (and therefore their IP phone) from location to location. The user simply connects their laptop into a network connection at any company site, customer site, or even a broadband Internet connection in a hotel, and the user can make and receive calls over their software-based IP phone using a USB headset connected to the laptop.

Although Cisco offers a couple software-based IP phones, it first introduced the Cisco IP SoftPhone, as shown in Figure 4-22. The Cisco IP SoftPhone offers the following features and characteristics:

- Requires extra software (specifically the Telephony Service Provider) to be installed on the PC
- G.711 and G.729a CODEC support
- Integrates with Microsoft NetMeeting

- Integrates with a Lightweight Directory Access Protocol (LDAP) directory

- Requires the creation of a user account

- No softkeys

- No XML support

Figure 4-22   Cisco IP SoftPhone

Cisco IP Communicator

In addition to the Cisco IP SoftPhone, Cisco also offers the Cisco IP Communicator as a software-based IP phone. Like the Cisco IP SoftPhone, the Cisco IP Communicator installs on a laptop or PC, allowing the user to take their IP phone with them from location to location. However, the Cisco IP Communicator, as shown in Figure 4-23, reflects the look and feel of a hardware-based IP phone (that is, the 7970G IP phone) more so than the Cisco IP SoftPhone. The Cisco IP Communicator offers the following features and characteristics:

- Does not require Telephony Service Provider (TSP) software

- G.711 and G.729a CODEC support

- Five softkeys

- Eight line/speed dial buttons

- XML support

Figure 4-23 Cisco IP Communicator

Cisco 7920

Many laptop computers today contain *wireless* network adapters, allowing a user to carry the laptop with them while still maintaining connectivity to a network. In the past few years, wireless technologies have found their way into many libraries, hotels, and airports around the country, and today wireless technology is springing up in some of the most unlikely places. For example, I recently connected to a wireless network at a bookstore and in a restaurant.

However, wireless technology (that is, IEEE 802.11b) isn't limited to PCs. Cisco now offers a wireless IP phone. This phone is not a "cordless" phone, as you might have in your home. The Cisco 7920 IP Phone, as shown in Figure 4-24, uses the same wireless technology your laptop uses to connect to wireless access points, allowing you to conduct untethered IP phone conversations. The 7920 boasts the following features:

- Pixel-based display
- G.711 and G.729a CODEC support
- Two softkeys
- Four-way rocker switch
- Hold and Mute keys

- Handset and ringer volume control

- Security features to prevent eavesdropping

- Six lines/speed dials

- 802.11b protocol support

Figure 4-24   Cisco 7920 Wireless IP Phone

Cisco 7936

Have you ever sat in a conference room and seen one of those big speakerphones (looking much like a spaceship) sitting in the middle of the conference room table? Those conference room speakerphones contain circuitry optimized for picking up multiple voices around the table. Cisco partnered with Polycom, a leading manufacturer of conference room speakerphones, to produce an IP telephony version of the Polycom speakerphone. Specifically, the Cisco IP Conference Station 7936 replaces a company's traditional conference room speakerphone. The 7936, as shown in Figure 4-25, offers the following features:

- Supports natural two-way conversations (unlike many legacy speakerphones)

- G.711 and G.729a CODEC support

- Three microphones for 360-degree room coverage

- No XML support

- Three softkeys

- No inline power support

Figure 4-25   Cisco IP Conference Station 7936

Selecting Features for IP Phones

The maturity of PBXs allows them to offer a suite of user features. To compete
with a PBX, an IP telephony solution must offer comparable features. Fortunately,
the Cisco CallManager platform offers most any feature found in today's modern
PBXs, and a few features not found. This section introduces you to a sampling of
the many features available in CallManager 4.x platforms.

Conferencing

A conference call allows multiple parties to simultaneously speak with each other.
The processing of mixing together different audio streams can put a strain on a
CCM server's resources. Therefore, some network designers dedicate a CCM to
conference call support. A dedicated CCM server supports up to 128 users in a

single conference call. For enhanced scalability and to reduce the conference call processing burden on the CCM server, hardware installed in various Cisco routers and switches can offload the conference call processing, making hardware conferencing the widely preferred method.

Annunciator

The Annunciator plays prerecorded announcements (for example, a .WAV file) to give callers information about why a call failed. For example, during a service interruption, a caller might hear, "A service disruption has prevented the completion of your call. In case of emergency, call your operator. This is a recording."

Transcoding

Transcoding resources (for example, DSP stored in Cisco routers or switches) convert back and forth between high-bandwidth CODECs (for example, G.711) and low-bandwidth CODECs (for example, G.729). Therefore, a call originating as a G.711 call could be converted into a G.729 call before going across a WAN connection. Such a resource might be needed if you have equipment (for example, an interactive voice response system) that only supports the G.711 CODEC, and you simultaneously want to use the G.729 CODEC over the IP WAN (for bandwidth preservation).

Music on Hold

When a caller is placed on hold, is being transferred, or is being conferenced in with another party, the CCM software can play *music on hold* (*MOH*) for the listener. CCM administrators can easily add MOH files by dragging and dropping either .WAV or .MP3 files into a designated folder on a CCM server (assuming the administrators have the licensing to do so).

note

Some Cisco routers have the ability to play MOH, thus eliminating the need for MOH traffic to cross the WAN.

Speed Dial and Abbreviated Dial

A speed dial button allows a caller to press a single button to reach a preconfigured destination. For example, you might have your "significant other's" phone number programmed in as one of your speed dial buttons. However, depending on a caller's IP phone model, the caller might need additional speed dials. Therefore, Cisco allows the administrator or the user to configure *abbreviated dial numbers*.

A Cisco IP Phone supports up to 99 speed dial entries, and users can enter a one- or two-digit number (that is, the abbreviated dial number) and then press the *ABBRDIAL* softkey to dial a preconfigured abbreviated dial number. For example, imagine you entered your dentist's phone number in your IP phone's 49th speed dial entry. Because your IP phone doesn't have 49 speed dial buttons, you dial 49 and then press the ABBRDIAL button to call your dentist. Keep in mind that the phone does not permit you to scroll through your abbreviated dial numbers, which is one drawback of abbreviated dial.

Auto Answer

The auto answer feature allows a phone to answer a call as soon as the call comes in. This feature might be useful for a call center environment, where customer service agents wear headsets and can start talking with an incoming caller immediately, without having to reach for the handset.

The CCM administrator can configure the auto answer feature to auto answer using either a headset or the built-in speakerphone, which brings to mind another possible application. If you have a Cisco IP Phone in your home, and you leave your teenage children alone for the weekend with the instruction not to have any parties, you could call your phone remotely. The IP phone, configured for auto answer, immediately answers using the speakerphone, and you listen in on what's happening in your home.

Call Forward

When you are in a meeting or away from your office, you might want your calls forwarded to voice mail or another phone number. The CCM supports three call-forwarding types: 1) Forward All (all calls forwarded), 2) Forward Busy (calls forwarded when you're on the phone), and 3) Forward No Answer (calls forwarded if you don't answer your phone after four rings).

Direct Transfer

The Direct Transfer feature allows you to join two parties together. Perhaps you have someone on hold, and you are talking with someone else. Pressing the *DirTrfr* softkey joins those parties together, without consuming any conferencing resources.

Call Join

Whereas the Direct Transfer featured allows you to join two calls, the Call Join feature allows you to join up to 15 active calls, in addition to yourself, in a conference call. The person who initiated the call, however, is the only person allowed to add participants to a call. The conference call remains active even if the call originator hangs up.

Immediate Divert to Voice Mail

The *Immediate Divert* (*iDivert*) softkey sends a call directly to voice mail. For example, you might be meeting with someone in your office, and your phone starts ringing. You don't want to disrupt your meeting by answering the phone, and you don't want to allow the phone to ring four times before the incoming calls are forwarded to voice mail. Pressing the *iDivert* softkey immediately forwards the incoming call to voice mail, minimizing the disruption to your meeting.

Multilevel Precedence and Preemption

Multilevel Precedence and Preemption allows high-priority calls from authenticated users to preempt lower-priority calls. For example, a national emergency might flood a company's phone system with calls. With Multilevel Precedence and Preemption, administrators assign designated users priority over any existing calls to, for example, coordinate emergency responses.

Malicious Call Identification

Users receiving malicious calls can press the *Malicious Call Identification* (*MCID*) softkey (or dial a feature code) to send an alarm notification to the CCM administrator. The MCID feature also flags malicious calls in the call accounting records and can send special messages to the primary rate interface (PRI) to hold the call up, allowing authorities to trace the call back to the originator.

Call Park

Call Park allows a caller to "park" a call in a location identified by a number. The parked call is retrievable from another phone. From the other phone, simply dial the number identifying the parked location to retrieve the call.

Call Pickup/Group Call Pickup

Consider a group of workers in the same department working in neighboring cubicles. These workers might need the ability to answer a call coming into a coworker's phone. This function is supported by the Call Pickup feature. The Group Call Pickup feature extends the ability of the Call Pickup feature, allowing a user to answer a call coming into another department's phone. For example, perhaps a receptionist serves both the accounting and payroll offices. The Group Call Pickup feature allows the receptionist to answer an incoming call for either of these call groups.

Call Back

When I call my mother from my home phone, if her line is busy, I hear a message from my local phone company saying they can notify me when her phone is no longer busy (for the low, low cost of 90 cents!) The Cisco CallManager Call Back feature offers a similar function for on-cluster calls (without the 90-cent charge).

Barge and Privacy

Did you ever call a company and hear a message similar to, "This call might be monitored for quality assurance"? The CCM software supports the ability for someone else to join a call (and perhaps monitor the call for quality assurance) with the Barge feature. However, there might be times when you don't want your boss barging in on your conversation. Perhaps you don't want someone listening when you're talking with your spouse, or worse yet, listening in on a phone interview with another company! The Privacy feature allows a user to prevent anyone from barging into a call, on a call-by-call basis.

The Cone of Silence: Securing Voice

Did you ever watch the old TV show *Get Smart*? When Maxwell Smart wanted to talk privately with the chief, Max insisted on using the "Cone of Silence," a transparent hood that descended over their heads. Today's IP telephony networks also need a cone of silence, a way to securely transmit conversations. Hacker tools proliferate in the Internet, and some tools can capture voice packets and convert a VoIP conversation to a .WAV file. Fortunately, Cisco introduced multiple security features in CallManager version 4.0, helping to keep private conversations private.

Three primary security goals include:

- Identity

- Integrity

- Privacy

Identity

In the world of security, identity verifies a user's credentials before the user receives permission to perform certain functions. A Cisco IP Phone and Cisco CallManager server can authenticate each other through the use of *certificates*. A certificate is a digital document containing information about the certificate's holder. But what's to prevent a hacker from creating a false certificate? A trusted third party, called a *certificate authority* (*CA*), vouches for the validity of a certificate.

Beginning with the Cisco 7970 IP Phone, Cisco installs certificates in a phone during the phone's manufacturing process. The CCM server uses a certificate created during installation. Phone models introduced prior to the 7970 use *Locally Significant Certificates* (*LSCs*), which are installed by the Cisco *Certificate Authority Proxy Function* (*CAPF*) software.

Integrity

Integrity confirms that data (or in our case, voice) hasn't been manipulated in transit. To illustrate the concept of integrity, let's say I send you a letter, and we agree that I'll write a number on the outside of the envelope. This number indicates the number of vowels contained in the letter. After you receive the envelope, you read through the letter, count the number of vowels, and compare that number with the number I wrote on the envelope. If the numbers match, you conclude the letter was not intercepted and manipulated in transit. Although IP networks use much more sophisticated methods of ensuring integrity, the concept remains the same.

Cisco IP telephony networks can provide integrity through image authentication (that is, making sure the phone's binary firmware file hasn't been tampered with), file authentication (that is, making sure the phone's configuration file hasn't been tampered with), and signal authentication (that is, making sure call signaling packets haven't been tampered with).

Privacy

Privacy involves encrypting (that is, scrambling) a packet's contents. If a hacker intercepted an encrypted packet, the packet would be of no value to the hacker. Examples of encryption technologies include *Triple Data Encryption Standard* (*3DES*) and *Advanced Encryption Standard* (*AES*). These encryption technologies involve complex mathematical functions, making a hacker's decryption attempts impractical.

Cisco leverages encryption technologies to encrypt signaling information and, in some cases, the actual voice packets. Signaling encryption scrambles the SCCP messages sent between a Cisco IP Phone and the Cisco CallManager. Examples of SCCP messages include dialed dual tone multifrequency (DTMF) digits and call status information. Encrypting voice packets is called *media encryption*. Media encryption uses the *Secure Real-Time Transport Protocol* (*SRTP*), which uses a form of the previously mentioned AES.

A Picture Is Worth a Thousand Words: Adding Video to Voice Calls

Cisco introduced video call support in version 4.0 of its CallManager software. Examples of video-capable Cisco IP Phones include the Cisco 7940G, 7960G, 7970G, and 7971G-GE IP Phones. However, Cisco continually introduces new IP phones and features. So, please check Cisco.com for the latest listing of video-capable phones.

The LCD on a Cisco IP Phone doesn't display the video in a video call. Rather, video appears on a PC attached to the IP phone, using the Cisco *VT Advantage* product, as shown in Figures 4-26 and 4-27.

Figure 4-26   Cisco VT Advantage Connection

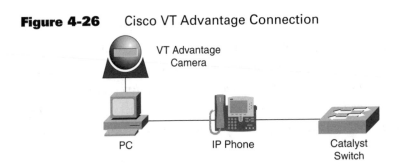

Figure 4-27   Cisco VT Advantage Application

The CCM communicates with video-capable Cisco IP Phones via SCCP, and if those IP phones attach to a PC running VT Advantage software, the IP phones can report their video capabilities back to the CCM using SCCP. If both endpoints (that is, the IP phones on each end of a conversation) support video calls, the endpoints can set up a video channel between themselves.

The Cisco VT Advantage product includes software and a camera, as shown in Figure 4-28. The camera connects to a USB port on a PC. The VT Advantage software installs on the PC connected to the camera, and that PC connects into the Ethernet switch port on an IP phone.

Figure 4-28   Cisco VT Advantage Camera

Adding video to a call requires callers to rethink their behavior during a call. I admit it. I've talked with people on the phone, and while my voice sounded calm and friendly, the expression on my face told a different story, my rolling eyes indicating my impatience with the other party. Video calls require a bit more decorum.

Consider the *mute* function on an IP phone. When you're in an audio-only call and you press the mute button, the other party stops hearing you, allowing you to have a private conversation in your office. Consider a situation where you're conducting an important business video call, and you press the mute button on your IP phone. If you want audio privacy, chances are, you want video privacy too. Fortunately, the Cisco VT Advantage product pauses the video of a video call when you press the mute button on an IP phone. Also, you can optionally configure the VT Advantage software to a receive-only mode, where you see video from the other party, but the other party doesn't see you.

Besides two-party video calls, the Cisco product line features multipoint control units (MCUs), which mix audio and video streams together to support video conference calls. Examples of the Cisco video MCUs include the IP/VC 3511 (supporting 15 simultaneous video conference participants), and the IP/VC 3540 (supporting up to 100 simultaneous conference participants), as shown in Figure 4-29.

Figure 4-29   Cisco IP/VC 3540 Multipoint Control Unit

The IP/VC 3540 MCU mixes the audio and video from conference participants. Cisco supports two options for viewing conference participants:

- **Voice activated**—The voice activated display mode shows the video of the conference participant currently speaking.

- **Continuous presence**—The continuous presence display mode continually shows up to four participants on a screen. However, if a conference contains more than four participants, off-screen participants (that is, participants that are not currently one of the four displayed participants) are displayed if they begin to speak.

Consider a situation where Phone A is video capable, and Phone A calls Phone B, which is not video capable. Because Phone B lacks video support, Phone A only sends audio to Phone B. However, let's say Phone B transfers the call to Phone C, which is video capable. Because both devices in the call (that is, Phone A and Phone C) now support video, the call, which once only used audio, starts to transmit both audio and video between the endpoints.

Because a video call requires more bandwidth than an audio-only call, during peak WAN usage, enough bandwidth might be available for an audio call but not for a video call. CCM administrators can configure Cisco IP Phones to retry a call as an audio-only call if a video call attempt fails.

note
Cisco CallManager also supports third-party H.323 video clients, allowing existing H.323 systems to leverage the power of Cisco CallManager features.

Cisco CallManager in the "Express" Lane

Some small office/home office (SOHO) environments lack sufficient IP phones to justify the purchase of CCM servers. Although these smaller offices might be able to register with a centralized CCM cluster using the IP WAN, some IP telephony designers instead recommend (for redundancy and scalability) the purchase of *Cisco CallManager Express* (*CME*) routers for these locations. The CME feature supports CCM-like functions on a router, as opposed to a dedicated server platform, thus reducing a customer's investment.

Administrators configure CME features via a router's IOS or optionally via a web interface. Depending on the router platform, a single CME router supports up to 240 IP phones. Examples of Cisco router models capable of running the CME feature include:

- 1760 (24 max IP phones)

- 2610XM (36 max IP phones)

- 2691 (72 max IP phones)

- 2851 (96 max IP phones)

- 3725 (144 max IP phones)

- 3745 (192 max IP phones)

- 3825 (168 max IP phones)

- 3845 (240 max IP phones)

While CME offers CCM-like call processing features in a router, *Cisco Unity Express* (*CUE*) offers voice mail and auto attendant features in a router. CUE, however, requires extra hardware. This extra hardware contains storage space for voice mail messages. IP telephony designers can select between two storage options for a CUE router:

- **Network Module (NM)**—The NM-CUE or NM-CUE-EC network modules each occupy a network module slot in a router and support up to 100 user mailboxes.

- **Advanced Integration Module (AIM)**—The AIM-CUE card mounts on a router's motherboard and supports up to 50 user mailboxes.

CUE hardware and software fully integrates into 2600XM, 2691, 2800, and 3800 Series routers. Although you can use CUE in conjunction with CME, you might also use CUE as your voice mail/auto attendant solution in a CCM server environment. Like the CCM server, administrators can configure both the CME and CUE via a web interface, as shown in Figure 4-30.

Figure 4-30   CME/CUE Administration Interface

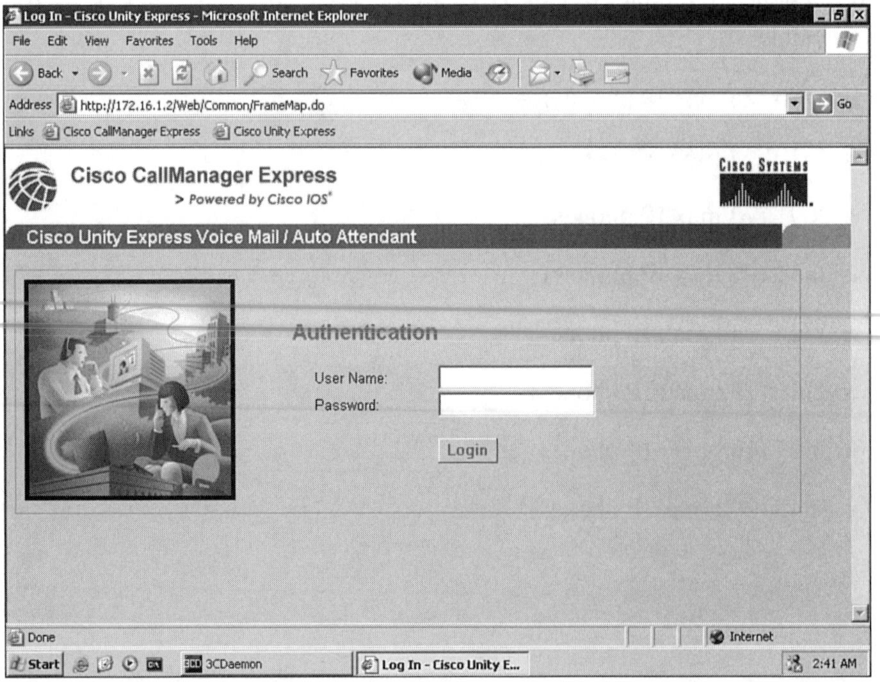

CUE's automated attendant function allows the router to answer incoming calls. Callers can then interact with CUE by, for example, entering extension numbers using their telephony keypad. Companies can create custom greetings and provide recorded answers to commonly asked questions (for example, directions and hours of operation). Also, administrators can configure CUE with a company's holiday and hours of operation information, giving callers different call treatment for times when the business is closed.

Similar to a CCM server environment, IP phones register with a CME router using SCCP. However, recall that before an IP phone registers, it typically gets an IP address from a DHCP server and downloads a configuration file from a TFTP server. In the CME environment, the CME router can function as both a DHCP server and a TFTP server, eliminating the need for an external server. Once the CME router establishes a call between a couple of IP phones, the IP phones communicate directly between themselves using the RTP, as shown in Figure 4-31.

Figure 4-31   IP Phone/CME Router Communication

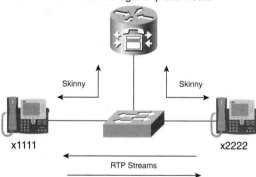

The CME router might also contain analog or digital interfaces (for example, FXO, *Foreign Exchange Station (FXS)*, *Integrated Services Digital Network (ISDN)*, or T1 interfaces) to send calls originating from an IP phone out to a PBX or to the PSTN.

Case Study: Your Turn to Do an Extreme Phone System Makeover

Based on your previous design of XYZ Company's phone system (as discussed in the previous chapter's case study) and based on your recommendations for the XYZ Company to migrate to a VoIP network, the XYZ Company asks you to provide it with yet another design. This time, the XYZ Company wants you to diagram how its telephony network would look with all of its phone switches (that is, PBXs and key system) replaced with Cisco CallManager servers and/or CME routers.

Recall the information in Table 1-3 (reproduced here in Table 4-5) concerning the XYZ Company from the case study in Chapter 1, "Touring the History Museum of Telephony."

Table 4-5   Case Study Design Requirements

Location	Number of Telephones	Features Required
Headquarters	4500	Voice mail A conference bridge capable of supporting a conference of 20 simultaneous participants
Remote Office 1	2000	Access to the corporate voice mail system Access to the corporate conference bridge Capability to support 72 simultaneous voice paths back to the headquarters
Remote Office 2	30	Access to the corporate voice mail system Access to the corporate conference bridge Capability to support 12 simultaneous voice paths back to the headquarters

Based on these criteria, design a pure IP telephony solution using the hardware and software products discussed in this chapter. Diagram and discuss your answer.

Design Diagram for XYZ Company:

Design Description for XYZ Company:

_____

_____

_____

_____

_____

_____

_____

_____

_____

_____

_____

_____

_____

Suggested Solution

Multiple design solutions satisfy the design requirements for this case study. The following suggested solution represents only one solution. So, don't be concerned if your solution varies from the suggested solution.

The XYZ Company wishes to replace its existing PBXs and key system with IP telephony components. The design from Chapter 3, "Paving the Pathway to a Voice over IP Network," introduced voice-enabled routers into the XYZ Company's network. We can now add Ethernet switches to the design and connect the voice-enabled routers and new IP phones to the Ethernet switches. We can configure the Ethernet switches to provide inline power to the attached IP phones and to provide auxiliary VLAN information to the IP phones.

We can remove the PBXs and key system. Because the XYZ Headquarters contains 4,500 IP phones, we select a CCM cluster for the headquarters location, using the Cisco 2:1 redundancy design, which requires a total of four CCM servers using MCS-7835H server platforms.

XYZ Remote Office 1 requires support for 2000 IP phones. A three-server CCM cluster, using MCS-7835H server platforms, meets this remote office's requirements.

XYZ Remote Office 2 only requires support for 30 IP phones. 30 IP phones probably don't justify the purchase of a CCM cluster. These 30 IP phones could register with the centralized CCM cluster (that is, the CCM cluster located at XYZ Headquarters). However, for redundancy and scalability reasons, this design recommends the use of a CME router at XYZ Remote Office 2. A 2610XM router supports up to 36 IP phones. Therefore, this design specifies that the 30 IP phones at XYZ Remote Office 2 register with a 2610XM-based CME router.

The XYZ Company's design requirements also called for voice mail support for all locations. Cisco CallManager interoperates with many legacy voice mail systems, even in the absence of a PBX. Therefore, the XYZ Headquarters and XYZ Remote Office 1 continue to use existing voice mail facilities. However, we decide to purchase a Cisco Unity Express (asynchronous interface module - Cisco Unity Express [AIM-CUE]) card to mount on the router's motherboard to support voice mail for XYZ Remote Office 2. The AIM-CUE supports up to 50 voice mail boxes.

The case study in Chapter 3 provisioned WAN links between XYZ locations. Therefore, the only remaining design requirement involves support for conference calling. The CCM environment supports either hardware-based or software-based conference calling. With hardware-based conference calls, DSPs, located in routers or switches, provide the processing power to mix multiple audio streams together. Software-based conference calling uses a CCM server to mix audio streams. This case study requires support for a conference call with 20 participants. A dedicated CCM server supports up to 128 conference participants. Therefore, this design specifies a software-based conference solution, using CCM servers for the XYZ Headquarters and XYZ Remote Office 1 locations. The XYZ Remote Office 2 location can use hardware resources (that is, DSPs) installed in the CME router for conferenc calling support. The suggested solution, as shown in Figure 4-32, represents a distributed deployment design, with one slight variation. XYZ Remote Office 2 uses a CME router, as opposed to a CCM cluster.

Figure 4-32   XYZ Company's Suggested Solution

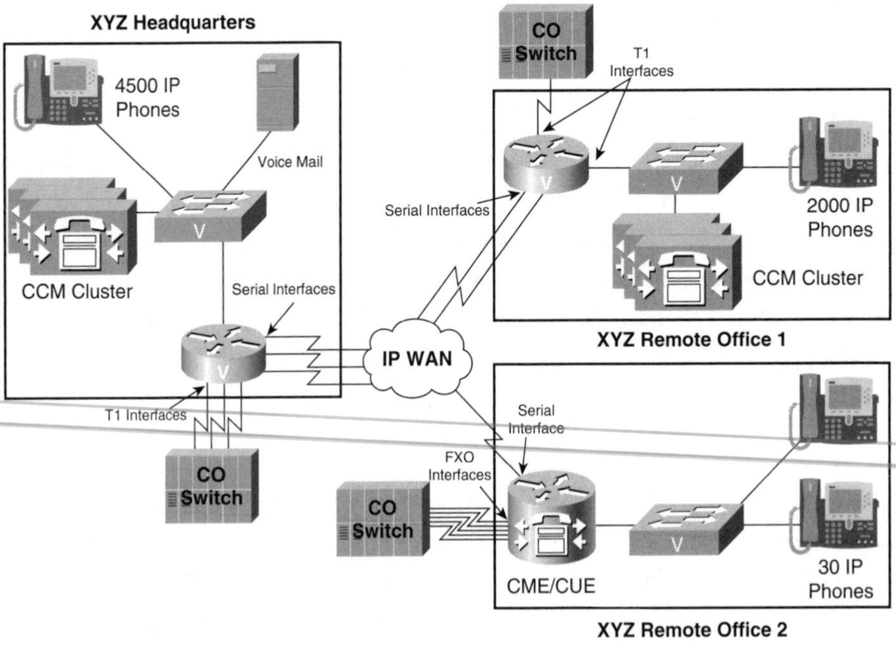

Chapter Summary

This chapter explained how Cisco CallManager servers replace many PBX functions in an IP telephony environment. For redundancy and scalability, we grouped CCM servers into clusters. We determined how many CCM servers were needed for a cluster, based on the number of supported IP phones and redundancy requirements.

Features available on Cisco IP Phones rival, and, in many cases, surpass, present-day PBX features; and this chapter explored the operation of many of the more popular IP phone features. Features available on various Cisco IP Phone models were also reviewed.

Cisco CallManager version 4.0 introduced support for video calls and enhanced security. This chapter discussed the VT Advantage product used for video calls and explored how CCM servers secure our voice transmissions through identity, integrity, and privacy mechanisms.

Finally, we discussed how a small- to medium-sized office could leverage the features offered by the CME and the CUE products. The CME feature allows an IOS router to support up to 240 IP phones, as opposed to supporting these IP phones with CCM servers. The CUE feature offers voice mail and autoattendant features within an IOS router.

Chapter Review Questions

1. What protocol does a Cisco IP Phone use to communicate with a Cisco CallManager server?

   a. RTP

   b. SCCP

   c. H.323

   d. MGCP

2. A logical grouping of Cisco CallManager servers is called a _____.

    a. Zone

    b. Region

    c. Location

    d. Cluster

3. Cisco CallManager servers restrict calls using _____ and _____. (Select two.)

    a. Locations

    b. Calling Search Spaces

    c. Device Pools

    d. Partitions

4. Which of the following products is designed to support enhanced 911 service?

    a. IVR

    b. CSS

    c. CER

    d. SRST

5. How much voltage powers a Cisco IP Phone?

    a. -24 VDC

    b. -48 VAC

    c. -24 VAC

    d. -48 VDC

6. Identify the wireless Cisco IP Phone model.

    a. 7920

    b. 7960

    c. 7914

    d. 7970

7. What feature does the VT Advantage product add to IP telephony?

    a. Enhanced security

    b. Video calls

    c. Diagnostic features

    d. Software-based transcoding

8. Which of the following protocols encrypts voice packets?

    a. SIP

    b. RTCP

    c. RAS

    d. SRTP

9. Which of the following supports voice mail and auto attendant functions within a router?

    a. CME

    b. CUE

    c. CCS

    d. SRST

10. Which of the following are true concerning Cisco CallManager Express (CME)? (Select two.)

    a. CME runs on a Windows 2000 platform

    b. CME runs on a router platform

    c. CME supports up to 240 IP phones

    d. CME supports up to 480 IP phones

What You Will Learn

After reading this chapter, you should be able to

- ✔ Explain the need for gateway control languages.

- ✔ Identify characteristics of H.323.

- ✔ List the features of MGCP.

- ✔ Describe the operation of SIP.

CHAPTER 5

Speaking the Gateways' Languages

The whole world hasn't migrated to *Voice over IP (VoIP)* telephony yet. Therefore, your VoIP networks need a portal to the rest of the world (that is, the public switched telephony network or public switched telephone network [PSTN]). Chapter 1, "Touring the History Museum of Telephony," introduced a VoIP *gateway*. Recall that a gateway acts as a threshold between a VoIP network and another type of network (for example, a *private branch exchange [PBX]* or the PSTN). For example, a gateway might have an Ethernet interface connecting to a VoIP network and a series of Foreign Exchange Office (FXO) or T1 interfaces connecting to the PSTN.

Gateways and *CCM* servers need a common language for communication; that is, a *protocol*. Think of gateway protocols as *languages of love* between VoIP devices. This chapter discusses the generic functions of these protocols and considers three specific gateway protocols:

- H.323
- MGCP
- SIP

Before delving into the specifics of individual gateway control protocols, first consider the general characteristics of gateway protocols.

Gateway Protocols: The Languages of Love

The ultimate goal of a gateway protocol on a VoIP network is to allow *Real-Time Transport Protocol (RTP)* streams (that is, streams of VoIP packets) to flow directly between endpoints. During the call setup process, each endpoint (for example, an FXO port in a gateway) needs to learn the IP address and User Datagram Protocol (UDP) port to use in order to get a phone call to the other end of the conversation.

Besides just setting up a call, you might optionally want to perform call administration and accounting features. These features can keep track of bandwidth usage on the *wide-area network (WAN)* and maintain call records, which can be used for billing or planning purposes. You might also need a way to obtain status information about a current call.

While your local gateway might know how to reach local phones, that local gateway might need to contact an external database of addresses to determine the location of a remote phone. This external database can learn about remote phones by having the gateway used by those remote phones register those phone numbers with the database. By having this central repository of phone number to IP address mappings, less configuration needs to be performed on each local gateway.

Consider the following example. A gateway located in Lexington, KY knows how to reach phone numbers in the 859 area code (that is, the area code of Lexington, KY). The Lexington gateway registers itself with an address database, as shown in Figure 5-1. When a gateway registers with a database, the gateway tells the database what the gateway's IP address is and what phone numbers the gateway can reach. In this example, the gateway has an IP address of 172.16.1.10.

Figure 5-1   Gateway Registration

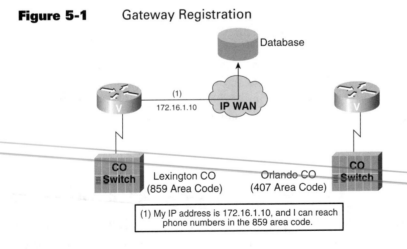

A caller attached to a gateway in Orlando, FL then wants to call a number in the 859 area code. However, the Orlando gateway lacks any information about the 859 area code. The Orlando gateway then asks the database how to get to the 859 area code. The database responds by saying, "You can reach phone numbers in the 859 area code by sending your packets to an IP address of 172.16.1.10," as shown in Figure 5-2. The Orlando gateway sets up a call with the Lexington gateway, using a gateway protocol (for example, H.323), and RTP packets begin to flow between the IP phones.

Figure 5-2   Gateway Resolution

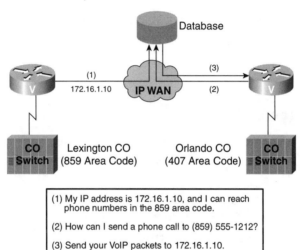

In the Cisco IP telephony environment, a CCM server acts as a database that can direct a gateway (for example, a Cisco voice-enabled router) to a remote gateway connected to the destination phone.

The Tried and True Language: H.323

H.323 represents the most mature of the three protocols considered in this chapter. However, the H.323 gateway protocol actually embodies multiple protocols. So, when you consider H.323, think of it as a collection of protocols, rather than a single protocol. For example, H.323 includes protocols to set up and tear down

VoIP calls, protocols to encode video transmissions, protocols to encode voice conversations, and even a data collaboration protocol for shared white boarding.

But for now, let's focus on just a couple of the H.323 protocols (used for VoIP calls), specifically:

- **H.225**—Performs call setup and *Registration, Admission, and Status (RAS)* functions.

- **H.245**—Performs call control, including exchanging gateway capabilities (for example, the supported coder decoders [CODECs]) between the end systems.

H.323 Pieces and Parts

In addition to the protocols that fall under the H.323 umbrella, H.323 also defines various hardware components, as shown in Figure 5-3.

Figure 5-3   H.323 Components

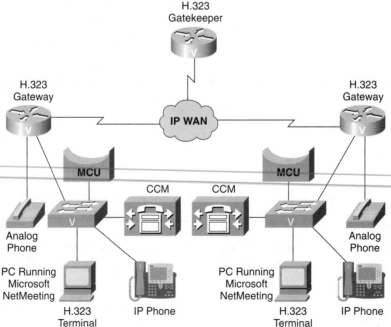

The following sections cover these components.

Terminals

An H.323 terminal acts as an endpoint in a conversation and communicates with another H.323 terminal. Notice that the Cisco IP phones are not considered terminals because these IP phones lack the full set of H.323 features. A PC running Microsoft NetMeeting does, however, act as an H.323 terminal.

Gateways

You can train your Cisco router to act as an H.323 gateway (using the appropriate *Cisco Internetwork Opertaing System [IOS]* software). An H.323 gateway translates back and forth between different types of audio formats (for example, VoIP and digital voice traveling over a T1 circuit).

Gatekeepers

Too many VoIP calls flowing over the WAN can *oversubscribe* (that is, require more bandwidth than is available) the WAN. To prevent WAN oversubscription, an H.323 gatekeeper can serve as a "traffic cop" for the IP WAN, keeping track of the available bandwidth. Before a call can travel across the IP WAN, an H.323 gateway or a CCM server can request permission from the H.323 gatekeeper. If WAN bandwidth is available for the call, the gatekeeper grants the connection request. However, if the WAN lacks sufficient bandwidth to support the call, along with all of the other existing calls, the gatekeeper can deny the connection request, thereby protecting the original voice calls from a bandwidth oversubscription that would be caused by an additional call.

Multipoint Control Unit

Technically, a conference call is a *multipoint call*, meaning that multiple endpoints participate in the same call. An H.323 *multipoint control unit (MCU)* handles the signaling to add and remove participants from a conference call, and the

MCU also mixes multiple audio and/or video streams together. The process of mixing audio and video streams requires processing power. Therefore, VoIP network designers often use dedicated hardware (for example, digital signal processors located in Cisco routers or switches) to act as conferencing resources.

H.323 Call Types

The previously mentioned gatekeepers are optional components because H.323 gateways can communicate directly between themselves. However, direct gateway-to-gateway calls suffer from scalability limitations. If you introduce gatekeepers into the network, the gateways communicate with gatekeepers using the RAS channel. Larger topologies might contain multiple gatekeepers, and those gatekeepers also communicate with each other using the RAS channel. Consider the following examples of how calls are completed in the following H.323 networks:

■ H.323 Gateway-to-Gateway Calls

■ H.323 Calls Using a Gatekeeper

H.323 Gateway-to-Gateway Calls

Direct gateway-to-gateway calls don't require a gatekeeper. Specifically, both gateways communicate directly with each other, as shown in Figure 5-4. First, H.225 performs the call setup, followed by H.245 performing a capabilities exchange. However, this H.225 and H.245 negotiation requires numerous packet exchanges between the gateways. Another, more efficient, option is *H.323 Fast Connect*, which performs the call setup and does a capabilities exchange in a single exchange of messages between the two gateways.

Figure 5-4   H.323 Call Setup without a Gatekeeper

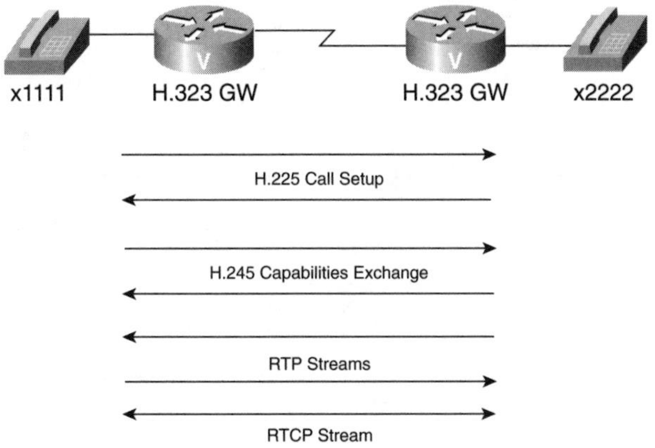

note

Figure 5-4 also shows a bidirectional *RTP Control Protocol (RTCP)* stream between the H.323 gateways. RTCP is a supervisory protocol for RTP and can provide information about the quality of the call.

H.323 Calls Using a Gatekeeper

In H.323 topologies containing a gatekeeper, the originating gateway (for example, a Cisco voice-enabled router) requests permission to place a call from the gatekeeper, using an admission request (ARQ) message, after which the gatekeeper might send an admission confirm (ACF) or an admission reject (ARJ) message. If the gatekeeper grants permission for the originating gateway to place the call, the call setup proceeds. The destination gateway also sends an ARQ to the gatekeeper. If permission for the destination gateway to set up the call is granted, the call setup proceeds as usual, using H.225 and H.245, after which RTP streams audio directly between the gateways. This call setup sequence is illustrated by the numbered steps in Figure 5-5.

Figure 5-5   H.323 Call Setup with a Gatekeeper

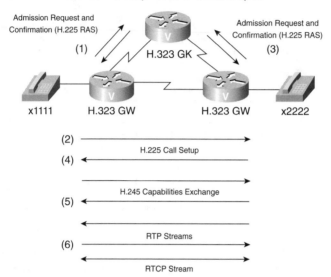

For even larger environments, you can have multiple gatekeepers involved in the call setup. The main difference with such a configuration is that when the first gatekeeper gets an admission request, that gatekeeper sends a location request (LRQ) and must receive a location confirm (LCF) from the remote gatekeeper before sending an ACF to the originating gateway.

To increase the availability of H.323 networks, you can configure multiple gate-keepers and/or gateways to service the same phone numbers. High availability technologies such as *Hot Standby Router Protocol (HSRP)*, where one router backs up another router, can also help maintain uptime in your H.323 network.

Cisco also offers a more scalable redundancy solution called *clustering*. With clustering, multiple gatekeepers belong to a group of gatekeepers called a *cluster*. When a gateway registers, the gateway is notified of a primary gatekeeper within the cluster to use, in addition to an alternate gatekeeper, which the gateway can use if the primary gatekeeper is unavailable.

Cisco's Very Own: MGCP

H.323 networks contain call-forwarding intelligence in multiple devices (for example, gateways) throughout the network. However, in a *Media Gateway Control Protocol vMGCP* network, the call-forwarding intelligence lives in a *call agent*. MGCP gateways lack call-forwarding intelligence. These gateways are minions to the call agent, forwarding dialed digits to the call agent and letting the call agent decide how to complete the call. In a Cisco environment, a call agent is a CCM server. Although Cisco originally developed MGCP, MGCP is now an industry standard (defined by RFC 2705 and RFC 2805).

Consider a couple of analog phones, each attached to Foreign Exchange Station (FXS) ports (in different routers). When a caller using one of these analog phones dials a number, the local router collects the dialed digits and forwards them to the call agent. The call agent assumes the responsibility for setting up the call. However, once the call is established, the call agent backs out of the way and allows the voice-enabled routers to stream RTP packets directly between themselves. This sequence is demonstrated by the numbered steps in Figure 5-6.

Figure 5-6   MGCP Call Setup

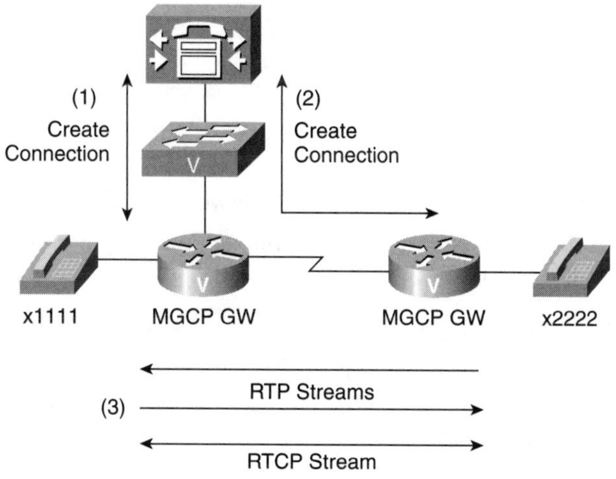

The call agent acts much like the referee in a boxing match. The two fighters come to the center of the ring. The referee talks with them about the rules (for example, "Let's have a clean fight") and then says "Box!" The referee backs out of the way and lets the fighters "communicate." An MGCP call agent does much the same thing, by establishing the rules for the communication and then backing out of the way once the call is set up. After the call setup is complete, the MGCP devices (for example, FXS ports connected to analog phones) stream RTP packets directly between themselves, without any intervention from the MGCP call agent.

MGCP networks contain *MGCP components* and *MGCP concepts*. MGCP components consist of the physical pieces of hardware making up an MGCP network, while the logical pieces of an MGCP network are MGCP concepts.

MGCP Components

The physical pieces (that is, MGCP components) comprising an MGCP network include

- Endpoints

- Gateways

- Call Agents

Endpoints

An endpoint is the interface between the VoIP network and the traditional telephony network. For example, consider an analog phone connecting to an FXS port in a router. By definition, the FXS port, not the analog phone, is the endpoint. Endpoint names look much like an e-mail address (for example, circuitID@mgcpgw.cisco-press.com) and are composed of two parts: the locally significant name of the endpoint (before the "@" sign) and the Domain Name System (DNS) name of the MGCP gateway (after the "@" sign).

Gateways

Like H.323 gateways, MGCP gateways convert audio between different network types (for example, between a VoIP network and the PSTN). MGCP categorizes various gateway types. For example a *residential gateway* supports devices typically found in residential environments, such as plain old telephone service (POTS) telephones.

Call Agents

A call agent contains the intelligence of an MGCP network and controls the gateways and their endpoints. An MGCP gateway can report *events* to the call agent, and the call agent can, for example, tell the endpoint what type of signal to send to the phone. Remember, in a Cisco IP telephony environment, a CCM server acts as an MGCP call agent.

MGCP Concepts

Recall that an MGCP concept is a logical piece of an MGCP network. Consider the following MGCP concepts:

- Call
- Event
- Signal

Call

A call forms when two or more endpoints interconnect.

Event

An MGCP call agent (for example, a CCM server) instructs an endpoint to watch for an event (that is, some activity occurring on the endpoint). As an example, an FXS port might watch for the event of an attached analog phone going off-hook.

Signal

A call agent instructs an endpoint to send a specific signal when a certain event occurs. For example, after the event of an analog phone going off-hook, the FXS port might send the *signal* of *dial tone* to the attached phone. Remember, the command for the FXS port to send the dial tone came from the MGCP call agent.

Making the MGCP Network More Fault Tolerant

To enhance the availability of an MGCP network, you might wish to deploy survivability strategies such as the following:

- **MGCP switchover and switchback**—MGCP switchover and switchback uses two or more CCMs. When an MGCP gateway does not see any MGCP messages from a CCM server for a period of time, the gateway sends packets called *keep alive packets*, to see whether the CCM server is accessible. If the MGCP gateway fails to receive a response, the gateway attempts to establish a connection with a backup CCM. If the primary CCM comes back up, the MGCP gateway can be configured to switch back to the primary.

- **MGCP gateway fallback**—MGCP gateway fallback works with *Survivable Remote Site Telephony (SRST)* to maintain a remote office that connects to a centralized CCM. If the WAN link, which the MGCP gateway uses to reach the CCM, fails, the gateway continues to operate, in a fallback mode, as an H.323 gateway.

The New Kid on the Block: SIP

Session initiation protocol (SIP) recently threw its hat into the ring to be a contender for the gateway protocol of choice. SIP designers envision the promise of vendor interoperability, the flexibility of network designers to select VoIP products from different vendors and have those products communicate via SIP. Cisco recently introduced a CallManager feature (that is, a SIP trunk) that permits a CCM environment to communicate with an SIP environment.

SIP uses the concept of inviting participants into sessions, and those sessions can be advertised by the Session Announcement Protocol (SAP). Like H.323, SIP distributes call-forwarding intelligence in devices throughout the network. These devices are called *user agents (UAs)*. Two types of UAs exist:

- User agent clients (UACs) initiate the connection by sending an INVITE message

- User agent servers (UASs) reply to INVITE messages

UAs include components such as IP phones. If the IP phone originates the call, the IP phone represents a UAC. However, when the IP phone receives a call, the IP phone acts as a UAS. Cisco provides SIP firmware, allowing an administrator to convert a Cisco 7960G IP Phone from a *Skinny Client Control Protocol* (*SCCP*) phone to an SIP phone.

A SIP network leverages various types of SIP servers:

- **Proxy Server**—Performs forwarding for a UAC

- **Registrar Server**—Registers the location of current clients

- **Redirect Server**—Informs the UA of the next server to contact

- **Location Server**—Performs address resolution for SIP proxy and redirect servers

SIP uses clear text for sending messages, which helps administrators troubleshoot network issues. The two types of SIP messages include

- **Request**—A message from a client to a server

- **Response**—A message from a server to a client

A request includes messages such as an INVITE (which requests a participant to join the session) or a BYE (which disconnects the current call). Conversely, a response message uses HTTP status messages. For example, have you ever attempted to connect to a website and received a "404 error" or a "500 error" message? Those HTTP responses are also used in the SIP environment.

For a SIP client to get the IP address of a SIP server, it has to resolve (that is, look up) a SIP address. These SIP addresses are actually URLs, which happen to begin with *sip:*, as opposed to *http:*. SIP addresses can include a variety of information such as username, password, hostname, IP address, and phone number information. Consider the following example of a SIP address:

> sip:18595551212@ciscopress.com;user=phone

In this example, the **user=phone** argument specifies that the user portion of the URL (that is, **18595551212**) represents a phone number and not a user ID.

SIP devices can dynamically make their addresses known by registering with a SIP registrar server. Once SIP devices have their addresses registered, a SIP client might have the ability to resolve a SIP address by itself, perhaps via DNS or through a local host table. However, a SIP client might use a SIP proxy server to query a SIP location database to resolve the SIP IP address. Consider a basic SIP call, where one SIP gateway communicates directly with another SIP gateway, without the use of proxy or redirect servers, as shown in Figure 5-7.

Figure 5-7   Basic SIP Call Setup

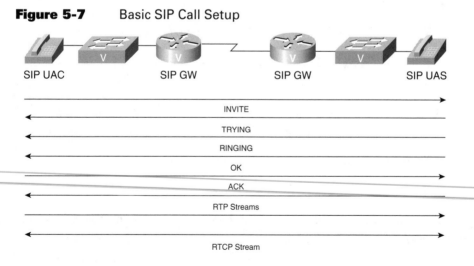

A basic SIP call setup begins when a SIP client sends an INVITE message to a SIP server (noting a SIP IP phone can act as either a UAC or a UAS, depending on whether it is originating or terminating the call). The destination server (that is, a UAS) responds if it is willing to join the session to which it has been invited. The originating client (that is, a UAC) sends an acknowledgement (that is, an ACK message) to the destination server. At this point, the RTP streams flow directly between the SIP gateways.

If you introduce a SIP proxy server into your topology, the call setup procedure is similar to that just discussed. However, the INVITE message goes to the proxy server rather than the destination UAS. The proxy server might consult a location server to learn the IP address of the final endpoint. The destination exchanges call parameters with the proxy server, which responds to the originating UAC. The UAC then forwards an ACK, via the proxy server, to the destination UAS, after which the RTP stream begins. Using a proxy server offers you the benefits of centralized call control and call setup management.

When a redirect server is used, the originating UAC sends an INVITE message to a redirect server, which might consult a location server to determine the path to the destination. The registrar server responds to the UAC with a "moved message," telling the UAC the IP address of the destination UAS. This operation is much like when you connect to a website, and you receive a message saying that the page you are looking for has moved to a new URL, and you are automatically redirected. Once the UAC learns the location of the destination UAS, a direct connection can be set up between the UAC and UAS. Therefore, the main purpose of a redirect server is to off-load the IP resolution process from the UAC.

If one of your SIP servers goes down, the voice network could be rendered unavailable. One way to provide redundancy is to have multiple instances of proxy and redirect servers. Therefore, the UAs can contain multiple server entries, and if the first server fails, the second server takes over.

Case Study: Your Turn to Be Trilingual

The case study in Chapter 4, "Meet the 'Brain' of the Voice over IP Network," directed you to design an IP telephony solution for the XYZ Company. Your next design decision involves selecting a gateway protocol for the gateways you specified in Chapter 4's case study. These gateways are the routers or switches located at each site that connect out to the local *central office (CO)* (that is, the PSTN).

Realize that your selection of a gateway protocol might differ from the suggested solution. Just know why you selected the gateway protocol.

Identify your gateway protocol recommendation for the XYZ Company (that is, **H.323**, **MGCP**, or **SIP**), and discuss the rationale for your selection in the following section.

Design Description for XYZ Company:

_____

_____

_____

_____

_____

_____

_____

_____

_____

_____

_____

_____

_____

Suggested Solution

Chapter 4's suggested solution used a distributed deployment model, with CCM clusters located at XYZ Headquarters and XYZ Remote Office 1. Also, XYZ Remote Office 2 contained a *CallManager Express (CME)* router, as shown in Figure 5-8.

Figure 5-8   Chapter 4's Suggested Solution

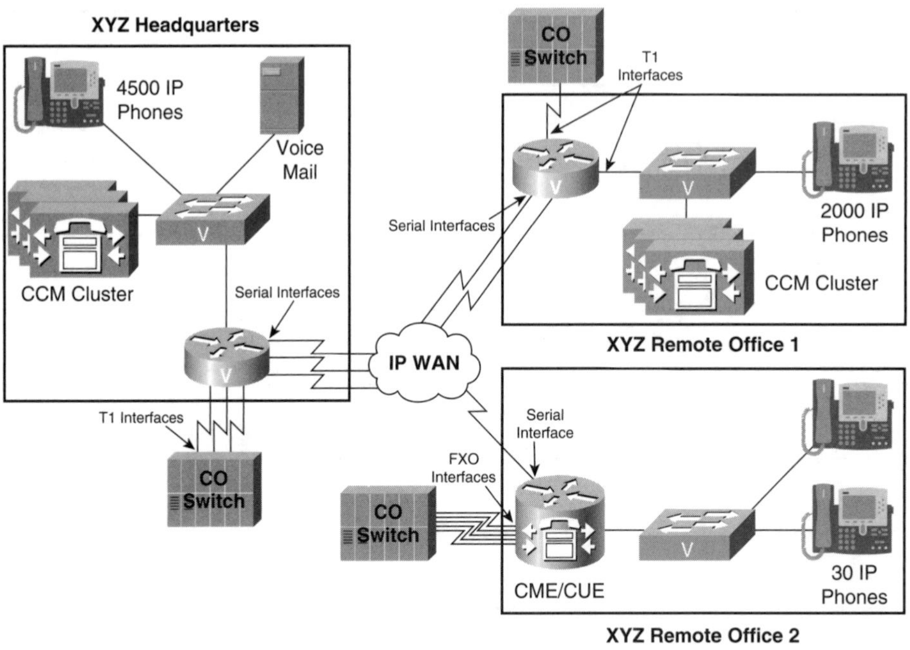

Because the suggested solution only contained Cisco call processing equipment (that is, the design did not use any third-party hardware) and because a distributed deployment model and a CME router were used, the suggested gateway protocol is **H.323**.

However, if XYZ Company used a centralized deployment model (that is, where all CCM servers reside at XYZ Headquarters), MGCP might be an appropriate gateway protocol choice. MGCP lends itself well to a centralized environment because the MGCP model specifies a centralized call agent with which remote MGCP gateways register. SIP is often used in a CCM environment when connecting a CallManager cluster to a third-party SIP solution.

Chapter Summary

This chapter discussed the need for gateway control protocols. For example, when an IP phone on an IP telephony network needs a connection with a phone on the PSTN, the phone call traverses a gateway. The gateway and the CCM server need a common language (that is, protocol) for communication.

Three gateway control protocols include H.323, MGCP, and SIP. H.323 represents the most mature of the gateway control protocols and is appropriate for a distributed deployment environment.

MGCP uses a call agent (for example, a CCM server) to store call-forwarding intelligence, while H.323 stores call-forwarding intelligence in gateways throughout the network.

SIP represents a newer gateway control protocol targeted at vendor interoperability. Cisco continues to enhance SIP features available in the CCM.

Chapter Review Questions

1. From the following list, identify three gateway control protocols.

    a. H.323

    b. SIP

    c. RTP

    d. MGCP

2. What H.323 component is responsible for performing a "capabilities exchange" between H.323 terminals?

   a. H.225

   b. T.120

   c. H.245

   d. G.711

3. Which H.323 devices prevent bandwidth oversubscription on the WAN?

   a. Terminals

   b. Gateways

   c. Gatekeepers

   d. MCUs

4. What message does an H.323 gateway send to an H.323 gatekeeper to request admission to the WAN?

   a. ARQ

   b. ACF

   c. ARC

   d. LRQ

5. Logical pieces of an MGCP network are called _____.

   a. MGCP terminals

   b. MGCP components

   c. MGCP gateways

   d. MGCP concepts

6. Which of the following is considered an MGCP component?

   a. Call

   b. Call agent

   c. Event

   d. Signal

7. In a Cisco IP telephony network, what acts as an MGCP call agent?

   a. Cisco CallManager

   b. Cisco Unity

   c. Cisco voice-enabled router

   d. Cisco voice-enabled switch

8. Which SIP component initiates a SIP connection by sending an INVITE message?

   a. UAS

   b. UAC

   c. SIP proxy server

   d. SIP redirect server

9. Identify the SIP server that informs the UA of the next server to contact.

   a. SIP proxy server

   b. SIP redirect server

   c. SIP location server

   d. SIP registrar server

10. What are the two types of SIP messages?

   a. Event

   b. Request

   c. Signal

   d. Response

What You Will Learn

After reading this chapter, you should be able to:

- ✔ Explain why QoS is critical on VoIP networks.

- ✔ Distinguish between *congestion management* and *congestion avoidance.*

- ✔ Describe how to limit the bandwidth used by specific traffic types.

- ✔ Identify strategies for maximizing available WAN bandwidth for VoIP traffic.

CHAPTER 6

Why Quality Matters

Traditionally, networks physically separated voice, video, and data traffic. These traffic types literally flowed over separate media (for example, leased lines or fiber optic cables). Today, however, network designers leverage the power of existing data networks to transmit voice and video, thus achieving significant cost savings by reducing equipment, maintenance, and even staffing costs.

Today's converged networks present a challenge, however. Specifically, multiple applications contend for bandwidth, and some applications (for example, voice) are more intolerant of delay, sometimes called *latency*, than other applications, such as FTP file transfers. A lack of bandwidth overshadows most quality problems.

A lack of bandwidth might cause packets to suffer from one or more of the following symptoms:

- **Delay**—Delay is the time required for a packet to travel from its source to its destination. You might have witnessed delay on the evening news, when the news anchor is talking via satellite to a foreign news correspondent. Due to the satellite delay, the conversation begins to feel unnatural.

- **Jitter**—Jitter results from the uneven arrival of packets. Imagine a *Voice over IP (VoIP)* conversation where packet 1 arrives followed by packet 2 20 milliseconds (ms) later. After another 70 ms packet 3 arrives, and then packet 4 arrives 20 ms behind packet 3. This variation in arrival times, called *jitter*, does not result from dropped packets. However, the jitter might sound like dropped packets (that is, gaps in the speech) from the listener's perspective.

- **Drops**—Routers and switches contain *buffers* to store packets when the network link (that is, the physical network connection) lacks sufficient bandwidth to transmit the packets at the moment. Packet drops occur when a link is congested and a buffer overflows. Some traffic types, such as web traffic, retransmit dropped packets. However, dropped voice and video packets are gone forever. These traffic types, which use User Datagram Protocol (UDP) for transmission, lack the ability to retransmit dropped packets. UDP is still preferred over Transmission Control Protocol (TCP) for voice, however, due to UDP's reduced overhead. And if you think about it, you wouldn't want voice packets retransmitted anyway, because voice packets arriving out of order would sound like gibberish.

Fortunately, *quality of service* (*QoS*) features available on Cisco routers and switches can recognize important traffic and then treat that traffic in a special way. For example, you might wish to allocate 128 kbps of bandwidth for VoIP traffic, and optionally give that traffic priority treatment. At the same time, you may want your web traffic to receive 64 kbps of non-priority bandwidth.

Too Many Swimmers in the Bandwidth Pool

Consider water flowing through a series of pipes with varying diameters. The water's flow rate through those pipes is limited to the water's flow rate through the pipe with the smallest diameter. Similarly, as a packet travels from its source to its destination, the packet's effective bandwidth is the bandwidth of the slowest link along that path, as shown in Figure 6-1.

Figure 6-1   Effective Bandwidth

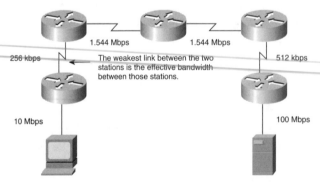

Because a lack of bandwidth represents the primary quality challenge in a network, the logical question is, "How can I increase available bandwidth?" A knee-jerk response to that question is often, "Add more bandwidth!" While there is no substitute for more bandwidth, extra bandwidth comes at a relatively high cost.

Compare your network to a highway system in a large city. During rush hour, the lanes of the highway are congested, but the lanes might be underutilized during other periods of the day. Instead of just building more lanes to accommodate peak traffic rates, highway engineers convert one or more existing lanes to *car pool lanes*. Cars with two or more riders can use the reserved car pool lane. The riders in these cars enjoy higher priority on the highway. Similarly, you can use QoS features to give your mission-critical applications higher-priority treatment in times of network congestion.

Being Politically Incorrect: Treating Special Traffic in a Special Way

The mission statement of QoS could read something like, "To categorize traffic and apply a policy to traffic categories, in accordance with a QoS policy." Specifically, there are three basic steps to QoS configuration:

Step 1   Determine network performance requirements for various traffic types. For example, consider these design guidelines for voice, video, and data traffic:

- Voice

  - No more than 150 ms of one-way delay

  - No more than 30 ms of jitter

  - No more than 1 percent packet loss

- Video

  - No more than 150 ms of one-way delay for interactive video applications (for example, video conferencing)

— No more than 30 ms of jitter

— No more than 1 percent packet loss

■ Data

Applications vary in their delay and loss requirements. Therefore, categorize data applications into predefined *classes* of traffic, where each class is configured with specific delay and loss characteristics.

Step 2   Categorize traffic into specific categories. For example, you might have a category named "Low Delay," and you decide to place voice and video packets in that category. You might also have a "Low Priority" class, where you place traffic such as music downloads from the Internet. As a rule of thumb, Cisco recommends you create no more than ten classes of traffic.

Step 3   Document your QoS policy, and make the policy available to your users. Then, for example, if a user complains that their network gaming applications are running slowly, you can point them to your corporate QoS policy, which describes how applications such as network gaming have *best-effort* treatment (that is, all other packet types take priority over these packet types).

Cisco allows you to fill your tool belt with multiple QoS tools (that is, *QoS mechanisms*). One goal of this chapter is to help you decide when to use one QoS tool versus another. All of the Cisco QoS features are categorized into one of three categories, as shown in Figure 6-2.

Figure 6-2   QoS Categories

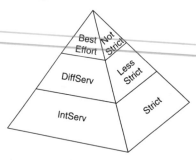

The following is an explanation of these categories:

- *Best-Effort* does not truly provide QoS. No reordering of packets occurs. Best-Effort uses the *first-in, first-out* (*FIFO*) queuing strategy, where packets are emptied from a queue (that is, a storage space on the router) in the same order they entered the queue.

- *Integrated Services (IntServ)*, often referred to as *Hard QoS*, can make strict bandwidth reservations. IntServ uses signaling among network devices to provide bandwidth reservations. Resource Reservation Protocol (RSVP) is an example of an IntServ approach to QoS. Because IntServ must be configured on every router along a packet's path, the main drawback of IntServ is its lack of scalability.

- *Differentiated Services (DiffServ)*, as the name suggests, differentiates between multiple traffic flows. Specifically, packets are *marked*, and routers and switches can then make decisions (for example, dropping or forwarding decisions) based on those markings. Because DiffServ does not make an explicit reservation, it is often called *Soft QoS*.

This chapter focuses on DiffServ, as opposed to IntServ or Best-Effort. Before examining the specific DiffServ QoS tools that can improve voice quality, first consider the following categories of QoS mechanisms:

- Classification
- Marking
- Congestion management
- Congestion avoidance
- Policing and shaping
- Link efficiency

Classification

Classification places traffic into different categories. Multiple characteristics can be used for classification. For example, point of presence 3 (POP3), Internet Message Access Protocol (IMAP), Simple Mail Transfer Protocol (SMTP), and

Microsoft Exchange traffic could all be placed in an "EMAIL" class, while traffic entering the router on any serial interface could be placed in the "SERIAL" class. Classification does not, however, alter any bits in the frame or packet.

Marking

Marking manipulates bits within a frame, cell, or packet telling the network how to treat that traffic. Marking alone does not change how the network treats a packet. Other tools (for example, queuing tools) can, however, reference those markings and make forwarding or dropping decisions based on those markings.

Congestion Management

When you hear the term *congestion management*, think *queuing*. These concepts are one and the same. When an interface's output software queue contains packets, the interface's queuing strategy determines how the packets are emptied from the queue, as shown in Figure 6-3. For example, some traffic types can be given priority treatment (that is, sent out of the queue first), and bandwidth amounts can be made available for specific classes of traffic (for example, voice or video traffic).

Figure 6-3   Queuing

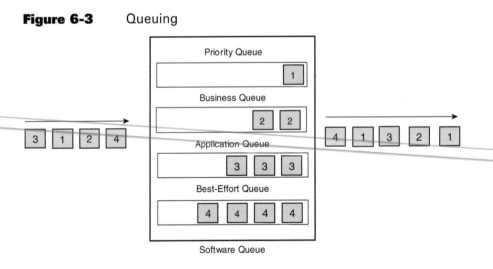

Queuing mechanisms determine in what order and in what quantity specific
packets are emptied from a queue.

Congestion Avoidance

If an interface's output queue fills to capacity, newly arriving packets are discarded (that is, *tail dropped*), regardless of the priority assigned to the discarded packet. To prevent this behavior, Cisco employs a congestion avoidance technique called *weighted random early detection (WRED)*. After the queue depth reaches a specific configurable level (that is, the minimum threshold) for a particular priority marking, WRED introduces the possibility of discard for packets with that priority marking. As the queue depth continues to increase, the possibility of discard increases until a configurable maximum threshold is reached. After the queue depth exceeds the maximum threshold for traffic with a specific priority, there is a 100 percent chance of discard for packets with that priority marking.

Policing and Shaping

Sometimes, instead of making a minimum amount of bandwidth available for specific traffic types, you might want to limit the available bandwidth. Both *policing* and *shaping* tools can accomplish this objective. Collectively, these tools are called *traffic conditioners*.

Policing can be used as packets go into or come out of a router, and policing typically discards packets exceeding the configured rate limit, which you can think of as a *speed limit* for particular traffic types. Because policing drops packets, resulting in retransmissions, policing is recommended for use on higher-speed interfaces (that is, greater than 2.048 Mbps).

Shaping buffers (that is, delays) traffic exceeding a configurable rate. Therefore, shaping is recommended for use on slower-speed interfaces (that is, equal to or less than 2.048 Mbps). Another distinction between shaping and policing is that policing can attempt to send packets exceeding a configured limit and mark those packets with a lower-priority marking.

Link Efficiency

To make the most of the limited bandwidth available on slower-speed links, you might choose to implement *compression* or *Link Fragmentation and Interleaving (LFI)*, as illustrated in Figure 6-4. Using header compression on smaller packets, such as voice packets, can dramatically increase a link's available bandwidth.

Figure 6-4   Link Efficiency Mechanisms

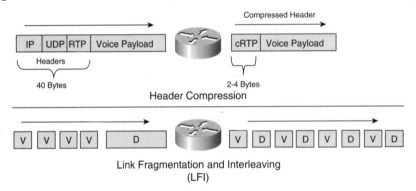

LFI addresses the issue of *serialization delay*, which is the amount of time required for a packet to exit an interface. A large data packet, for example, on a slower-speed link (that is, less than 768 kbps) could create excessive delay for a voice packet, due to the time required for the data packet to exit the interface. LFI fragments large packets and interleaves smaller packets in amongst the fragments, reducing the serialization delay the smaller packets experience.

Giving Voice Top Priority

Before QoS mechanisms can treat voice with high priority, these QoS mechanisms must recognize voice packets. This chapter considers the very popular DiffServ model of QoS. DiffServ, as the name suggests, literally differentiates between packet types and marks those packets. Once a packet is marked, the next router or the next switch in the packet's path can examine the marking and immediately know how to treat the packet.

The first question might be, "How is a voice packet recognized as a voice packet?" This recognition process is called *classification*. For example, you might recognize Telnet, FTP, and HTTP traffic and categorize those applications together in a specific class of traffic. You might place voice packets in a separate class. Cisco routers and switches are very flexible in their ability to recognize different packet types. For example, to recognize voice traffic, you could use access control lists (ACLs), which can, for example, match traffic based on source and destination IP addresses, in addition to source and destination port numbers. Also, the Cisco Network Based Application Recognition (NBAR) feature can classify traffic by examining traffic characteristics up to and including the application layer (for example, the name of a graphics file being downloaded as part of a web page). NBAR's deep packet inspection can interrogate packet characteristics and recognize application signatures. While classification groups common types of traffic, classification doesn't alter the classified packets in any way.

While classification is great, you probably do not want to configure classification on every router. Therefore, once the traffic is classified, you can *mark* the traffic. After a router marks a packet, other routers and switches in the network can reference those markings and make decisions (that is, forwarding or dropping decisions) based on those markings.

As a metaphor, consider the frequent flyer programs offered by many major airlines. After traveling on enough flights and accumulating enough miles, you achieve the designation of a *frequent flyer*, which might come with such perks as priority boarding. However, as you approach the gate agent, does the gate agent require you to prove your frequent flyer status by showing your boarding passes from all your previous flights? Not at all. Instead, after you achieve frequent flyer status (that is, you are *classified* as a frequent flyer), the airline gives you a *marking*, such as a luggage tag indicating your frequent flyer status. Therefore, as you approach the gate agent, you only need to show your marking (e.g., luggage tag or an actual marking on your boarding pass). The same theory holds true in a network. Once packets are classified (achieving frequent flyer status in this metaphor), the packets simply show their marking (a luggage tag in our metaphor) to subsequent routers or switches without the need for reclassification at each router and each switch along the packets' path.

The next logical question might be, "How is a packet marked?" Inside an Internet Protocol version 4 (IPv4) header, there is a byte (that is, 8 bits) called the *Type of Service (ToS)* byte. You can mark packets, using bits within the ToS byte, using either *IP Precedence* or *Differentiated Service Code Point (DSCP)* markings, as shown in Figure 6-5.

Figure 6-5   ToS Byte

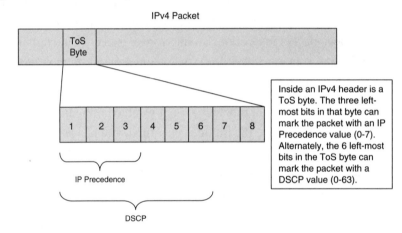

IP Precedence uses the three left-most bits in the ToS byte. With 3 bits at its disposal, IP Precedence markings range from 0 to 7. However, 6 and 7 should not be used because those values are reserved for network use.

For more granularity, you might choose DSCP, which uses the six left-most bits in the ToS byte. Six bits yield 64 possible values (0–63). The challenge with so many values at your disposal is that the value you choose to represent a certain level of priority might be treated very differently by a router or switch under someone else's administration.

For example, let's say that in my network, I mark high-priority traffic with a DSCP value of 26. However, you decide to mark high-priority traffic in your network with a DSCP value of 39. In fact, your network considers a DSCP value of 26 to have the priority of dirt. Do you see the problem? We're just arbitrarily selecting values, without any common frame of reference.

To maintain relative levels of priority among devices, the *Internet Engineering Task Force (IETF)*, a standards body, selected a subset of DSCP's 64 possible values for use. These values are called *Per Hop Behaviors (PHBs)* because they indicate how each router hop along the path from the source to the destination treats packets.

All PHBs fall into one of four categories:

- Default

- Expedited Forwarding (EF)

- Assured Forwarding (AF)

- Class Selector (CS)

Default

Traffic only needing best-effort treatment can be marked with the *Default* PHB, which simply means the six left-most bits in the packet's ToS byte (that is, the DSCP bits) are all 0s (that is, a DSCP value of 0).

Default PHB = 000000 (in binary) = 0 (in decimal)

Expedited Forwarding

The EF PHB has a DSCP value of 46. Latency-sensitive traffic, such as voice, typically receives a PHB marking of EF.

EF PHB = 101110 (in binary) = 46 (in decimal)

Assured Forwarding

The AF PHB represents the broadest category of PHBs. Specifically, AF PHBs represent 12 different PHB values, as shown in Table 6-1.

Table 6-1   Assured Forwarding PHBs

PHB	Low Drop Preference	Medium Drop Preference	High Drop Preference
Class 1	AF11 (10) 001010	AF12 (12) 001100	AF13 (14) 001110
Class 2	AF21 (18) 010010	AF22 (20) 010100	AF23 (22) 010110
Class 3	AF31 (26) 011010	AF32 (28) 011100	AF33 (30) 011110
Class 4	AF41 (34) 100010	AF42 (36) 100100	AF43 (38) 100110

Notice the assured forwarding PHBs are grouped into four classes. Examining these DSCP values in binary reveals that the three left-most bits of all the Class 1 AF PHBs are 001 (that is, a decimal value of 1); the three left-most bits of all the Class 2 AF PHBs are 010 (that is, a decimal value of 2); the three left-most bits of all the Class 3 AF PHBs are 011 (that is, a decimal value of 3); and the three left-most bits of all the Class 4 AF PHBs are 100 (that is, a decimal value of 4). Because IP Precedence-aware devices examine these three left-most bits, an IP Precedence-aware router interprets all Class 1 DSCP values as an IP Precedence value of 1. The same applies to Class 2, 3, and 4 PHB values.

Each AF PHB class contains three distinct values, which indicate a packet's *drop preference*. Higher values in an AF PHB class are more likely to be discarded during periods of congestion. For example, an AF13 packet is more likely to be discarded than an AF11 packet.

Voice packets typically receive a PHB value of EF, while call setup traffic uses a PHB value of CS3. Also, interactive video often uses a value of AF41.

Class Selector

CS PHBs provide complete backward compatibility with IP Precedence values because, just like IP Precedence, CS PHBs have 0s in the fourth, fifth, and sixth bits of the ToS byte, as shown in Table 6-2. For example, imagine your router uses DSCP markings, but you are sending packets to a router that only understands IP Precedence markings. Such a scenario provides a great opportunity to use CS markings. You could send a packet marked with a DSCP value of 40, which is 101000 in binary. When that packet is received by an IP Precedence-aware router, the packet's IP Precedence value will be interpreted as 5, because only the three left-most bits are considered, and because 101 in binary equals 5 in decimal.

Table 6-2   Class Selector (CS) PHBs

PHB	Decimal Value	Binary Value	IP Precedence Value
CS0	0	**000**000	0
CS1	8	**001**000	1
CS2	16	**010**000	2
CS3	24	**011**000	3
CS4	32	**100**000	4
CS5	40	**101**000	5
CS6	48	**110**000	6
CS7	56	**111**000	7

Thus far, you've examined packet markings using the ToS byte in an IPv4 header. These markings (that is, DSCP and IP Precedence markings) are considered Layer 3 markings (that is, markings occurring at the Network Layer of the OSI Model). However, you can also mark traffic at Layer 2 of the OSI Model (that is, the Data Link Layer). For example, you can mark frames traveling over an Ethernet trunk with a Layer 2 class of service (CoS) value, as illustrated in Figure 6-6.

Figure 6-6   Class of Service (CoS) Marking

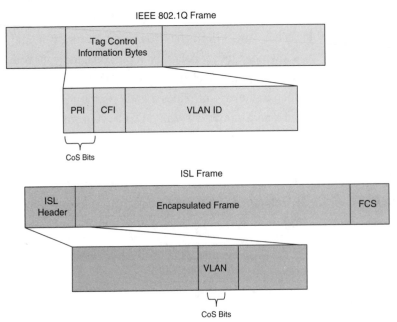

CoS values range from 0–7, although Cisco recommends that you never use 6 or 7, because 6 and 7 are reserved for network use. The bits used to create the CoS marking depend on the type of trunk being used:

- **IEEE 802.1Q Trunk**—Uses 3 bits in a Tag Control byte to mark a CoS value

- **ISL Trunk**—Uses 3 bits in the ISL header to mark a CoS value

note

Marking frames flowing over an IEEE 802.1Q trunk is referred to as *IEEE 802.1p*.

Layer 2 markings can also extend to the WAN. Consider a Frame Relay network. A Frame Relay header contains a bit called the *Discard Eligible (DE)* bit, which identifies frames that the service provider can drop during periods of congestion. You can leverage the DE bit to identify less important traffic you send to the Frame Relay service provider. Similarly, you can mark the *Cell Loss Priority (CLP)* bit in an Asynchronous Transfer Mode (ATM) cell to identify less important ATM traffic.

A major design issue to keep in mind is that a CoS marking (that is, a Layer 2 marking) sent over an Ethernet trunk does not pass through a router. So, if you only use CoS markings to identify traffic priorities, those CoS markings need *remarking* to Layer 3 markings before the traffic passes through a router. Otherwise, the traffic emerges from the router with a CoS value of 0, as shown in Figure 6-7.

Figure 6-7   Without CoS Remarking

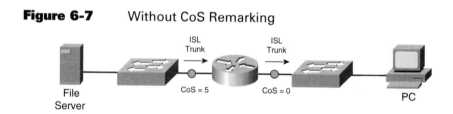

While Cisco recommends marking traffic as close to the source as possible, you typically don't want end users setting their own priority markings. Therefore, you can use your Catalyst switches to create a *trust boundary*, which is a point in the network that does not trust incoming markings. An exception to having a wiring closet switch acting as a trust boundary would be a Cisco IP phone connected to the switch. Because Cisco IP phones mark packets, you can extend a trust boundary to the phone.

Classification and marking serve as the initial steps in ensuring voice quality. However, classification and marking alone do not alter traffic behavior. Once a router or a switch marks traffic, other QoS mechanisms can reference those markings and make forwarding or dropping decisions based on those markings.

Feeling a Little Congested?

When a device, such as a switch or a router, receives traffic faster than it can be transmitted, the device attempts to buffer (that is, store) the extra traffic until bandwidth becomes available. This buffering process is called *queuing* or *congestion management*. Routers contain both a hardware queue and a software queue. The router automatically determines the size of the hardware queue, and the first packet to go into the hardware queue is the first packet to exit it. However, after the hardware queue fills to capacity, the software queue accommodates additional packets, and you can use queuing mechanisms to influence the order in which various traffic types are emptied from the software queue, as shown in Figure 6-8.

Figure 6-8   Software Queue

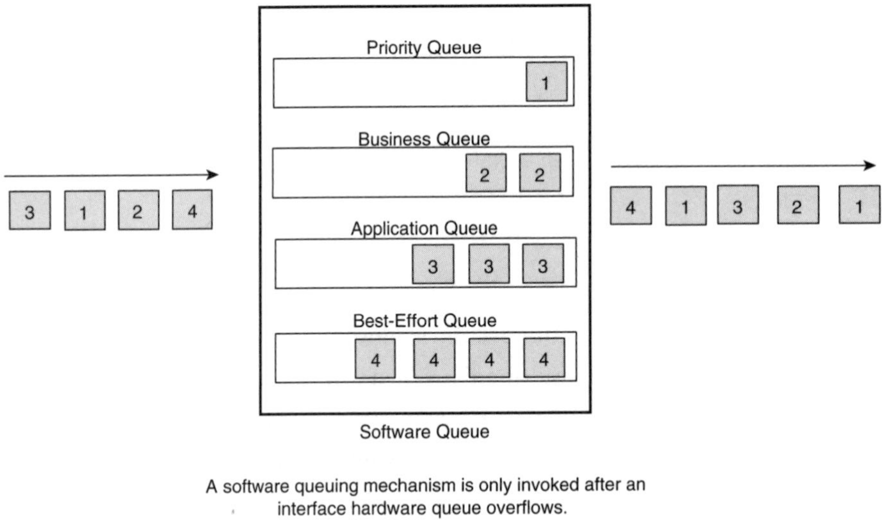

Software Queue

A software queuing mechanism is only invoked after an
interface hardware queue overflows.

Congestion occurs not just in the WAN but also in the LAN. Mismatched interface speeds, for example, could result in congestion on a high-speed LAN. Aggregation points in the network can also result in congestion. For example, perhaps multiple workstations connect to a switch at FastEthernet speeds (that is, 100 Mbps), and these workstations simultaneously transmit to a server also connected to the same switch via FastEthernet. Such a scenario can result in traffic backing up in a queue.

Cisco routers and switches support multiple queuing mechanisms. Before delving into modern queuing methods, such as *Low Latency Queuing (LLQ)*, first consider a few of the Cisco legacy queuing mechanisms.

First-In, First-Out (FIFO) Queuing

FIFO queuing does not truly perform any QoS operations. As FIFO's name suggests, the first packet to come into the queue is the first packet sent out of the queue, as shown in Figure 6-9. Routers use FIFO queuing in their hardware queue. FIFO in the software queue works just like FIFO in the hardware queue (that is, no packet manipulation occurs). Interfaces running at speeds greater than 2.048 Mbps use FIFO queuing by default.

Figure 6-9   First-In, First-Out (FIFO) Queuing

FIFO queuing does not perform any packet reordering.

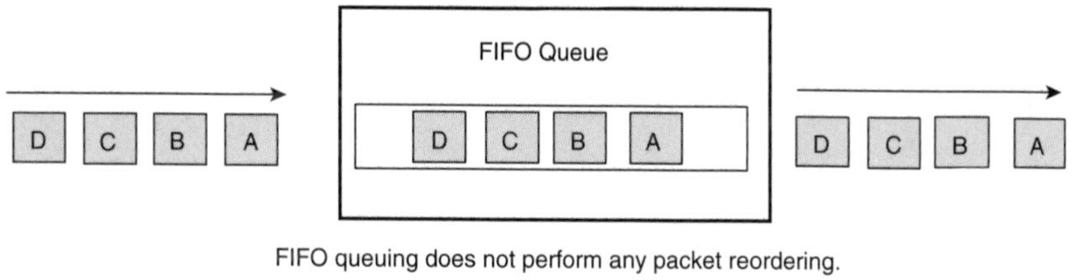

While FIFO is widely supported on all IOS platforms, it can starve out traffic by allowing bandwidth-hungry flows to take an unfair share of the bandwidth. For example, if FTP file transfer packets and voice packets simultaneously reside in a queue, the bandwidth-hungry nature of FTP could starve out the voice packets, causing noticeable gaps in the voice.

Weighted Fair Queuing (WFQ)

WFQ is enabled by default on slow-speed interfaces (that is, 2.048 Mbps and slower). WFQ allocates a queue for each flow, for as many as 256 flows by default. WFQ uses IP Precedence values to provide a weighting to Fair Queuing (FQ).

When emptying the queues, FQ does *byte-by-byte* scheduling. Specifically, FQ looks 1 byte deep into each queue to determine whether an entire packet can be sent. FQ then looks another byte deep into the queue to determine whether an entire packet can be sent. As a result, smaller traffic flows and smaller packet sizes have priority over bandwidth-hungry flows with large packets.

In the following example, three flows simultaneously arrive at a queue. Flow A has three packets, which are 128 bytes each. Flow B has a single 96-byte packet. Flow C has a single 70-byte packet. After 70 byte-by-byte rounds, FQ can transmit the packet from Flow C. After an additional 26 rounds, FQ can transmit the packet from Flow B. After an additional 32 rounds, FQ can transmit the first packet from Flow A. Another 128 rounds are required to send the second packet from Flow A. Finally, after a grand total of 384 rounds, the third packet from Flow A is transmitted, as shown in Figure 6-10.

Figure 6-10   Fair Queuing

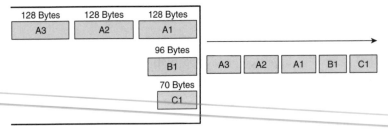

Output Queue

With WFQ, packets' IP Precedence values influence how the packets are emptied from a queue. Consider the previous scenario with the addition of IP Precedence markings. In this scenario, Flow A's packets are marked with an IP Precedence of 5, while Flow B and Flow C have default IP Precedence markings of 0. The order of packet servicing with WFQ is based on *sequence numbers*, where packets with the lowest sequence numbers are transmitted first.

Sequence numbers remind me of my barbershop. My barbershop has a sign reading, "Please take a number." I can pull a number from a dispenser, and when they call my number, it's my turn to get my hair cut. Sequence numbers work the same way. Each packet in the queue is assigned a sequence number, and lower numbers get to go first, just like customers in my barbershop.

The sequence number is the *weight* of the packet multiplied by the number of byte-by-byte rounds that must be completed to service the packet, just as in the FQ example. The Cisco IOS calculates a packet's weight differently depending on the router's IOS version. In older versions of the Cisco IOS (prior to IOS 12.0(5)T), the formula for weight was

$$\text{WEIGHT (pre IOS } 12.0(5)T) = 4096 / (\text{IP Prec.} + 1)$$

In more recent versions of the IOS, the formula for weight is

$$\text{WEIGHT (newer IOS versions)} = 32768 / (\text{IP Prec.} + 1)$$

Using the pre-IOS 12.0(5)T formula (to make the math simpler), the sequence numbers for the previously described packets are

$$A1 = 4096 / (5 + 1) * 128 = 87,381$$

$$A2 = 4096 / (5 + 1) * 128 + 87381 = 174,762$$

$$A3 = 4096 / (5 + 1) * 128 + 174762 = 262,144$$

$$B1 = 4096 / (0 + 1) * 96 = 393,216$$

$$C1 = 4096 / (0 + 1) * 70 = 286,720$$

Therefore, after applying the weight, WFQ empties packets from the queue in the following order: A1 – A2 – A3 – C1 – B1, as shown in Figure 6-11. Compare that WFQ packet order with the FQ packet order of C1 – B1 – A1 – A2 – A3.

Figure 6-11   Weighted Fair Queuing

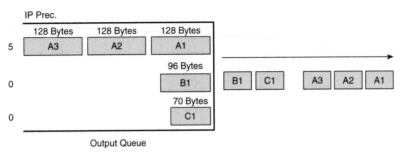

Sequence Number* = 4096 / (IP Prec. + 1)

* In IOS 12.0(5)T and later, the Sequence Number = 32768 / (IP Prec. + 1).

Priority Queuing (PQ)

Unlike FIFO and WFQ, priority queuing allows you to specify high-priority traffic and instruct the router to send that traffic first. Priority queuing places traffic into one of four queues (that is, High, Medium, Normal, and Low). Each queue receives a different level of priority, and higher-priority queues must be completely emptied before any packets are emptied from lower-priority queues, as shown in Figure 6-12. This behavior can starve out lower-priority traffic.

Figure 6-12   Priority Queuing

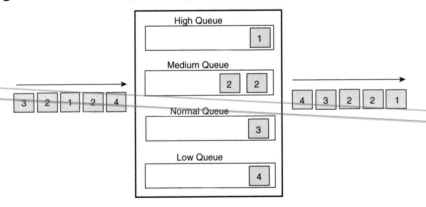

Priority queuing completely empties higher-priority queues
before emptying lower-priority queues.

To better understand priority queuing, consider an analogy. Imagine you want to purchase portable MP3 players for all your friends and family this holiday season. For illustrative purposes only, assume an MP3 player costs $1 at Wal-Mart, $10 at K-Mart, $100 at Target, and $1000 at Circuit City. From where do you buy your first MP3 player? Probably Wal-Mart.

From where do you buy your second MP3 player? Do you want to spread the wealth around, and buy the second MP3 player from K-Mart? Based on the price difference, you're going to buy your second, third, and fourth MP3 players from Wal-Mart, too. In fact, you'll keep buying MP3 players from Wal-Mart until Wal-Mart is out of stock.

Once Wal-Mart is out of MP3 players, and you still need to buy more, where do you go? Based on the prices, you'll probably buy your next MP3 player from K-Mart.

Let's jump to the end of the story and ask, "When would you ever buy an MP3 player from Circuit City?" Based on our *very* fictitious prices, you would only buy an MP3 player from Circuit City when Wal-Mart, K-Mart, and Target were all out of stock.

The same logic applies to priority queuing. As long as the *High* queue contains packets, no packets from the *Medium*, *Normal*, or *Low* queues are transmitted. Packets from the Medium queue can only be sent when the High queue is completely empty, and the only time packets are transmitted from the Low queue is when the High, Medium, and Normal queues are all empty. While priority queuing can offer special traffic, such as voice, high-priority treatment, priority queuing's strict approach tends to starve out lower-priority traffic.

Class-Based Weighted Fair Queuing (CB-WFQ)

The WFQ mechanism makes sure no traffic is starved out, unlike PQ. However, neither WFQ nor PQ makes a specific amount of bandwidth available for defined traffic types. You can, however, specify a minimum amount of bandwidth to make available for various traffic types using the CB-WFQ mechanism.

CB-WFQ can specify bandwidth amounts for up to 64 classes of traffic. Traffic for each class goes into a separate queue. Therefore, one queue (for example, for CIT-RIX traffic) might be overflowing, while other queues are still accepting packets.

Therefore, CB-WFQ gives you the benefit of specifying an amount of bandwidth to give to different traffic classes, something you cannot do with WFQ or PQ. Also, CB-WFQ does not starve out lower-priority traffic as PQ does. The only major downside to CB-WFQ is its lack of a priority queuing mechanism. PQ can give priority treatment to specific traffic, such as voice traffic, while CB-WFQ cannot. A slight modification to CB-WFQ called LLQ fixes this issue.

Low Latency Queuing (LLQ)

LLQ bears a strong resemblance to CB-WFQ. In fact, LLQ is almost identical in its configuration to CB-WFQ. However, LLQ can instruct one or more traffic classes to direct traffic into a priority queue. Realize that when you place packets in a priority queue, you are not only allocating a bandwidth amount for that traffic, but you are also policing (that is, limiting the available bandwidth) for that traffic. The policing option is necessary to prevent high-priority traffic from starving out lower-priority traffic, as PQ might do.

Note that if you tell multiple traffic classes to give priority treatment to their packets, all priority packets go into the same queue. Therefore, priority traffic could suffer from having too many priority classes. Also, be aware that packets queued in the priority queue cannot be fragmented, which is a consideration for slower-speed links (that is, link speeds less than 768 kbps). LLQ, based on all of these benefits, is the Cisco preferred queuing method for latency-sensitive traffic, such as voice and/or video.

Consider an example. Imagine you have two routers interconnected with a 512 kbps link, as shown in Figure 6-13. This link carries web traffic, voice traffic, and a few other traffic types. However, you want to ensure that your web traffic receives at least 128 kbps of bandwidth over that link. You want your voice traffic to have up to 256 kbps of the link's bandwidth. You also want voice traffic to receive priority treatment, meaning the voice packets get sent first, up to a limit of 256 kbps to prevent starving out other traffic types. Also, if the voice traffic doesn't happen to need all of its 256 kbps of bandwidth at the moment, other applications can enjoy some of that unused bandwidth. Such a scenario can be realized using LLQ as your queuing method.

Figure 6-13   Low-Latency Queuing Example

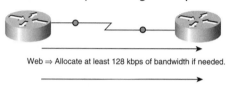

Web ⇒ Allocate at least 128 kbps of bandwidth if needed.

Voice ⇒ Allocate up to 256 kbps of *priority* bandwidth.

While CB-WFQ allocates a specific bandwidth amount, LLQ can allocate *priority* bandwidth amounts for specified traffic classes.

Catalyst-Based Queuing

This section, thus far, focused on router queuing approaches. However, some Cisco Catalyst switches also support their own queuing method, called *Weighted Round Robin (WRR)*. For example, a Catalyst 2950 switch contains four queues, and WRR can be configured to place frames with specific CoS markings into specific queues (for example, CoS values 0 and 1 might be placed in queue number 1).

Weights can be assigned to the queues, influencing how much bandwidth frames with various markings receive. The queues are then serviced in a round robin fashion, where a certain number of frames are forwarded from queue number 1, followed by a certain number of frames being forwarded from queue number 2, and so on.

On the Catalyst 2950, queue number 4 can be designated as an *expedite* queue, which gives priority treatment to frames, such as voice frames, in that queue. Specifically, the expedite queue must be empty before any additional queues are serviced. This behavior, much like priority queuing's behavior, can lead to protocol starvation.

Consider a WRR example, as illustrated in Figure 6-14. Imagine you assign a weight of 1 to queue number 1, a weight of 2 to queue number 2, a weight of 3 to queue number 3, and a weight of 4 to queue number 4. The weight specifies how many packets are transmitted from a queue during a round robin cycle. Specifically, during a single round robin cycle, one packet is transmitted from queue number 1. Two packets are transmitted from queue number 2, followed by three packets from queue number 3. Finally, four packets are sent from queue number 4. The round robin cycle then begins again.

Figure 6-14   Weighted Round Robin Example

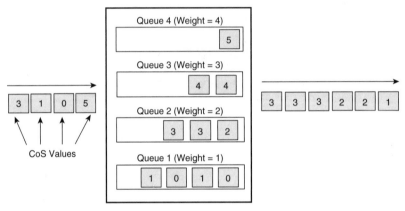

WRR *weights* queues to determine the relative amount of bandwidth available to each queue. In this example, Queue 4 has twice the available bandwidth of Queue 2.

Throwing Packets out the Window

Recall from your early studies of networking technology how *TCP windowing* functions. A sender sends a single segment, and if the sender receives a successful acknowledgement from the receiver, the sender sends two segments (that is, a *windows size* of 2). If those two segments are successfully acknowledged, the sender sends four segments, and so on, increasing the window size exponentially.

However, if a segment is dropped, the TCP flow goes into *TCP slow start*, where the window size is reduced to 1. The TCP flow then exponentially increases its window size until the window's size reaches half of the window size when congestion originally occurred. At that point the TCP flow's window size increases linearly.

TCP slow start is relevant to QoS because when an interface's output queue is completely full, all newly arriving packets are discarded (that is, tail dropped), and all those TCP flows simultaneously go into TCP slow start.

Note that the process of multiple TCP flows simultaneously entering TCP slow start is called *global synchronization* or *TCP synchronization*. When TCP synchronization occurs, a link's bandwidth is underutilized, resulting in wasted bandwidth.

Random Early Detection (RED)

To find a solution for global synchronization, we need look no further than my favorite Star Trek movie, *Star Trek II: The Wrath of Khan*. Remember the scene near the end of the movie where Spock is in the radiation chamber, and he's dying? He sacrificed his life to save the ship. Spock tells Kirk that this action was only logical, because the good of the many outweighs the good of the few, or the one. By the same logic, a QoS mechanism called *random early detection (RED)*, sacrifices a few packets for the good of the many packets. To prevent a queue from completely filling to capacity, resulting in the tail drop of all packet flows, RED randomly discards a few packets. As a queue's depth (that is, the number of packets in the queue) increases, RED begins discarding packets more aggressively.

Three parameters influence when RED discards a newly arriving packet:

- Minimum threshold

- Maximum threshold

- Mark probability denominator

The *minimum threshold* specifies the number of packets in a queue before the queue considers discarding packets. After the queue depth exceeds the minimum threshold, RED introduces the possibility that a packet will be discarded, and the probability of discard increases until the queue depth reaches the *maximum threshold*, as shown in Figure 6-15. After a queue depth exceeds the maximum threshold, all other packets attempting to enter the queue are discarded.

Figure 6-15   Random Early Detection (RED)

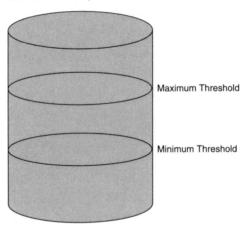

Maximum Threshold

Minimum Threshold

Output Queue

The probability of packet discard when the queue depth equals the maximum threshold is *1/(mark probability denominator)*. For example, if the mark probability denominator were set to 10, when the queue depth reached the maximum threshold, the probability of discard would be 1/10 (that is, a 10 percent chance of discard).

The minimum threshold, maximum threshold, and mark probability denominator comprise a *RED profile*. As shown in Figure 6-16, there are three distinct ranges in a RED profile: 1) no drop, 2) random drop, and 3) full drop. The probability of discard at the maximum threshold equals 1/MPD. Therefore, in the figure, the probability of discard with the average queue depth of 45 packets equals 1/5 = .2 = 20 percent.

Figure 6-16   RED Drop Ranges

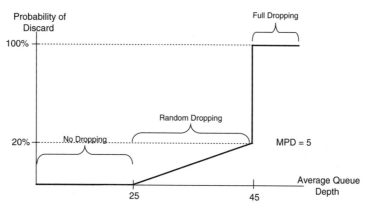

RED proves most useful on router interfaces where congestion is likely. For example, a WAN interface might be a good candidate for RED.

Weighted RED (WRED)

Cisco routers do not support RED, but fortunately Cisco routers support something better, WRED. Unlike RED, WRED creates a RED profile for each priority marking. For example, a packet marked with an IP Precedence value of 0 might have a minimum threshold of 20 packets, while a packet with an IP Precedence of 1 has a minimum threshold of 25 packets. In this example, packets with an IP Precedence of 0 would start to be discarded before packets with an IP Precedence of 1 as the queue begins to fill up.

Explicit Congestion Notification (ECN)

WRED discards packets, which is one way for the router to tell its neighbors that it's congested. However, Cisco routers can now indicate a congestion condition by signaling, using an approach called *Explicit Congestion Notification (ECN)*.

ECN uses the two last bits in an IP v4 header's ToS byte to indicate whether or not a device is ECN-capable and if so, whether or not congestion is being experienced, as shown in Figure 6-17. When ECN lets a router know that congestion is being experienced, the router can reduce its TCP transmission rate by transmitting fewer packets at a time before expecting an acknowledgement from the receiving device.

Figure 6-17   Explicit Congestion Notification

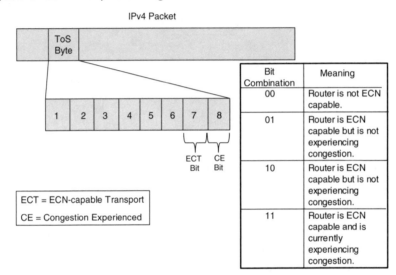

Cisco routers can use ECN as an extension to WRED and mark packets exceeding a specified queue threshold value. If the queue depth is at or below the WRED minimum threshold, the packets are sent normally, just as with WRED. Also, if the queue depth is above the WRED maximum threshold, all packets are dropped, just as with WRED.

However, if the queue depth is currently somewhere in the range from just above the minimum threshold through the maximum threshold, one of three things might happen:

■ If both endpoints are ECN-capable, the ECT and CE bits are set to a 1 and sent to the destination, indicating that the transmission rate should be reduced.

- If both endpoints do not support ECN, the normal WRED behavior occurs.

- A packet with its ECN and CE bits marked might reach a destination router that already has a full queue. In such an instance, the notification is dropped.

Setting Speed Limits on Traffic

Instead of allocating bandwidth for applications, there are instances when you might wish to restrict the amount of bandwidth available for specific traffic. For example, you might want to set a *speed limit* for users on your network downloading MP3 music files from the Internet.

QoS mechanisms that limit bandwidth are called *traffic conditioners*. The two categories of traffic conditioners are *policing* and *shaping*. While both these approaches limit bandwidth, the mechanisms' operation varies:

- **Policing**—Policing typically limits bandwidth by discarding any traffic exceeding a specified rate. However, policing can also remark traffic exceeding the specified rate and attempt to send the traffic anyway. Because policing's drop behavior causes TCP retransmits, policing is recommended for higher-speed interfaces. Also, note that policing can be applied inbound or outbound on an interface.

- **Shaping**—Shaping limits excess traffic, not by dropping traffic, but by buffering it. This buffering of excess traffic can lead to delay. Due to this delay, shaping is recommended for slower-speed interfaces. Unlike policing, shaping lacks the ability to remark traffic. As a final contrast, shaping can only be applied in the outbound direction on an interface.

The question becomes, how do you send traffic out of an interface at a rate less than the physical clock rate of the interface? Many people have the misconception that if they had some sort of police radar gun that could measure the speed of packets exiting an interface, they could point the radar gun at the packets leaving the interface; and the packets would be leaving at a rate slower than the line rate after configuring policing or shaping. That's not possible! Entering a few commands in a router's configuration does not alter the speed configured on an external channel service unit (CSU)/data service unit (DSU).

Here's the secret. For this to be possible, policing and shaping tools don't transmit all of the time. Specifically, these traffic conditioning mechanisms send a certain number of bits or bytes at line rate, and then they stop sending until a specific timing interval (for example, 1/8 of a second) elapses. Once the timing interval is reached, the interface again sends a specific amount of traffic at line rate, and then it stops and waits for the next timing interval. This process continually repeats, allowing an interface to send an *average* bandwidth that might be below the physical speed of the interface. This average bandwidth is called the Committed Information Rate (CIR). The number of bits (the unit of measure used with shaping tools) or bytes (the unit of measure used with policing tools) that is sent during a timing interval is called the committed burst (Bc). The timing interval is written as Tc. Note, however, that because the router does not send partial frames, if the transmission of a frame begins during a timing interval, the entire frame will be transmitted even if the size of the frame causes more than Bc bits or bytes to be sent during that timing interval.

For example, imagine you have a physical line rate of 128 kbps, but a CIR of only 64 kbps. Also assume there are eight timing intervals in a second (that is, $Tc = 1/8$ of a second = 125 ms), and during each of those timing intervals, 8000 bits (that is, the Bc value) are sent at line rate. Therefore, over the period of a second, 8000 bits are sent (at line rate) eight times, for a grand total of 64,000 bits per second, which is the CIR, as shown in Figure 6-18.

Figure 6-18   Shaping Example

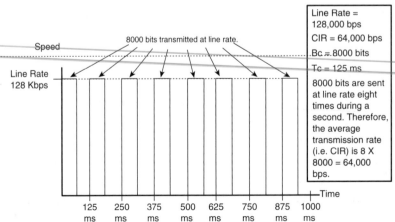

What if you don't need to send Bc bits (or bytes) during a timing interval? Perhaps you simply don't have enough traffic to need the bandwidth at the moment. There is an option to *bank* those bits, and use them during a future timing interval. The parameter that allows this storing of unused potential bandwidth is called the Excess Burst (Be) parameter. The Be parameter in a shaping configuration specifies the maximum number of bits that can be sent in excess of the Bc during a timing interval, if those bits are indeed available. For those bits to be available, they must have gone unused during previous timing intervals. Policing tools, however, use the Be parameter to specify the maximum number of bytes that can be sent during a timing interval. Therefore, in a policing configuration, if the Bc equals the Be, then no excess bursting occurs. If excess bursting does occur, then policing tools consider this excess traffic as exceeding traffic (that is, breaking the speed limit). Policing tools consider traffic not exceeding the specified CIR as conforming traffic. As part of your policing configuration, you can specify what action to take when traffic conforms to the CIR and what other action to take when the traffic exceeds the CIR.

To get a bit mathematical for a moment, the relationship between the Tc, Bc, and CIR is given by the formula:

$$CIR = Bc\ /\ Tc$$

Alternately, the formula can be written as

$$Tc = Bc\ /\ CIR$$

Therefore, if you want a smaller timing interval, which can reduce delay for voice packets, you could configure a smaller Bc.

To illustrate the operation of traffic conditioners, consider the metaphor of a *token bucket*, where a router places Bc tokens in the bucket during each timing interval. Also, the bucket's capacity equals Be tokens. In a policing configuration, traffic requiring no more than the Bc number of bits or bytes to be transmitted is called conforming traffic. Traffic requiring more than the Bc number of bytes is said to be exceeding traffic, as shown in Figure 6-19.

Figure 6-19   Token Bucket

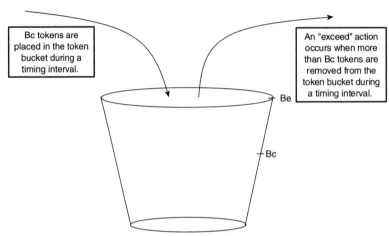

Bc tokens are placed in the token bucket during a timing interval.

An "exceed" action occurs when more than Bc tokens are removed from the token bucket during a timing interval.

Be

Bc

Consider a policing example, where there are currently 500 bytes in the token bucket. A packet comes through requiring 300 bytes. The bytes are removed from the bucket, and the packet is sent. Then, before the bucket replenishes with more tokens, another 300-byte packet comes along. Because there are only 200 bytes remaining in the bucket, the packet cannot be sent and is discarded. This illustration describes how policing functions with a *single token bucket*. However, Cisco also supports a *dual token bucket*, as shown in Figure 6-20.

Figure 6-20   Dual Token Bucket

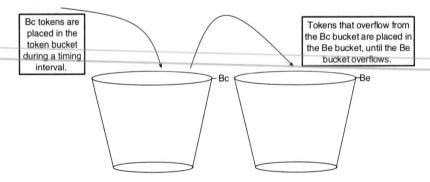

Bc tokens are placed in the token bucket during a timing interval.

Tokens that overflow from the Bc bucket are placed in the Be bucket, until the Be bucket overflows.

Bc

Be

Using a dual bucket metaphor, the first bucket has a depth of Bc, and the second bucket has a depth of Be. If a packet can be forwarded using bytes in the Bc bucket, the packet is said to be *conforming*. If the packet cannot be forwarded using the bytes in the Bc bucket, but it can be forwarded using the bytes in the Be bucket, the traffic is said to be *exceeding*. If the packet cannot be forwarded using either of the buckets individually, the traffic is said to be *violating*. Realize, however, a violating packet might still be transmitted if it can be forwarded using the combined tokens (that is, bytes) in both the Bc and Be buckets.

Instead of policing traffic to a single rate, Cisco also supports *dual-rate policing*, as shown in Figure 6-21. With dual rate policing, the router still uses two token buckets. The first bucket is the Committed Information Rate (CIR) bucket, and the second bucket is the Peak Information Rate (PIR) bucket. These buckets are replenished with tokens at different rates, with the PIR bucket being filled at a faster rate.

Figure 6-21   Dual Rate Token Bucket

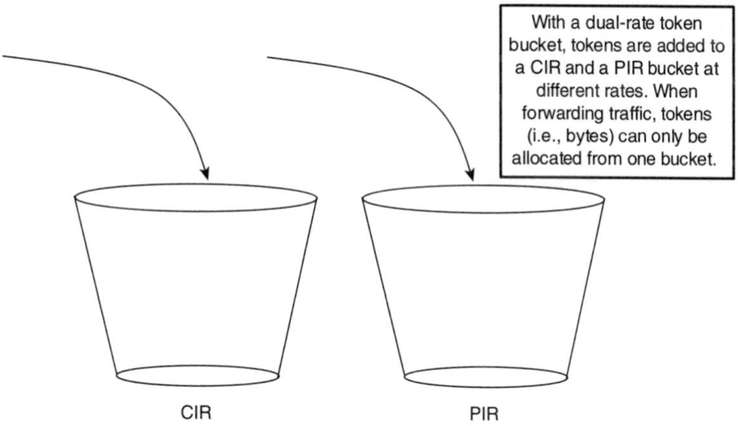

With a dual-rate token bucket, tokens are added to a CIR and a PIR bucket at different rates. When forwarding traffic, tokens (i.e., bytes) can only be allocated from one bucket.

CIR   PIR

When a packet arrives, a dual-rate policer checks to see whether the PIR bucket has enough tokens (that is, bytes) to send the packet. If the PIR bucket lacks sufficient tokens, the packet is said to be *violating*, and the packet is discarded. Otherwise, the policer checks to see whether the CIR bucket has enough tokens to forward the packet. If the packet can be sent using the CIR bucket's tokens, then the packet is conforming. If the CIR bucket's tokens are not sufficient, but the PIR bucket's tokens are sufficient, the packet is said to be *exceeding*, and the exceed action (for example, transmit the packet with a DSCP value of AF11) is applied.

With a policing mechanism, you can specify various actions to perform based on whether a packet is conforming, exceeding, or violating. Examples of these actions include

- **Transmit**—Sends the packet

- **Drop**—Discards the packet

- **Mark**—Sets priority bits for the packet

- **Multiaction**—Performs more than one action, such as marking the packet with a DSCP value of AF12, and setting the CLP bit to a 1

To illustrate how you might use policing in a network, consider the following example. Imagine you wish to restrict HTTP traffic to 100 kbps and Telnet traffic to 50 kbps, as illustrated in Figure 6-22. By limiting the bandwidth of these applications, you make sure these applications don't starve out other, more important traffic, such as voice.

Figure 6-22   Policing

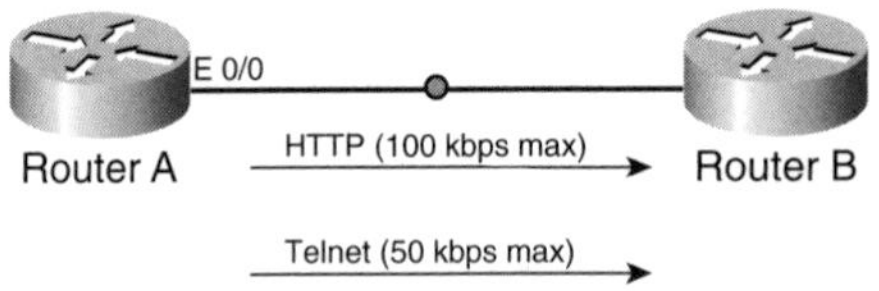

Router A   HTTP (100 kbps max) →   Router B

E 0/0

Telnet (50 kbps max) →

Shaping Frame Relay Networks

On Frame Relay networks, not only might you need to shape your traffic, but you also might need your router to respond to congestion occurring in the service provider's cloud. When a service provider becomes congested and needs to discard frames, the service provider can choose to first discard frames that have their

Discard Eligible (DE) bit set to a 1. The service provider might also request that the sending router slow its transmission rate by marking the Backward Explicit Congestion Notification (BECN) bit to a 1, in a frame going back to the sender, as shown in Figure 6-23. When BECN marking occurs, if the originating router is configured to respond to BECNs, the originating router reduces its CIR by 25 percent. If the router receives another BECN in the next time interval, it decreases its transmission rate by 25 percent of the current rate. This behavior can continue until the rate drops to the router's configured minimum CIR, the rate below which the router refuses to go.

Figure 6-23   Backward Explicit Congestion Notification

When Router A receives a frame marked with a
BECN bit, it reduces its CIR by 25 percent.

You might, however, encounter a situation where the vast majority of the traffic flowing over the Frame Relay network flows in only one direction, from one router to another router (that is, with little, if any, return traffic). In such a situation, the service provider cannot mark a BECN bit in a frame going back to the sender because there are no (or very few) frames going back to the sender. To remedy this situation, the service provider can mark the Forward Explicit Congestion Notification (FECN) bit in a frame destined for the receiver. If the receiving router is configured to respond to FECNs, it generates a meaningless frame, called a *Q.922 test frame*, and sends the frame back to the sender. This test frame allows the service provider the opportunity to mark that frame's BECN bit, in an attempt to make the sender slow its transmission rate, as shown in Figure 6-24.

Figure 6-24   Forward Explicit Congestion Notification

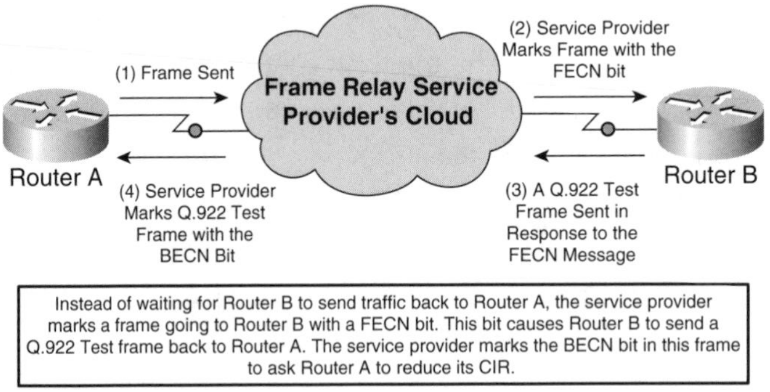

After a sender slows its transmission rate due to BECNs, 16 timing intervals must elapse before the sender begins to increase its transmission rate. When the sender does increase its transmission rate, it does so at a much more cautious pace than when it reduced its rate. Specifically, the sender only increases its transmission rate by (Be + Bc)/16 bits per timing interval.

Doing More with Less (Bandwidth)

Bandwidth on WAN links is regarded as a precious commodity because customers typically pay their service provider recurring monthly fees for that WAN bandwidth. Therefore, a VoIP design goal is to make the most efficient use of the WAN's scarce bandwidth. This section addresses QoS mechanisms that make your traffic better stewards of WAN bandwidth. Specifically, this section introduces you to compression technologies, which send fewer bits across the link, and link fragmentation and interleaving technologies, which fragment large payloads to reduce the serialization delay experienced by smaller payloads. First, let's discuss compression. The two broad categories of compression include

- **Payload Compression**—Reduces the payload size, using approaches such as the STAC, Predictor, or MPPC

- **Header Compression**—Reduces the size of TCP and/or RTP headers

The goal of compression technologies is to increase the throughput over a WAN link, while reducing packet delay. However, particularly with payload compression approaches (that is, when the actual data, not just the header, is compressed), the time required by lower-end routers (for example, 2600 Series routers) to run the compression algorithm might actually increase the overall delay. Fortunately, these routers might support hardware acceleration modules, which you can add to dramatically improve the router's ability to perform compression in a timely manner. For example, a Compression Advanced Integration Module (CAIM) is available to offload compression tasks from 2600 Series routers.

This chapter, however, focuses on header compression. With header compression, the header of a packet shrinks from approximately 40 bytes in size to approximately 3 to 5 bytes (for TCP header compression) or 2 to 4 bytes (for *RTP header compression [cRTP]*), as illustrated in Figure 6-25. Compressing 40 bytes down to as little as 2 bytes might seem nearly impossible. Back in the early 90s, hard drive compression swept the industry. I remember the thrill I felt after running compression software on my 80 MB hard drive, giving me approximately 160 MB of usable storage space! (Ah…how times have changed…) I was very satisfied to receive a 2:1 compression ratio. So, how do header compression technologies offer 20:1 compression ratios? Here's the secret. The routers are not technically doing compression.

Figure 6-25   RTP Header Compression

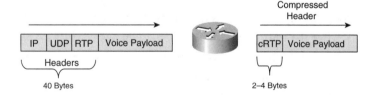

Header compression technology makes the observation that most information contained in a packet's header remains the same during the session (for example, during a phone call). Consider the source and destination IP addresses in the header. Those addresses don't change during a session. What about TCP or UDP port numbers? Usually, they don't change either. The payload type information contained in an RTP packet doesn't change. So, why send the same information in every single packet? Header compression technology saves a tremendous amount of bandwidth by not sending this repetitive information. A compressed voice header, for example, only carries such information as UDP checksums and a session context ID (CID), which identifies the flow that the packet is a part of.

Another QoS mechanism useful for slower link speeds is *Link Fragmentation and Interleaving (LFI)*. Consider a 1500-byte data frame being sent out of a 64-kbps serial interface. The interface, in this case, needs 187 ms just to place that data frame on the wire. If there is a smaller voice packet sitting behind that data frame, the voice frame experiences excessive delay before it is ever placed on the wire, resulting in jitter. LFI mechanisms fragment larger payloads to specified fragment sizes and then interleave the smaller payloads in among the fragments, greatly reducing the serialization delay experienced by the smaller payloads, as shown in Figure 6-26.

Figure 6-26   Link Fragmentation and Interleaving

As a metaphor, imagine you're driving your super-fast sports car, and you pull up behind one of those big triple tractor-trailers at a traffic light. These triple tractor-trailers connect three separate trailers to a single tractor (that is, a truck pulling three trailers). After the traffic light turns green, the massive tractor-trailer slowly enters the intersection. Meanwhile, you're being delayed and are possibly about to experience road rage. However, what if the trucking company had taken those three trailers and placed each one of them behind a separate tractor? If it had, there would be three separate tractor-trailer vehicles on the road. In your sports car, you might be able to pass one or two of those tractor-trailers and, as a result, get through the traffic light quicker. That's exactly what LFI mechanisms do.

LFI mechanisms break up the big payload (the triple tractor-trailer in our metaphor) and interleave the relatively tiny voice packets in amongst those fragments (your sports car passing some of the individual tractor-trailers in our metaphor), resulting in decreased serialization delay and improved voice quality.

The three primary LFI mechanisms supported by Cisco are

- **Multilink PPP (MLPPP)**—Used on PPP links

- **FRF.12**—Used on Voice over IP over Frame Relay (VoIPovFR) links

- **FRF.11 Annex C**—Used on Voice over Frame Relay (VoFR) links

The serialization delay goal when configuring an LFI mechanism is delay in the range of 10 to 15 ms. To determine the serialization delay for a specific frame size on a specific link speed, use the formula:

Serialization Delay = (Frame_Size * 8) / Link_Speed

The reason the frame size gets multiplied by eight is to convert bytes into bits. Consider a frame size of 512 bytes on a link speed of 128 kbps:

Serialization Delay = (512 * 8) / 128 = 32 ms

This calculation shows that 32 ms elapse while a 512-byte frame exits on a 128-kbps interface.

Automatically Configuring QoS with AutoQoS

Optimizing a QoS configuration for VoIP can be a daunting task. Fortunately, Cisco added a feature called AutoQoS to many of its router and switch platforms to automatically generate router-based or switch-based VoIP QoS configurations. With a single command, AutoQoS can analyze a router interface (that is, determine the interface's bandwidth and encapsulation type) and apply appropriate QoS features, such as LLQ, LFI, cRTP, Classification, Marking, and Simple Network Management Protocol (SNMP) notifications, which could alert an administrator in the event of too many dropped voice packets.

On a switch platform, AutoQoS can enable such features as WRR (for queuing), configuring CoS queue mapping (for example, placing voice traffic in a high-priority queue), and interface trust states (for example, where the switch only trusts incoming CoS markings if a Cisco IP Phone is connected to the interface).

Case Study: Your Turn to Use Your New "Quality of Service" Tools

In Chapter 3, "Paving the Pathway to a Voice over IP Network," you recommended an amount of bandwidth to interconnect XYZ Headquarters with XYZ Remote Office 1 and XYZ Remote Office 2. Based on your bandwidth recommendations from the Chapter 3 case study, in the following space, specify appropriate QoS mechanisms to deploy on the XYZ Headquarters router, XYZ Remote Office 1 router, and XYZ Remote Office 2 router.

QoS Recommendation for XYZ Company:

Suggested Solution

The suggested solution provided in Chapter 3 specified two T1 circuits (1.544 Mbps each) between XYZ Headquarters and XYZ Remote Office 1. The suggested bandwidth between XYZ Headquarters and XYZ Remote Office 2 was 512 kbps, as shown in Figure 6-27.

Figure 6-27   XYZ Company's Suggested Solution

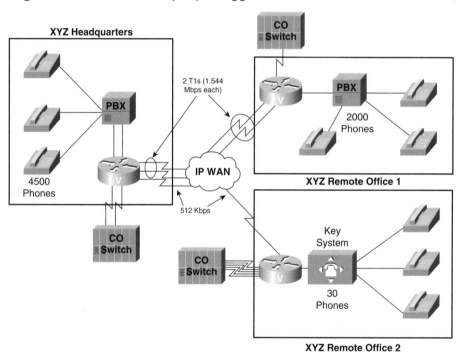

Link efficiency mechanisms, such as LFI and cRTP, benefit slower link speeds (that is, less than 768 kbps). Based on the suggested bandwidth amounts, this solution recommends the following QoS mechanisms:

Link between XYZ Headquarters and XYZ Remote Office 1

- LLQ
- WRED

Link between XYZ Headquarters and XYZ Remote Office 2

- LLQ

- WRED

- cRTP

- MLP

WRED causes TCP packets to retransmit. However, RTP uses UDP. Therefore, while WRED benefits data traffic classes, WRED should not be applied to the voice traffic class. Also, note the suggested solution contains no policing or shaping mechanisms. However, if you determined that an application at one of XYZ Company's sites dominates the WAN bandwidth, a policing or shaping mechanism might be appropriate.

Chapter Summary

The chapter described the need for QoS mechanisms on a converged network (for example, a network that transports voice, video, and data). Cisco recommends that packets be classified and marked as close to the source as possible.

However, classification and marking used in isolation don't alter a packet's behavior. Other QoS mechanisms (for example, queuing, policing, and WRED) can examine a packet's marking and make forwarding or dropping decisions based on those markings.

Queuing mechanisms determine which packets stored in a queue get forwarded first and how much bandwidth those packets receive. Cisco routers typically take advantage of LLQ as their queuing mechanisms in a voice environment. Catalyst switches, however, often use WRR as their queuing mechanism of choice.

As a router's output queue begins to fill up, WRED can randomly discard lower-priority packets to prevent a queue from filling to capacity. While WRED can benefit many data applications, voice network designers typically don't use WRED for voice traffic classes because the packet drops caused by WRED's packet discards impact voice packets (which use UDP instead of TCP) differently than TCP-based data packets (which go into a TCP slow start).

Not all QoS mechanisms make a minimum amount of bandwidth available for traffic classes. Some QoS mechanisms, such as policing and shaping, limit the amount of bandwidth certain applications can use. Policing typically limits an application's bandwidth by dropping packets that exceed a specified bandwidth limit. Policing might alternately mark packets with a lower-priority marking, as opposed to dropping those packets. Shaping is a kinder and gentler approach, because shaping temporarily stores excess packets and attempts to transmit those packets at a later time, when sufficient bandwidth is available.

On lower-speed WAN links (that is, less than 768 kbps), Cisco recommends link efficiency mechanisms such as LFI and cRTP. LFI tools include MLP for Point to Point Protocol (PPP) links, FRF.12 for VoIPovFR links, and FRF.11 Annex C for VoFR links (that is, links that send voice traffic out a particular permanent virtual circuit instead of sending voice traffic to a remote IP address). Each of these LFI mechanisms fragment large data packets and interleave small voice packets in amongst the fragmented data packets. cRTP header compression takes a 40-byte voice header and logically compresses the header down to only 2 or 4 bytes in size, thus reducing the WAN bandwidth required to transmit a voice conversation.

Realize that these QoS mechanisms are not meant to be used in isolation. Rather, many QoS tools complement each other. For example, you might benefit from using LLQ, cRTP, and WRED, and shaping all on the same router interface.

Chapter Review Questions

1. Which of the following results from an uneven arrival of packets?

   a. Packet loss

   b. Tail drop

   c. Jitter

   d. TCP retransmits

2. As a design recommendation, voice packets should have a maximum one-way delay of

   a. 10 ms

   b. 15 ms

   c. 150 ms

   d. 250 ms

3. Which of the following Per-Hop Behaviors (PHBs) has the highest drop probability?

   a. AF41

   b. AF12

   c. AF11

   d. AF13

4. Identify the *congestion management* QoS mechanism from the following.

   a. LLQ

   b. WRED

   c. LFI

   d. Policing

5. Which of the following QoS mechanisms begins to discard lower-priority packets as a router's output queue starts to fill to capacity?

    a. LLQ

    b. WRED

    c. LFI

    d. Policing

6. Which of the following queuing mechanisms offer a priority queue? (Select two.)

    a. WRR

    b. LLQ

    c. FIFO

    d. WFQ

7. Which of the following QoS mechanisms can either discard or remark packets exceeding a specified bandwidth limit?

    a. LLQ

    b. WRED

    c. LFI

    d. Policing

8. What is the typical size of a voice packet's header, before compression?

    a. 2 bytes

    b. 4 bytes

    c. 26 bytes

    d. 40 bytes

9. Select the appropriate Link Fragmentation and Interleaving (LFI) tool for Voice over IP over Frame Relay (VoIPovFR) links.

   a. MLP

   b. FRF.12

   c. FRF.11 Annex C

   d. cRTP

10. Traffic shaping's timing interval (Tc) can be calculated from which of the following formulas?

   a. Tc = Bc / CIR

   b. Tc = CIR * Bc

   c. Tc = CIR / Bc

   d. Tc = (Bc + CIR) / Bc

What You Will Learn

After reading this chapter, you should be able to

- ✔ Identify key benefits offered by the Cisco Unity messaging solution.

- ✔ List conference calling product options.

- ✔ Describe Cisco call center applications.

VoIP Supporting Roles

Previous chapters in this book walked you through the migration from a traditional telephony network (that is, based on a corporate *private branch exchange [PBX]* system) to a *Voice over IP (VoIP)* network, where voice packets travel over a data network. However, the story doesn't end there. In order for VoIP telephony systems to compete with well-entrenched legacy telephony systems, VoIP must offer much more than just the ability to place a phone call.

Today's PBX users expect features such as voice mail and conference calling. Some businesses use large call centers for their customer support departments. Therefore, VoIP technologies must step up to the challenge and not only match existing supplementary features, but exceed those features.

Fortunately, Cisco offers a suite of value-added enhancements to its basic Cisco CallManager-centric voice solution. This chapter delves into several applications you might consider in your design, beginning with the VoIP answer to voice mail.

Leave a Message at the Beep: the Cisco Answer to Unified Messaging

Answering machines are dwindling in American households these days, in favor of voice mail service provided by the local telephone company. If you're talking on your home phone and another call comes in (assuming you don't have call waiting), the other caller receives a busy signal and can't leave a message on your answering machine. However, if you've subscribed to a voice mail service, callers can leave you messages while you're on the phone.

Telephony designers for businesses recognized the benefits of voice mail long ago, and many existing PBX systems offer voice mail to PBX users. As businesses migrate from their PBX systems to VoIP systems, almost all designs require voice mail functionality.

Which Came First, the Voice Mail System or the CCM?

Fortunately, in many cases, companies don't need to throw out their existing voice mail system just because they replace their PBX with a *Cisco CallManager (CCM)*. The CCM might still be able to leverage the business's existing investment in a voice mail system using the *Simplified Messaging Desk Interface (SMDI)* protocol.

Many legacy voice mail systems connect into PBX analog station ports. Similarly, businesses can connect many of these legacy voice mail systems into ports on some Cisco gateways. For example, the Cisco Catalyst 6000 and 6500 Series switches support a Communication Media Module, which can accommodate a 24-port Foreign Exchange Station (FXS) module, and the CCM can communicate with the Catalyst 6000/6500 Series switch via SMDI, allowing the legacy voice mail ports to be used by the CCM, as shown in Figure 7-1.

Figure 7-1   Legacy Voice Mail Integration

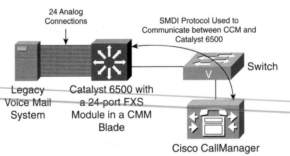

One-Stop Messaging

PBX users typically rely on their PBX voice mail system for voice messages, on their e-mail server for voice mail messages, and their fax machine for fax messages. Fortunately, Cisco offers a product called *Cisco Unity* that acts as a single repository for all these various message types.

Current versions of Cisco Unity run on a Windows Server 2003 platform and leverage Microsoft's Exchange software to store voice mail, e-mail, and fax messages. Unity can be configured such that users only need to check their single Unity mailbox to retrieve all their messages (that is, voice mail, e-mail, and fax messages). In order to retrieve their messages, Unity users don't need to be seated at a computer. Users can access their Unity message store via a phone and, for example, have their e-mail read to them, thanks to Unity's text-to-speech conversion feature.

note
Cisco also makes a version of Unity available for Lotus Domino, as opposed to Microsoft Exchange.

Unity consists of three primary components:

- **Unity server**—The Unity server represents the application itself. Current versions of Unity run on a Windows Server 2003 platform, such as a Cisco *Media Convergence Server (MCS)*.

- **Directory server**—The directory server maintains user account information. The directory server is a component of the messaging system being integrated with Unity (for example, Lotus Domino or Microsoft Exchange).

- **Message store**—As the name suggests, the message store is the physical storage space for e-mail, voice mail, and fax messages. The message store is a component of the messaging system being integrated with Unity.

Although all three components can reside on the same server, in larger environments, these components might be distributed across multiple servers for increased scalability. Although not required, a Unity messaging system can coexist with the CCM in an IP telephony environment, as shown in Figure 7-2.

Figure 7-2   Unity and CCM Integration

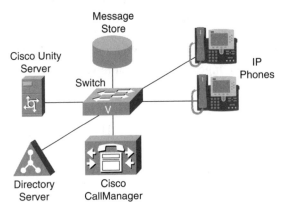

Consider a scenario. You're traveling, and you want to check your e-mail from a telephone. You call into your corporate messaging system (which uses Cisco Unity), and you can instruct the messaging system to *read* you your e-mail. Unity, using text-to-speech conversion technology, audibly reads you the text in your e-mails. Although it would be nice, Unity does not describe what the graphics in your e-mail look like. After you listen to your e-mails, Unity can let you listen to your voice mail. Perhaps later in the day, you're working on your laptop computer at the airport (using wireless network connectivity). You can log into your company's Unity system and retrieve your fax messages, including graphics.

Advanced Messaging with a PBX

As mentioned earlier, when a company migrates away from a PBX system to a CCM system, the company's IP telephony design doesn't immediately need to include Unity. Similarly, a company might migrate its voice mail solution to Unity, while retaining its existing PBX. The Cisco *Unity PBX-IP Media Gateway (PIMG)* offers one approach to making such integration possible. The PIMG contains eight ports, which connect back to the PBX, and a network connection, which allows the PIMG to communicate with Unity using the *session initiation protocol (SIP)*, as discussed in Chapter 5, "Speaking the Gateways' Languages." Up to six PIMGs can be stacked, offering a total of 48 simultaneous conversations between the PBX and Unity, as shown in Figure 7-3. Unity supports several other integration options as well (for example, digital set emulation).

Figure 7-3   PBX and Unity Integration

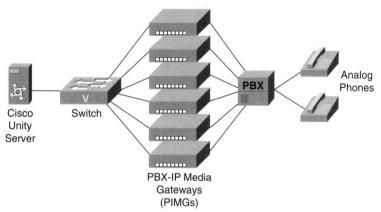

Cisco
Unity
Server

Switch

PBX

Analog
Phones

PBX-IP Media
Gateways
(PIMGs)

Have Your People Call My People: Creating a Conference Call

Chapter 4, "Meet the 'Brain' of the Voice over IP Network," discussed conference calling support in an IP telephony environment. A CCM server supports conference calling (that is, mixing multiple audio streams together into a single conversation). For more scalability, a CCM can leverage digital signal processors (DSPs) located in Cisco routers or switches.

However, for companies with frequent conference calling needs, CCM administrators might want to empower specific users to set up conference calls. The Cisco *Conference Connection* application gives specific users rights to configure their own conferences via a web interface. Although Cisco continually evolves its products, just to give you a frame of reference, Cisco Conference Connection version 1.2 supports up to 180 conference participants.

After a conference coordinator (for example, an office manager with rights to configure conferences) schedules a conference, the Cisco Conference Connection can send e-mail notifications to conference participants. The Cisco Conference Connection application runs on an MCS. However, the Cisco Conference Connection cannot coexist on an MCS with the CCM application.

While the Cisco Conference Connection application serves audio conferencing needs, the Cisco *MeetingPlace* application supports audio and video conferencing, in addition to web collaboration, as shown in Figure 7-4. Conference scheduling integrates with Microsoft Outlook and Lotus Notes.

Figure 7-4　　Cisco MeetingPlace

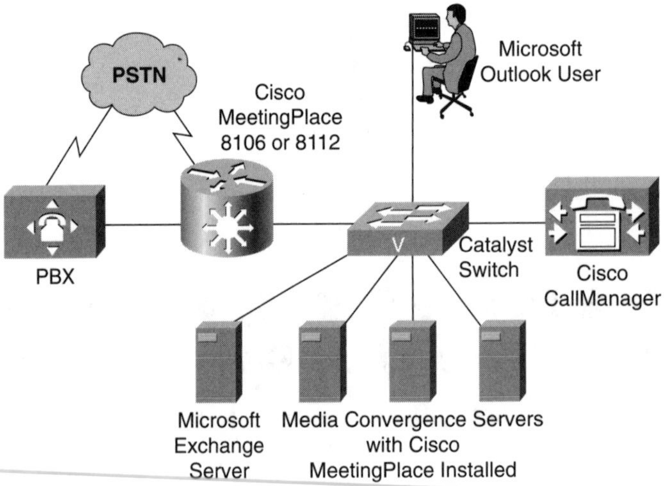

For example, imagine you wanted to set up a video conference. From within Microsoft Outlook, you can open up your Outlook calendar, select the starting time for the meeting, and click the **MeetingPlace** tab, as shown in Figure 7-5. You can then specify conference options, such as the conference duration, the number of audio participants, and the number of video participants.

Figure 7-5   MeetingPlace Integration with Microsoft Outlook

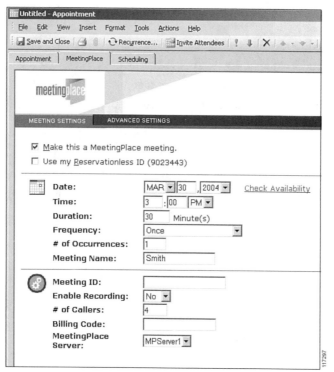

After clicking **Send**, the necessary audio, video, and web resources are allocated. Meeting participants using Microsoft Outlook have the meeting appear in their Outlook calendar. Meeting participants not using Microsoft Outlook receive an e-mail notification instead.

Perhaps you need to reschedule the meeting to a later time in the day. With MeetingPlace, you only need to drag and drop the event from one time on your Outlook calendar to another time. Fifteen minutes before the conference begins, by default, conference participants receive a meeting reminder, and they simply click the **Connect Me** button in the appointment appearing in their Outlook calendar to join the conference. In the background, MeetingPlace connects the participant to appropriate audio, video, and web resources. Even conference participants lacking computer access can dial into the conference from a phone and participate in the audio portion of the conference.

I've participated in meetings with attendees I didn't personally know. Someone would speak, and I wondered who spoke. Fortunately, MeetingPlace graphically identifies the speaking party. MeetingPlace also uses icons to indicate each conference participant's capabilities (that is, audio, video, and/or web capabilities).

Conference moderators control which participants can speak. As another personal example, I've participated in conferences where someone would put the conference on hold, in order to make another call, and guess what all of the conference participants heard. That's right. Music on hold! MeetingPlace allows conference moderators to eliminate such disruptions.

MeetingPlace participants can select how they want to view conference participants using video. For example, a participant can view the video from up to four other participants. Alternately, a participant might only want to view video from the speaking party.

Conference participants can share applications on their computer for demonstration purposes. One participant also can allow another participant to control an application on their computer. For example, imagine you're in a conference, and you are showing the conference participants how you designed your VoIP network by sharing your Microsoft Visio application (that is, a graphical design program used for such things as designing computer networks). Another participant might say, "Hey, I've got a great idea! Let me show you how to distribute the servers in your cluster." You could then share your Microsoft Visio application, which is running on your local computer, with the other conference participant. The other participant could then add additional components to your Visio design because they could take control of the Visio application running on your computer.

MeetingPlace participants can open up chat windows with each other, much like an instant messaging application. Breakout sessions can also be created on the fly. If not all of the invited participants are able to attend the conference at the scheduled time, MeetingPlace can record the conference and make synchronized audio and video playback of the conference available over the web.

Your Call Is Very Important to Us: The Cisco Answer to Call Centers

Have you ever purchased a product and had to call the manufacturer's customer support department? If so, your call probably went into a call center, where multiple customer service agents sat in their cubicles, anxious to give you excellent customer service!

The Cisco IP telephony solution supports call center environments on small, medium, and even large scales. Features commonly found in call center environments include

- **Automatic Call Distribution (ACD)**—ACD technologies dictate how incoming calls are spread across customer service agents working in a call center. For example, consider a small call center with three customer service agents: Dave, Doug, and Gary. If the telephone numbers assigned to these agents are configured in a *round robin* hunt group, the first call to come into the call center goes to Dave. While Dave is on the phone, another call comes in, and it is forwarded to Doug. Meanwhile, Dave completes his call and hangs up. Another call comes in and, due to the round robin configuration of the hunt group, is forwarded to Dave, who has the first telephone number in the hunt group. Meanwhile, Gary props his feet up on his desk and reads the newspaper. Such an approach doesn't seem fair, especially for Dave. Fortunately, ACD technologies can distribute calls more fairly. As an example, ACD can forward an incoming call to the phone number that has remained idle the longest.

- **Interactive Voice Response (IVR)**—IVR systems allow callers to interact with a database and use their telephone keypad to input information, such as a Social Security number or a personal identification number (PIN). As an example, I used to work with the telephone and data network at a university, and we installed an IVR system for the university's students. Students could call into the IVR system and perform such functions as registering for classes, verifying their housing information, and checking their grades.

- **Computer Telephony Integration (CTI)**—CTI technologies can gather information from incoming callers (for example, via caller ID or by having the caller enter their account number via their telephone keypad) and present information about the caller on a customer service agent's computer display. For example, I called into an investment company where my wife and I have a few mutual funds, and I wanted to change my monthly automatic deposits. After the customer service agent assisted me with my request, he told me my daughters were going to be starting college in a certain number of years and recommended that we discuss a 529 college savings plan. How did the customer service agent know the age of my daughters? Through computer telephony integration. After I entered my account information via my telephone's keypad, my account information, including information about my family, displayed on the customer service agent's computer display.

Cisco offers a couple of call center products. The *Cisco IP Contact Center (IPCC) Express Edition* targets small- and medium-sized business, while the *IPCC Enterprise Edition* meets call center needs for larger enterprises.

Cisco IPCC Express Edition

The Cisco IP Call Center Express Edition application provides a call center solution for small- to medium-sized businesses. Specifically, IPCC Express Edition supports up to approximately 200 customer service agents. The IPCC Express Edition application comes in three flavors to meet a spectrum of call center needs:

- **Standard**—The IPCC Express Edition Standard application provides basic contact management functions and is appropriate for an internal help desk, as an example.

- **Enhanced**—The IPCC Express Edition Enhanced application meets the requirements for small- to medium-sized contact centers and includes such features as skills-based routing (that is, routing calls to agents with specific areas of expertise), priority queuing (that is, the ability to handle more important calls quicker than less important calls), computer telephony integration, silent monitoring (that is, allowing a customer service manager to listen in on calls coming into the call center), and barge-in (that is, allowing a customer service manager to join an existing call between a customer and an agent).

- **Premium**—The IPCC Express Edition Premium application offers all features contained in the Enhanced edition plus a few bonus features, including e-mail and fax notification services (that is, allowing information to be e-mailed or faxed to customers), Hypertext Transfer Protocol (HTTP)/*extensible markup language (XML)* integration (that is, the ability to retrieve data stored on an enterprise web server), and optional automatic speech recognition (that is, the ability for a caller to speak their information instead of pressing keys on a telephone's keypad).

Cisco IPCC Enterprise Edition

While the IPCC Express Edition serves small- to medium-sized businesses, the IPCC Enterprise Edition might be appropriate for larger enterprise customers needing a more robust solution. The IPCC Enterprise Edition supports up to 2000 agents per CCM cluster. However, call center designs accommodate multiple CCM clusters, meaning the IPCC Enterprise Edition solution can scale to thousands of seats.

Figure 7-6 shows components of the IPCC Enterprise Edition solution.

Figure 7-6   Cisco IP Contact Center Enterprise Edition

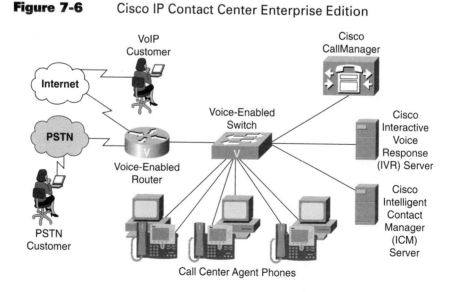

The following is a description of the components of the IPCC Enterprise Edition solution:

- **Cisco Intelligent Contact Manager (ICM)**—The ICM provides ACD functionality.

- **Cisco CallManager (CCM)**—The CCM, as described in Chapter 4, provides call processing for an IP telephony environment.

- **Cisco IP Interactive Voice Response (IVR), Cisco IP Queue Manager, or Cisco Internet Service Node (ISN)**—When purchasing the IPCC Enterprise Edition, customers can select which application they want to perform functions such as IVR and call queuing.

Case Study: Your Turn to Pick Add-On Features

The case study presented in Chapter 1, "Touring the History Museum of Telephony," gave the telephony requirements for the XYZ Company, as shown in Table 7-1.

Table 7-1   Case Study Requirements

Location	Number of Telephones	Required Features
Headquarters	4500	Voice mail A conference bridge capable of supporting a conference of 20 simultaneous participants
Remote Office 1	2000	Access to the corporate voice mail system Access to the corporate conference bridge Capability to support 72 simultaneous voice paths back to the headquarters
Remote Office 2	30	Access to the corporate voice mail system Access to the corporate conference bridge Capability to support 12 simultaneous voice paths back to the headquarters

In previous chapters, you specified hardware, software, and bandwidth requirements to meet XYZ Company's design guidelines, with the exception of voice mail and conference calling applications. This final case study challenges you to complete the design by recommending an IP telephony-based voice mail and conferencing solution for the XYZ Company. In the following space, describe and justify your recommendation.

Design Description for XYZ Company:

Suggested Solution

Multiple solutions exist for this case study. So, don't be concerned if your solution varies from the suggested solution. The suggested solution from Chapter 4 recommended the use of a Unity Express module for XYZ Remote Office 2. However, XYZ Headquarters and XYZ Remote Office 1 continued to use XYZ Company's existing voice mail system.

This solution recommends the installation of a Cisco Unity server, located at XYZ Headquarters, to provide a converged messaging solution. With Cisco Unity, XYZ Company's employees can retrieve their e-mail, voice mail, and fax messages from Unity's single repository.

To meet the conference calling design requirement, this solution recommends a Cisco MeetingPlace server. Although XYZ Company only needs audio conferencing currently, if in the future XYZ Company decides to add video to its conference calls, Cisco MeetingPlace can support audio, video, and web conferencing.

Chapter Summary

This chapter introduced a collection of value-added features for an IP telephony environment using CCM servers for call processing. The Cisco Unity converged messaging system offers a single repository for multiple messaging types (that is, e-mail, voice mail, and fax messaging). Users can, for example, retrieve their voice mail and even e-mail from a telephone, using Unity's text-to-speech conversion feature.

The Cisco Conference Connection and MeetingPlace applications offer conference calling solutions for businesses, allowing meeting coordinators to easily schedule a meeting, allocate necessary resources, and notify meeting participants. MeetingPlace, the newer of the conference applications, also supports video and web conferencing, and MeetingPlace integrates with Microsoft Outlook's calendaring feature. MeetingPlace offers a graphical interface that allows conference participants to readily identify the speaking party. In a video conference, MeetingPlace can display a video feed from up to four other participants. Alternately, Meeting-Place can display a single video feed showing the participant currently speaking.

Review Questions

1. A company installs a CCM server while migrating to an IP telephony solution. However, the company wants to leverage its existing investment in a voice mail system. The company connects analog ports on its existing voice mail system to a 24-port FXS module in a CMM blade installed in a Catalyst 6500 Series switch. What protocol, running between a CCM server and the Catalyst 6500 Series switch, allows a CCM server to use the company's existing voice mail system?

   a. SCCP

   b. SMDI

   c. SIP

   d. SMTP

2. Identify the three components of a Unity installation, including required third-party products.

   a. Directory Server

   b. CCM Server

   c. Message Store

   d. Unity Server

3. What device allows a Unity server to act as the voice mail system for a legacy PBX?

   a. ATA

   b. 7914 Expansion Module

   c. Catalyst 6500 PFC

   d. PIMG

4. Approximately how many conference participants are supported by the Cisco Conference Connection version 1.2 application?

   a. 80

   b. 180

   c. 280

   d. 380

5. Which of the following technologies dictates how calls coming into a call center are distributed among the customer service agents?

   a. CTI

   b. ACD

   c. IVR

   d. COS

6. Which of the following applications supports audio and video conferencing?

   a. Conference Connection

   b. Unity

   c. IP IVR

   d. MeetingPlace

7. Identify the three versions of the Cisco IPCC Express Edition application.

   a. Basic

   b. Standard

   c. Enhanced

   d. Premium

8. Which of the following applications provides automatic call distribution functionality for the Cisco IPCC Enterprise Edition application?

   a. IP IVR

   b. ICM

   c. ISN

   d. CCM

9. The Cisco IPCC Express Edition application supports up to approximately how many agents?

   a. 100

   b. 200

   c. 500

   d. 800

10. The Cisco IPCC Enterprise Edition application supports up to approximately how many agents per CCM (Cisco CallManager) cluster?

   a. 100

   b. 200

   c. 500

   d. 2000

Answers to Chapter Review Questions

Chapter 1

1. What are the names of the two wires used by a traditional home phone to carry voice traffic and signaling information? (Select two.)

   a. Ground

   b. **Tip**

   c. Magneto

   d. **Ring**

2. Who invented the first direct dial-telephone switch?

   a. Thomas Watson

   b. **Almond Brown Strowger**

   c. Alexander Graham Bell

   d. Harry Nyquist

3. Which type of telephone switch is most appropriate for a business needing to support 10,000 phones?

   a. CO switch

   b. Key system

   c. **PBX**

   d. Ethernet switch

4. Identify three types of signaling used on PSTN networks.

   a. Information

   b. Address

   c. Fallback

   d. Supervisory

5. How many voice channels can be carried over a T1 circuit in a traditional PSTN/PBX environment?

   a. 16

   b. 24

   c. 30

   d. 64

6. "Dial tone" is an example of which type of signaling?

   a. Information

   b. Address

   c. Fallback

   d. Supervisory

7. Which of the following are potential advantages of a VoIP network? (Select three.)

   a. Reduced dedicated circuit costs

   b. More mature technology than PBX/key system approaches

   c. Lays a foundation for more advanced services

   d. Reduced physical plant costs

8. How much voltage does a telephone switch apply across the tip and ring wires?

   a. -48 volts of DC

   b. -48 volts of AC

   c. +90 volts of DC

   d. +90 volts of AC

9. Which VoIP component is used to forward calls between different types of networks?

   a. Call agent

   b. Gatekeeper

   c. **Gateway**

   d. MCU

10. Which VoIP component is used to mix multiple audio streams?

   a. Call agent

   b. Gateway

   c. Gatekeeper

   d. **MCU**

Chapter 2

1. Which of the following best describes an *analog* waveform?

   a. A waveform represented by a series of 1s and 0s

   b. **A continuously varying waveform**

   c. A waveform after it passes through the G.711 CODEC

   d. A waveform after it passes through the G.729 CODEC

2. According to the *Nyquist Theorem*, if you are digitizing music, and the highest frequency being sampled is 20 kHz, what is the minimum number of samples that should be taken per second?

   a. 10,000

   b. 20,000

   c. **40,000**

   d. 80,000

3. Undersampling an analog wave (that is, not taking enough samples to accurately reproduce the wave) can result in:

   a. **Aliasing**

   b. Glare

   c. Gaussian distribution

   d. Linear quantization

4. G.711 is an example of which type of CODEC?

   a. **PCM**

   b. ADPCM

   c. CS-ACELP

   d. LD-CELP

5. Which of the following CODECs includes VAD (Voice Activity Detection)?

   a. G.729

   b. G.729a

   c. **G.729b**

   d. G.711

6. Which of the following is a voice quality measurement that uses a "trained ear?"

   a. **MOS**

   b. PSQM

   c. GoS

   d. PSQM

7. The process of assigning numeric values to PAM (pulse amplitude modulation) samples is called:

   a. Aliasing

   b. Oversampling

   c. Glare

   d. **Quantization**

8. A solid hour of voice conversation is the definition of which of the following terms?

   a. GoS

   b. PSQM

   c. **Erlang**

   d. Centum Call Second

9. A company's monthly phone bill indicates that the company's total phone usage for the month was 10,000 minutes. Estimate the number of call minutes during the "busy hour."

   a. **68 call minutes**

   b. 87 call minutes

   c. 360 call minutes

   d. 22 call minutes

10. Which of the following CODECs produces the best voice quality?

   a. G.723

   b. **G.711**

   c. G.729

   d. G.726

Chapter 3

1. Approximately how many minutes of downtime per year does a network experience if it has the "five nines" of availability?

   a. 53 minutes

   b. 46 minutes

   c. 16 minutes

   d. **5 minutes**

2. Which of the following offer Layer 3 redundancy in a network? (Select the two best answers.)

   a. 802.1w

   b. **VRRP**

   c. **HSRP**

   d. RSTP

3. An analog phone can connect to which of the following router interfaces?

   a. BRI

   b. FXO

   c. E&M

   d. **FXS**

4. The wall jack in your home, where you plug in your analog telephone, can connect to which of the following router interfaces?

   a. BRI

   b. **FXO**

   c. E&M

   d. FXS

5. Identify two valid framing types for a T1 circuit.

   a. AMI

   b. **SF**

   c. B8ZS

   d. **ESF**

6. Select the type of line coding that replaces a byte containing eight 0s with two bipolar violations.

   a. AMI

   b. SF

   c. **B8ZS**

   d. ESF

7. How many channels does a T1 circuit have?

    a. 16
    b. **24**
    c. 30
    d. 32

8. What channel on an ISDN circuit carries signaling information?

    a. A
    b. B
    c. C
    d. **D**

9. Which of the following parameters are configurable on an FXS interface? (Select the two best answers.)

    a. **Signal type**
    b. Ring number
    c. **Ring frequency**
    d. Dial type

10. An ISDN BRI circuit has how much usable bandwidth (that is, not including the D channel)?

    a. 56 kbps
    b. 64 kbps
    c. **128 kbps**
    d. 256 kbps

Chapter 4

1. What protocol does a Cisco IP Phone use to communicate with a Cisco Call-Manager server?

   a. RTP

   b. SCCP

   c. H.323

   d. MGCP

2. A logical grouping of Cisco CallManager servers is called a _____.

   a. Zone

   b. Region

   c. Location

   d. Cluster

3. Cisco CallManager servers restrict calls using _____ and _____. (Select two.)

   a. Locations

   b. Calling Search Spaces

   c. Device Pools

   d. Partitions

4. Which of the following products is designed to support enhanced 911 service?

   a. IVR

   b. CSS

   c. CER

   d. SRST

5. How much voltage powers a Cisco IP Phone?

   a. -24 VDC

   b. -48 VAC

   c. -24 VAC

   d. -48 VDC

6. Identify the wireless Cisco IP Phone model.

    a. **7920**

    b. 7960

    c. 7914

    d. 7970

7. What feature does the VT Advantage product add to IP telephony?

    a. Enhanced security

    b. **Video calls**

    c. Diagnostic features

    d. Software-based transcoding

8. Which of the following protocols encrypts voice packets?

    a. SIP

    b. RTCP

    c. RAS

    d. **SRTP**

9. Which of the following supports voice mail and autoattendant functions within a router?

    a. CME

    b. **CUE**

    c. CCS

    d. SRST

10. Which of the following are true concerning Cisco CallManager Express (CME)? (Select two.)

    a. CME runs on a Windows 2000 platform

    b. **CME runs on a router platform**

    c. **CME supports up to 240 IP phones**

    d. CME supports up to 480 IP phones

Chapter 5

1. From the following list, identify three gateway control protocols.

   a. **H.323**

   b. **SIP**

   c. RTP

   d. **MGCP**

2. What H.323 component is responsible for performing a "capabilities exchange" between H.323 terminals?

   a. H.225

   b. T.120

   c. **H.245**

   d. G.711

3. Which H.323 device prevents bandwidth oversubscription on the WAN?

   a. Terminals

   b. Gateways

   c. **Gatekeepers**

   d. MCUs

4. What message does an H.323 gateway send to an H.323 gatekeeper to request admission to the WAN?

   a. **ARQ**

   b. ACF

   c. ARC

   d. LRQ

5. Logical pieces of an MGCP network are called _____.

   a. MGCP terminals

   b. MGCP components

   c. MGCP gateways

   d. **MGCP concepts**

6. Which of the following is considered an MGCP component?

 a. Call

 b. **Call agent**

 c. Event

 d. Signal

7. In a Cisco IP telephony network, what acts as an MGCP call agent?

 a. **Cisco CallManager**

 b. Cisco Unity

 c. Cisco voice-enabled router

 d. Cisco voice-enabled switch

8. Which SIP component initiates a SIP connection by sending an INVITE message?

 a. UAS

 b. **UAC**

 c. SIP proxy server

 d. SIP redirect server

9. Identify the SIP server that informs the UA of the next server to contact.

 a. SIP proxy server

 b. **SIP redirect server**

 c. SIP location server

 d. SIP registrar server

10. What are the two types of SIP messages?

 a. Event

 b. **Request**

 c. Signal

 d. **Response**

Chapter 6

1. Which of the following results from an uneven arrival of packets?

   a. Packet loss

   b. Tail drop

   c. **Jitter**

   d. TCP retransmits

2. As a design recommendation, voice packets should have a maximum one-way delay of

   a. 10 ms

   b. 15 ms

   c. **150 ms**

   d. 250 ms

3. Which of the following Per-Hop Behaviors (PHBs) has the highest drop probability?

   a. AF41

   b. AF12

   c. AF11

   d. **AF13**

4. Identify the *congestion management* QoS mechanism from the following.

   a. **LLQ**

   b. WRED

   c. LFI

   d. Policing

5. Which of the following QoS mechanisms begins to discard lower-priority packets as a router's output queue starts to fill to capacity?

   a. LLQ

   b. **WRED**

   c. LFI

   d. Policing

6. Which of the following queuing mechanisms offer a priority queue? (Select two.)

   a. WRR

   b. LLQ

   c. FIFO

   d. WFQ

7. Which of the following QoS mechanisms can either discard or remark packets exceeding a specified bandwidth limit?

   a. LLQ

   b. WRED

   c. LFI

   d. Policing

8. What is the typical size of a voice packet's header, before compression?

   a. 2 bytes

   b. 4 bytes

   c. 26 bytes

   d. 40 bytes

9. Select the appropriate Link Fragmentation and Interleaving (LFI) tool for Voice over IP over Frame Relay (VoIPovFR) links.

   a. MLP

   b. FRF.12

   c. FRF.11 Annex C

   d. cRTP

10. Traffic shaping's timing interval (Tc) can be calculated from which of the following formulas?

   a. Tc = Bc / CIR

   b. Tc = CIR * Bc

   c. Tc = CIR / Bc

   d. Tc = (Bc + CIR) / Bc

Chapter 7

1. A company installs a CCM server while migrating to an IP telephony solution. However, the company wants to leverage its existing investment in a voice mail system. The company connects analog ports on its existing voice mail system to a 24-port FXS module in a CMM blade installed in a Catalyst 6500 Series switch. What protocol, running between a CCM server and the Catalyst 6500 Series switch, allows a CCM server to use the company's existing voice mail system?

    a. SCCP

    b. **SMDI**

    c. SIP

    d. SMTP

2. Identify the three components of a Unity installation, including required third-party products.

    a. **Directory Server**

    b. CCM Server

    c. **Message Store**

    d. **Unity Server**

3. What device allows a Unity server to act as the voice mail system for a legacy PBX?

    a. ATA

    b. 7914 Expansion Module

    c. Catalyst 6500 PFC

    d. **PIMG**

4. Approximately how many conference participants are supported by Cisco's Conference Connection version 1.2 application?

    a. 80

    b. **180**

    c. 280

    d. 380

5. Which of the following technologies dictates how calls coming into a call center are distributed among the customer service agents?

   a. CTI

   b. ACD

   c. IVR

   d. COS

6. Which of the following applications supports audio and video conferencing?

   a. Conference Connection

   b. Unity

   c. IP IVR

   d. MeetingPlace

7. Identify the three versions of the Cisco IPCC Express Edition application.

   a. Basic

   b. Standard

   c. Enhanced

   d. Premium

8. Which of the following applications provides automatic call distribution functionality for the Cisco IPCC Enterprise Edition application?

   a. IP IVR

   b. ICM

   c. ISN

   d. CCM

9. The Cisco IPCC Express Edition application supports up to approximately how many agents?

   a. 100

   b. 200

   c. 500

   d. 800

10. The Cisco IPCC Enterprise Edition application supports up to approximately how many agents per CCM (Cisco CallManager) cluster?

   a. 100

   b. 200

   c. 500

   d. **2000**

Next Steps: Where Do I Go From Here?

This book provided you with a glimpse into the world of Voice over IP (VoIP). You learned the theory surrounding VoIP operation, identified many of the components used in VoIP networks, and worked through various VoIP design case studies. At this point, you might be anxious to take the next step: learning to configure a VoIP network.

Basic Router and Switch Configuration

If you do want to configure VoIP networks, Cisco Press offers a wealth of resources. Realize, however, that before you start configuring VoIP networks, you must first know how to perform basic router and switch configuration. Therefore, as an initial step toward your configuration goals, consider the following titles from Cisco Press:

- *CCNA Self-Study: Introduction to Cisco Networking Technologies (INTRO) 640-821, 640-801*

- *CCNA Self-Study: Interconnecting Cisco Network Devices (ICND) 640-811, 640-801*, 2nd Edition

You might prefer to take live courses, in addition to or instead of reading these texts. If so, the following introductory courses are available from Cisco Learning Partners:

- Introduction to Cisco Networking Technologies (INTRO) v2.0

- Interconnecting Cisco Network Devices (ICND) v2.2

Visit the following website to find authorized training resources:
http://www.cisco.com/go/authorizedtraining

Combined, these books and courses help prepare you for the following exams, which lead to the Cisco Certified Network Associate (CCNA) certification:

■ 640-801 CCNA

or

■ 640-821 INTRO and 640-811 ICND

IP Telephony Certifications

Once you master fundamental router and switch configuration tasks, you can begin to focus specifically on voice technologies. Table B-1 provides a listing of Cisco IP Telephony certifications along with required exams and associated Cisco Learning Partner courses.

Table B-1   Cisco IP Telephony Certifications

Certification	Required Exams	Learning Partner Courses
CCVP (Cisco Certified Voice Professional)	CCNA Certification 642-642 QoS 642-432 CVOICE 642-425 IPTT 642-444 CIPT 642-452 GWGK	Quality of Service (QoS) Cisco Voice over IP (CVOICE) IP Telephony Troubleshooting (IPTT) Cisco IP Telephony Part 1 (CIPT1) Cisco IP Telephony Part 2 (CIPT2) Implementing Cisco Voice Gateways and Gatekeepers (GWGK)
Cisco IP Telephony Design Specialist	CCDA Certification 642-414 IPTD 642-642 QoS	IP Telephony Design (IPTD) Implementing Cisco Quality of Service (QoS)
Cisco IP Telephony Express Specialist	CCDA or CCNA Certification 642-432 CVOICE 642-642 QOS 642-143 IPTX	Cisco Voice over IP (CVOICE) Implementing Cisco Quality of Service (QoS) IP Telephony Express (IPTX)

Table B-1   Cisco IP Telephony Certifications *(continued)*

Cisco IP Telephony Operations Specialist	CCNA Certification 642-425 IPTT 642-642 QOS	IP Telephony Troubleshooting (IPTT) Implementing Cisco Quality of Service (QoS)
Cisco IP Telephony Support Specialist	CCNP Certification 642-444 CIPT 642-432 CVOICE 642-642 QOS	Cisco IP Telephony Part 1 (CIPT1) Cisco IP Telephony Part 2 (CIPT2) Cisco Voice over IP (CVOICE) Implementing Cisco Quality of Service (QoS)
Cisco IP Contact Center Express Specialist	CCNA Certification 642-161 IPCCX	IPCC Express and IP IVR Deployment (CRSD)
Cisco Unity Design Specialist	CCDA Certification MCSE: Messaging on Windows Server 2000; or MCSE: Messaging on Windows Server 2003 642-071 CUDN	Cisco Unity Design and Networking (CUDN) Unified Communications System Engineer (UCSE)
Cisco Unity Support Specialist	MCSE: Messaging on Windows Server 2000; or MCSE: Messaging on Windows Server 2003	Unified Communications System Engineer (UCSE)

Cisco continually updates its certification tracks. So, please visit the following URL for the most current information:

http://www.cisco.com/go/certification

In addition to the Cisco Learning Partner courses listed in Table B-1, Cisco Press offers multiple books on IP Telephony. Please visit the Cisco Press website at http://www.ciscopress.com for a complete listing of its IP telephony publications.

Glossary A

A

Active Directory (AD)   Microsoft's directory system, which consolidates a network's user and device information.

address signaling   The process of transmitting dialed digits.

a-Law   A companding (that is, COMpressing exPANDING) algorithm used in countries outside the U.S. and Japan, which has a superior signal-to-noise (S/N) ratio for lower-volume samples, as compared to u-Law.

aliasing   Reconstructing samples incorrectly due to a lack of sufficient samples being taken.

alternate mark inversion (AMI)   An approach of representing binary 1s as voltages with alternating polarities.

amplitude   The volume of a waveform.

analog   A continuously varying waveform.

auxiliary VLAN   The VLAN (that is, subnet) used to carry voice packets.

availability   A measurement indicating the likelihood that the network is up and functioning.

B

Backup and Restore System (BARS)   A Cisco backup application used for backing up data on a Cisco CallManager publisher.

backup CallManager server   A CallManager server that IP phones only register with if the phones' primary CallManager server becomes inaccessible.

B-channel   An ISDN *bearer* channel, which carries voice, data, or video.

binary   A series of 1s and 0s, which can represent data, voice samples, or video samples.

bipolar 8-zero substitution (B8ZS)   A method of encoding binary 1s and 0s that represents a byte containing all 0s by creating a couple of bipolar violations at specific bit positions.

bipolar violation   An error that occurs when two consecutive voltages have the same polarity.

broadcast storm   Occurs when broadcast packets circle the network forever, consuming bandwidth and switch processor resources.

buffer   A storage space inside of a router.

Busy Hour Call Attempts (BHCA)   The maximum number of active calls in a phone system during the busiest hour of the day.

busy signal   A combination of a 480 and 620 Hz tone, with on/off times of .5 sec/.5 sec, which indicates to the caller that the called party is on the phone.

C

call agent   Contains the call-forwarding intelligence for an MGCP network.

call detail record   An accounting record that contains details about calls placed on a network.

call minute   One minute of phone usage, which equals 1/60th of an Erlang.

caller-ID   Allows a called party to see who is calling them.

calling search space   A list of partitions in which a device (for example, an IP phone) is allowed to look when matching dialed digits.

CallManager Express (CME)   A Cisco IOS feature that supports CCM-like functions on a router, as opposed to a dedicated server platform.

capacitor   An electrical component that passes alternating current but blocks direct current.

central office (CO)   Where the local telephone company's phone switch is housed.

certificate   A digital document containing information about the certificate's holder.

certificate authority (CA)   A trusted third party that vouches for the validity of a certificate.

Certificate Authority Proxy Function (CAPF)   Software that installs a Locally Significant Certificate (LSC) on Cisco IP phones released prior to the 7970G model.

Cisco CallManager (CCM)   Cisco software running on a Media Convergence Server, which performs call processing functions in an IP telephony environment.

Cisco Emergency Responder (CER)   A Cisco software product that provides E-911 (Enhanced 911) service for an IP telephony network.

Cisco Internetwork Operating System (IOS)   The operating system on Cisco routers, and some Cisco Catalyst switches, used to configure network operation.

Cisco Unity Express (CUE)   A hardware module that offers voice mail and autoattendant features in a router.

cluster   A logical grouping of Cisco CallManager servers.

codebook   A dynamically created database containing sound patterns commonly used during a conversation (for example, the *ing* sound*).*

coder decoder (CODEC)   An algorithm that encodes and decodes waveforms (for example, G.711 and G.729).

co-lo   When a carrier to leases space for its equipment in a CO.

Conference Connection   A Cisco application that gives specific users rights to configure their own conferences via a web interface.

congestion management   A QoS technology that intelligently queues packets.

converge   The process of recovering from a link failure where traffic begins to flow over a backup link.

converged network   A network environment where voice, data, and/or video coexist.

D

Data Connection (DC) Directory   A user directory included with the Cisco CallManager software.

D-channel   An ISDN channel that carries signaling information, using the Q.931 protocol.

device unit   Represents the amount of work a CCM can perform.

dial peer   A configuration option that tells a router how to reach specific phone numbers.

dial plan   A set of instructions for reaching various phone numbers.

difference signal   A sample representing the difference between a digital sample and the previous sample, which consumes less bandwidth than sending an entire sample.

dual tone multifrequency (DTMF)   Two simultaneous frequencies that are interpreted as a dialed digit.

E

Ear and Mouth (E&M)   An analog interface present in many of today's PBX systems.

Erlang   One solid hour of conversation (that is, 60 minutes of phone usage).

Extended Superframe   A grouping of 24 standard 193-bit frames into a single frame.

extensible markup language (XML)   A programming language that offers an alternative method of sending text and pictures over a network, as opposed to HTML.

F

Fast Link Pulse (FLP)   A tone sent from a Cisco Catalyst switch to detect the presence of a device, such as an IP phone, that requires power.

first-in, first-out (FIFO)   A queuing strategy that sends packets out of a queue based on the order in which they entered the queue.

five nines   99.999 percent uptime, which equates to five minutes of downtime per year.

Foreign Exchange Office (FXO)   An analog port on a gateway that connects to an office (that is, a phone switch, such as a PBX or a switch in the local CO).

Foreign Exchange Station (FXS)   An analog connection on a gateway that connects to a station, such as an analog phone, fax machine, or speaker phone.

forklift upgrade   Replaces an existing telephone system with an IP telephony system in a single step, as opposed to a phased migration.

framing bit   A single bit that indicates the end of a frame.

frequency response   The range of frequencies reproduced or transmitted.

G

gatekeeper   A device, such as a Cisco router, that keeps track of available WAN bandwidth and permits or denies call attempts based on the available WAN bandwidth.

gateway   A router that converts back and forth between a VoIP network and another type of telephony network (such as a PBX or the PSTN network).

glare   The act of picking up a phone before it rings in an attempt to make a phone call and realizing someone else is on the other end of the line.

grade of service (GoS)   A measurement indicating the acceptable percentage of rejected calls during the busiest hour of the day.

ground start   Lets a phone switch know a phone went off-hook by applying a ground potential to the ring lead.

H

H.225   A protocol that performs call setup and RAS (Registration, Admission, and Status) functions.

H.245   A protocol that performs call control, including exchanging gateway capabilities (for example, the supported CODECs) between H.323 end systems.

H.323   A suite of protocols that supports audio, video, and data collaboration.

Hot Standby Router Protocol (HSRP)   A Cisco-proprietary protocol that allows one router to back up another router.

I

information signaling   Provides a caller information about the status of their call (for example, ring back or a busy signal).

Integrated Services Digital Network (ISDN)   A common channel signaling technology available as a Basic Rate Interface (BRI) connection or a Primary Rate Interface (PRI) connection.

Internet Protocol (IP)   The protocol that runs over the Internet and uniquely identifies components with IP addresses.

interoffice trunk   A connection from one phone switch to another.

IP Contact Center Enterprise Edition   A collection of Cisco IP telephony applications for a call center that supports up to 800 agents per Cisco CallManager (CCM) cluster.

IP Contact Center Express Edition   A Cisco call center application that supports up to approximately 200 agents and is available in three variants: Standard, Enhanced, and Premium.

J

jitter   An uneven arrival of packets.

K

keepalive   Packets sent periodically to determine whether a remote device is operational.

key system   A privately owned phone switch used by small businesses.

L

latency   Packet delay.

line coding   The set of rules that dictates how binary 1s and 0s are electrically transmitted over a wire.

Link Fragmentation and Interleaving (LFI)   A QoS mechanism that reduces serialization delay by fragmenting large payloads and interleaving small payloads in among the fragments.

liquid crystal display (LCD)   The technology used by many Cisco IP phones to display XML pages, line appearances, and softkey settings.

local loop   The connection from your home to the local central office, made up of tip and ring wires.

Locally Significant Certificate (LSC)   Digital certificates used by Cisco IP phones released prior to the 7970G model.

look ahead buffer   A storage area used by a CODEC to see whether a voice sample matches a pattern already in a dynamically created codebook, which allows the codebook location to be transmitted instead of the actual sample, thus reducing required bandwidth.

loop start signaling   Lets a phone switch know a phone went off-hook by current flow through the local loop.

Low Latency Queuing (LLQ)   A queuing technology that can give priority treatment to specific traffic types, such as voice.

M

mean time between failure (MTBF)   The average time between a component's failures.

mean time to repair (MTTR)   The average time required to repair or replace a specific faulty component.

Media Access Control (MAC) address   A globally unique 48-bit address assigned to a network interface card.

Media Convergence Server (MCS)   The server hardware used by Cisco CallManager servers.

Media Gateway Control Protocol (MGCP)   A gateway control protocol that stores call-forwarding intelligence in a centralized call agent, such as a Cisco CallManager.

MeetingPlace   A Cisco software application that supports audio and video conferencing, in addition to web collaboration.

metropolitan-area network (MAN)   A high-speed network servicing a large metropolitan area, which typically uses fiber optics to interconnect sites.

MGCP components   The physical pieces of hardware making up an MGCP network.

MGCP concepts   The logical pieces of an MGCP network.

midspan   An inline patch panel that provides power to IP phones over the non-Ethernet wires.

multiframe   A grouping of 16 standard E1 frames.

Multilink PPP (MLPPP)   Combines one or more physical PPP links into a single logical link.

N

Nyquist Theorem   A rule stating that when sampling an analog waveform, the sample rate needs to be at least twice as high as the highest frequency being sampled.

O

oversampling   Sampling voice by taking more than the required number of samples per second, thus consuming more bandwidth than necessary.

oversubscribe   To require more bandwidth than is available.

P

partition   Defines a set of route patterns and/or directory numbers. Phones that can reach one route pattern within a partition can reach all route patterns within the partition.

party line   A legacy type of telephony connection that allows more than one home to share the tip and ring wires going back to a CO.

permanent virtual circuit (PVC)   A virtual path through a Frame Relay or an ATM network.

policing   A QoS mechanism that limits bandwidth used by an application, typically by dropping excess packets.

power brick   An external power supply for a Cisco IP phone.

Power over Ethernet (PoE)   The IEEE 802.3af standard for powering network devices over an Ethernet cable.

primary CallManager server   A CallManager server that IP phones register with by default.

private branch exchange (PBX)   A privately owned phone switch used by a large business.

protocol   A set of rules that determines how information is exchanged.

Public Safety Answering Point (PSAP)   Contains a public database of 911 information.

public switched telephone network (PSTN)   The national public telephone system.

publisher   A CallManager server that contains a read/write copy of the CallManager database and sends updates to subscriber servers.

pulse amplitude modulation (PAM)   A sampling method that takes samples consisting of a single frequency (that is, the carrier frequency), with amplitudes (that is, volumes) equaling the amplitudes of the sampled waveform at the instance of the sampling.

pulse code modulation (PCM)   The process of converting pulse amplitude modulation (PAM) samples into a digital format, which is used by the G.711 CODEC.

pulse dialing   Opens and closes a tip and ring circuit very rapidly, which represents dialed digits to a telephone switch.

Q

Q.931   The protocol used on an ISDN circuit's D-channel as a signaling protocol.

quality of service (QoS)   A suite of mechanisms capable of treating special types of traffic in a special way.

quantization   The process of assigning a number to an amplitude.

quantization error   Noise resulting from inaccuracies in converting an analog waveform to a digital signal.

R

RTP Control Protocol (RTCP)   A supervisory protocol for RTP that can provide information about the quality of a call.

Real-Time Transport Protocol (RTP)   The protocol that carries voice packets.

Registration, Admission, and Status (RAS)   The protocol used to communicate with a Cisco H.323 gatekeeper.

reliability   A measurement indicating the likelihood that a packet can successfully traverse a network without being dropped.

replication   The process of copying database information from a publisher server to subscriber servers.

ring back   The ringing sound heard by a caller to indicate that the dialed phone is ringing.

ring cadence   The ringing pattern that specifies the on-off duration in a ring pattern.

ring number   The number of rings received on an FXO port before the port answers a call.

ringing   A type of supervisory signaling that lets a called party realize they are receiving a call.

robbed-bit signaling   Used with channel-associated signaling, where framing bits are *robbed* from a Super Frame or an Extended Superframe and used for signaling bits.

root bridge   A switch in the Layer 2 network running the Spanning Tree Protocol that serves as the point to which other switches forward traffic.

round robin   A type of hunt group, where incoming calls are sent to the first available number in a list of numbers.

RTP Header Compression (cRTP)   A QoS mechanism that logically compresses the size of a voice packet's header down to only 2 or 4 bytes.

run-time   CallManager data including such information as calls in progress, gateway and IP phone registration, and information about DSP resources.

S

sampling   The process of taking snapshots, or samples, of an analog voice waveform and representing those snapshots in binary.

Secure Real-Time Transport Protocol (SRTP)   A protocol that transports encrypted voice packets.

session initiation protocol (SIP)   A gateway control protocol that uses the concept of inviting participants into a session.

shaping   A QoS mechanism that limits the bandwidth used by an application, typically by delaying excess packets.

signaling   Information about a phone's status or a call's status (for example, ringing, loop start signaling, or a busy signal).

signaling protocol   A set of rules used to communicate call setup information.

Signaling System 7 (SS7)   The signaling protocol used between PSTN switches.

Simplified Messaging Desk Interface (SMDI)   A protocol that runs between a Cisco CallManager server and a Catalyst switch, allowing a legacy voice mail system to be used in an IP telephony environment.

Skinny Client Control Protocol (SCCP)   The protocol used to communicate between Cisco IP phones and Cisco CallManager servers.

softkey   A key on an IP phone that can serve different functions at different times (for example, hold, transfer, or conference).

Spanning Tree Protocol (STP)   A mechanism for preventing Layer 2 switching loops, while allowing redundant Layer 2 network connections.

station   A device used to interface with the telephony network, such as an analog phone or fax machine.

subscriber   A CallManager server that contains a read-only copy of the CallManager database and receives updates from a publisher server.

Super Frame   A grouping of 12 standard 193-bit frames into a single frame.

Survivable Remote Site Telephony (SRST)   A technology that allows a router at a remote site to take over call processing functions from the Cisco CallManager if the IP WAN goes down.

T

tail drop   Discarding packets because a queue overflows.

TCP connect   A message sent to set up a connection between a Cisco IP phone and a backup CallManager server.

time-division multiplexing (TDM)   A process of sending multiple conversations on a single connection by giving different time slices to different conversations.

tip and ring   A pair of wires leaving your phone, going into your RJ-11 wall jack, and traveling back to the telephone switch at your local central office.

toll bypass   The process of sending voice calls across an IP WAN, as opposed to sending calls over a long-distance network.

traffic engineering   The process of calculating the required amount of bandwidth (or number of trunks in a PBX environment) to accommodate a specific call volume.

trunk   A connection used to tie PBXs together. A trunk also defines an interswitch connection used to carry traffic from multiple VLANs.

U

u-Law   The most commonly used companding (that is, COMpressing exPANDING) algorithm in North America and Japan, which has lower idle channel noise compared to a-Law companding.

Uninterruptible Power Supply (UPS)   A power backup device that allows network components to continue functioning in the event of a power failure.

Unity   The Cisco flagship converged messaging solution, offering a single repository for voice, e-mail, and fax messages.

Unity PBX-IP Media Gateway (PIMG)   A device that allows a Cisco Unity messaging system to be used in a legacy PBX environment.

user agent (UA)   A SIP device that contains call-forwarding intelligence, such as a User Agent Client (that is, a SIP device that places calls) or a User Agent Server (that is, a SIP device that receives a call).

V

virtual LAN (VLAN)   A logical grouping of switch ports connected to devices in a common subnet.

Voice over IP (VoIP)   The process of sending voice traffic across a network by encapsulating voice traffic in IP packets.

VT Advantage   A Cisco software and hardware product that supports video calls, using a camera attached to a PC, which is attached to a Cisco IP phone.

W

weighted random early detection (WRED)   A QoS mechanism that prevents a router's queue from filling to capacity.

wide-area network (WAN)   A network that interconnects geographically separated networks.

INDEX

Numerics

3DES (Tripe Data Encryption Standard), 141

8-bit samples, 41

A

ABBRDIAL button, 136

abbreviated dial numbers, 136

access control lists (ACLs), 187

accounting, 158

accounts, CCO, 45

ACD (Automatic Call Distribution), 235

ACF (admission control) messages, 163

ACLs (access control lists), 187

AD (Active Directory), 100

Adaptive Differentiated PCM (ADPCM), 43

additional switch ports (IP Phones), 121

addresses, signaling, 6, 15–17

administration, call, 158

admission confirm (ACF) messages, 163

admission reject (ARJ) messages, 163

admission request (ARQ) messages, 163

ADPCM (Adaptive Differentiated PCM), 43

Advanced Encryption Standard (AES), 141

Advanced Integration Module (AIM), 146

AF (Assured Forwarding), 190

agents

call, 18, 165–167

UAs, 169

AIM (Advanced Integration Module), 146

a-Law, 41

aliasing, 37

AMI (alternate mark inversion), 77

amplitudes, 39

analog. *See also* interfaces

converting

calculating bandwidth, 49–54

case study, 54–58

compressing, 42–49

sampling, 36–42

interfaces, 70

announcements, 135

Annunciator, 135

F

Fair Queuing (FQ), 196

Fast Link Pulse (FLP), 120

fault tolerance

components, 65

MGCP, 168

FECN (Forward Explicit Congestion Notification), 213

FIFO (first-in, first-out) queuing strategies, 183, 195

FLP (Fast Link Pulse), 120

Foreign Exchange Office (FXO) ports, 73

Foreign Exchange Station (FXS) ports, 71

Forward Explicit Congestion Notification (FECN), 213

forwarding calls, 137

FQ (Fair Queuing), 196

Frame Relay

PVC, 84

shaping, 212

frames, multiframes, 82

framing bits, 76

frequencies

analog, 39

DTMF, 16

of rings, 72

FXO (Foreign Exchange Office) ports, 73

FXS (Foreign Exchange Station) ports, 71

G

gatekeepers, 19, 110, 161

gateways, 70

case study, 172

gateway-to-gateway calls (H.323), 162

PIMG, 230

protocols, 157–159

H.323, 159–164

MGCP, 165–168

SIP, 168–171

registration, 158

resolution, 158

glare, 12

global synchronization, 203

GoS (grade of service), 49–51

ground start signaling, 13, 72

Group Call Pickup feature (IP Phone), 138

grouping CCMs, 102

M

Q

R

S

W–X

SEARCH THOUSANDS OF BOOKS FROM LEADING PUBLISHERS

Safari® Bookshelf is a searchable electronic reference library for IT professionals that features more than 2,000 titles from technical publishers, including Cisco Press.

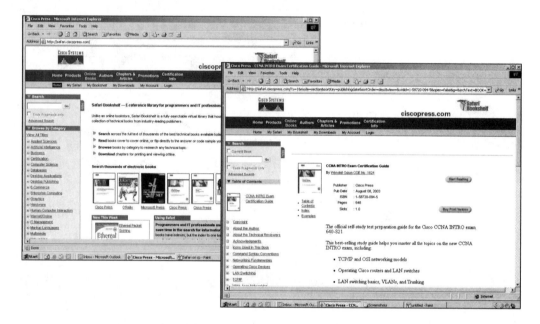

With Safari Bookshelf you can

- **Search** the full text of thousands of technical books, including more than 70 Cisco Press titles from authors such as Wendell Odom, Jeff Doyle, Bill Parkhurst, Sam Halabi, and Karl Solie.

- **Read** the books on My Bookshelf from cover to cover, or just flip to the information you need.

- **Browse** books by category to research any technical topic.

- **Download** chapters for printing and viewing offline.

With a customized library, you'll have access to your books when and where you need them—and all you need is a user name and password.

CISCO SYSTEMS

Cisco Press

SAVE UP TO 30%

Become a member and save at **ciscopress.com**!

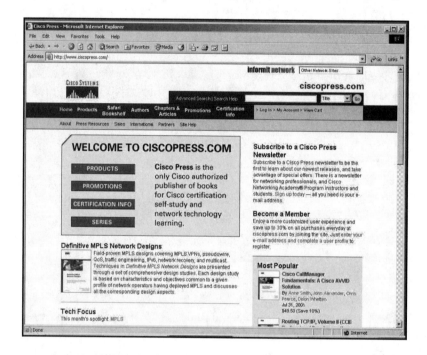

Complete a **user profile** at ciscopress.com today to become a member and benefit from **discounts up to 30% on every purchase** at ciscopress.com, as well as a more customized user experience. Your membership will also allow you access to the entire Informit network of sites.

Don't forget to subscribe to the monthly Cisco Press newsletter to be the first to learn about new releases and special promotions. You can also sign up to get your first **30 days FREE on Safari Bookshelf** and preview Cisco Press content. Safari Bookshelf lets you access Cisco Press books online and build your own customized, searchable electronic reference library.

Visit **www.ciscopress.com/register** to sign up and start saving today!

The profile information we collect is used in aggregate to provide us with better insight into your technology interests and to create a better user experience for you. You must be logged into ciscopress.com to receive your discount. Discount is on Cisco Press products only; shipping and handling are not included.

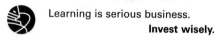

Learning is serious business.
Invest wisely.

DISCUSS
NETWORKING PRODUCTS AND TECHNOLOGIES WITH CISCO EXPERTS AND NETWORKING PROFESSIONALS WORLDWIDE

VISIT NETWORKING PROFESSIONALS
A CISCO ONLINE COMMUNITY
WWW.CISCO.COM/GO/DISCUSS

THIS IS THE POWER OF THE NETWORK. now.

CISCO SYSTEMS

Safari®

BOOKS ONLINE

ENABLED

THIS BOOK IS SAFARI ENABLED

INCLUDES FREE 45-DAY ACCESS TO THE ONLINE EDITION

The Safari® Enabled icon on the cover of your favorite technology book means the book is available through Safari Bookshelf. When you buy this book, you get free access to the online edition for 45 days.

Safari Bookshelf is an electronic reference library that lets you easily search thousands of technical books, find code samples, download chapters, and access technical information whenever and wherever you need it.

TO GAIN 45-DAY SAFARI ENABLED ACCESS TO THIS BOOK:

- Go to **http://www.ciscopress.com/safarienabled**

- Enter the ISBN of this book (shown on the back cover, above the bar code)

- Log in or Sign up (site membership is required to register your book)

- Enter the coupon code found in the front of this book before the "Contents at a Glance" page

If you have difficulty registering on Safari Bookshelf or accessing the online edition, please e-mail customer-service@safaribooksonline.com.